# WHAT DO I DO NOW?

EILEEN NECHAS

DENISE FOLEY

A FIRESIDE BOOK

A DIVISION OF SIMON AND SCHUSTER

NEW YORK ■ LONDON ■ TOKYO ■ SYNDEY ■ TORONTO ■ SINGAPORE

FIRESIDE
Simon & Schuster Building
Rockefeller Center
1230 Avenue of the Americas
New York, New York 10020

DESIGNED BY DIANE STEVENSON/SNAP•HAUS GRAPHICS
Manufactured in the United States of America

10  9  8  7  6  5  4  3  2  1

Library of Congress Cataloging-in-Publication Data
Nechas, Eileen
    What do I do now? / Eileen Nechas, Denise Foley.
        p.  cm.
    "A Fireside book."
    Includes index.
    1. Child rearing.  2. Child psychology.  3. Children—Health and hygiene.
I. Foley, Denise.  II. Title.
HQ769.N333  1992
649'.1—dc20                                                          92–16458
                                                                          CIP

ISBN 0-671-76848-4

# CONTENTS

*won't share, is manipulative or spoiled, whines endlessly, has tan-trums, bangs her head, says a dirty word. Using time-out for behav-ior problems, page 173.*

## PART FOUR ▪ FOR PARENTS ONLY

# ACKNOWLEDGMENTS

First, our heartfelt thanks go to the hundreds of parents who wrote or called us to share their experiences and to offer their tips for raising kids. Their enthusiasm and ingenuity constantly amazed and inspired us and made going to the post office the high point of the day.

We are also deeply indebted to three people whose technical help and enthusiastic support made us confident that we were giving our readers the best parenting information possible. George Sterne, M.D., who was our medical consultant at *Children* magazine, graciously agreed to fill the same position on this book. Despite his very busy schedule, George took the time to read every chapter for accuracy—even the letters!—and offered incisive and helpful criticism and guidance as we went along. Robert Mendelson, M.D., and his wife, Lottie Mendelson, R.N., M.S., P.N.P., who were regular columnists for *Children*, read the finished product and offered their suggestions for improving the book both medically and editorially. In addition to reviewing the book and writing the foreword, they solicited the experiences of the hundreds of parents they come in contact with in their practice and without being asked, served as our cheering section. Their unflagging support, enthusiasm, and friendship frequently lifted our spirits.

Thanks, too, to Marsha Walker, R.N., for her helpful advice on the breast-feeding chapter.

We'd also like to thank the other experts who so willingly took the time to talk to us, often at length, about their areas of expertise, and especially those who distributed our survey to their patients and clients. Our heartfelt thanks go to (in no particular order): Cynthia G. Last, Ph.D., Michael K. Levine, M.D., Patrick Burke, M.D., Ph.D., Heber Simmons, D.D.S., Patricia Keener, M.D., Alan S. Bellack, Ph.D., Kenneth Gordon, M.D., Renee A. Cohen, Ph.D., Henri Parens, M.D., Nancy Samalin, M.S., Quentin Van Meter, M.D., Joel Steinberg, M.D., Lynn Embry, Ph.D., Shirley Zussman, Ed.D., Edward Christophersen, Ph.D., Anne Bernstein, Ph.D., Raymond Karasic, M.D., Lonnie Carton, Ph.D., William Carey, M.D., Jay Belsky, Ph.D., William Koch, M.D., Sarah J. Fernsler, M.D., Natalie Elman, M.A., Louise Derman-Sparks, Ph.D., Susan Weissman, M.S.W., Marcia Lasswell, Ph.D., Jerome Karasic, M.D., Charles Schaeffer, Ph.D., Maureen R. Keefe, Ph.D., William Sobesky, Ph.D., James Garbarino, Ph.D., Sirgay Sanger, M.D., Dennis D. Embry, Ph.D., John Thompson, M.S.W., Linda Dunlap, Ph.D., Lynn Henderson, Joanna Lerman, M.S.W., Martin Stein, M.D., Joseph Zanga, M.D., Michael Lewis, Ph.D., Barry Zuckerman, M.D., Barry E. Guitar, Ph.D., Carolee Howes, Ph.D., Richard Ferber, M.D., Anne Armstrong, R.N., Darlene McCown, Ph.D., R.N., P.N.P., James McKendry, M.D., Jeffrey Fogel, M.D., James Uphoff, Ed.D., Michael Jellinek, M.D., Barbara Willer, Ph.D., and Louise Bates Ames, Ph.D.

Thanks also to our editor at Fireside, Sheridan Hay, whose skillful editing and insightful suggestions polished the finished product and who paid us the ultimate compliment by actually using what she read in this book with her two-year-old. We'd also like to thank Toni Sciarra, our first editor at Prentice Hall Press, whose suggestions helped shape this book. Special thanks go to our agent, Connie Clausen, and her former assistant Vera Fickey, whose faith in this project and in us buoyed us from the start.

For their help in reaching parents, our gratitude goes to the editors of *Mothering* magazine, *Los Angeles Parent*, *Big Apple Parents Paper*, *Grand Rapids Parent*, *Seattle Child*, *Chicago Parent*, and the National Organization of Mothers of Twins Clubs.

Thanks also to:

Camille Bucci, for her research help;

The public relations staffs of the American Academy of Pediatrics, the American Psychological Association, and The National Association for the Education of Young Children for helping us reach the right people;

Gloria Hage, Rita Nederostek, Barbara Fexa, Robin Lapadula, and Susan Ritter, who speedily provided us with transcripts of dozens of hours of taped interviews;

The editorial staff of *Children* magazine—Jeff Meade, Maria Mihalik, Paris Mihely-Muchanic, Ann Michael, Cathy Morgan, Susan Snyder, Linda Miller, and Amy Gottlieb—for their love, inspiration, and moral support, not to mention for giving us the time of our lives;

Georgene Bleiler, Jennifer Blythe, Kristy Belcher, and Mary Costello for baby-sitting;

Our husbands, Jim Nechas and Ed Rogan, for their love and support;

And our children, Dale and Julie Mazer, Sacha and Jon Nechas and Patrick Rogan, for teaching us everything we know about kids. And last, but not least, the best mother, Freda Tucker.

# FOREWORD

*by Lottie Mendelson, R.N., M.S., P.N.P., and Robert Mendelson, M.D.*

Welcome to parenting. And welcome to a very special book written by parents and professionals that helps explain what parenting is all about. We first got to know the authors several years ago when we wrote a column for *Children* magazine, the high-quality parenting publication they edited. We became familiar with their hands-on approach to parenting, which we liked because it was similar to our own. We always hoped that they (or someone) would write a book like this, and here it is. The style, approach, and practical attitudes of the authors are reflected page by page in what we feel will become one of the "must have" books for the thinking and caring parent.

Most of us become parents by choice. Most of us have preconceived notions of what kinds of parents we'll be, and what our children will be like. Most of us start out frightened and excited (not to mention fatigued), but we realize it's an amazing experience, a wondrous gift and a thrilling challenge. Along the way we'll be chewing and digesting a lot of theories and philosophies about how to do the job right—theories and philosophies that will no doubt change and evolve as our children teach *us* what parenting is really all about.

This book is truly a gift to and from parents—a gift of sharing information, experiences, and ways of parenting. The delightful, easy-to-read style makes the very valuable contents even easier to absorb and appreciate. In fact, this is the kind of book you will want to read for pleasure as well as knowledge. You'll learn that as parents you are the ones who know your child best. You'll be encouraged to trust your instincts, and you'll be given the resources to make informed decisions regarding your child's environment, health, and welfare. We believe the more information and education you acquire regarding this lifelong job, the better parent you will be.

From beginning to end, this book discusses questions most parents ponder at one time or another. It gives answers from both the "experts" and other parents. Denise and Eileen have even shared some of their personal trials of child-raising throughout the book, too. You'll find the kind of advice you can use right now, the kinds of ideas that have worked for other parents faced with the same anxieties and issues that you're now facing. And with its friendly conversational tone, you'll enjoy reading all of it or just looking up specific topics whenever you need to.

Chapters dealing with eating, sleeping, potty training, and temper tantrums, for example, are particularly full of information and tactics to use right now. Is there a parent who hasn't encountered at least some of these situations? The authors suggest you choose your battles carefully, however. In other words, decide which ones are important enough to be "wars." Parents who make a big deal or crisis out of everything are miserable and so are their children. Kids need fun, laughter, positive strokes, and a certain amount of freedom to grow. And they need to know you love them even when you don't like their behavior, choice, or action.

Throughout the book, Denise and Eileen encourage you to rely on your common sense, good judgment, and experience to choose what works best for you and your family. The authors remind you that what works one day may not work the next day on the very same child. That's why there are always alternative solutions to whatever sticky situation you find yourself in.

We are happy to recommend this book to all parents as a resource for basic information regarding parenting and as a tool that will facilitate further questioning and discussion. Reading this book can help you understand and believe that although all children are unique, their behaviors and problems rarely are. And that whatever your current sticky situation is, there's a solution somewhere in these pages that will help ease you out of it.

*Lottie Mendelson, R.N., M.S., P.N.P., is a pediatric nurse practitioner in Portland, Oregon.*

*Robert Mendelson, M.D., is a clinical professor of pediatrics at the Oregon Health Sciences University and has practiced pediatric and adolescent medicine in Portland for twenty-six years.*

# INTRODUCTION

## BEFORE YOU BEGIN THIS BOOK

The idea for this book—and its title—grew out of our relationship not as writing partners but as friends who were mothers. Five years ago, I was a new mother of a son who cried for hours on end, napped irregularly, and took to breast-feeding like a cat to water. I read everything I could get my hands on—books, articles, professional journals—but it wasn't enough. I was beginning to believe that either my son was "off the charts" or that I was truly the incompetent, ham-handed mother I believed myself to be.

I can remember the day I slipped into Eileen's office—at the time, we were the top editors of *Children*, a national magazine for parents—and told her my problems. "Okay," I said, "I've read it all. *What do I do now?*"

Eileen told me what had worked for her when she was raising her two daughters. But I walked out of her office with more than just some advice from a seasoned parent. I came out with a warm sense of well-being and relief. I was not an incompetent mother. My son was normal. There were days when Eileen, an experienced mother and stepmother of four, wanted to board the next nonstop to Brazil, too! I was not alone.

The experience started both of us thinking about the kind of help parents need when they're new at the job. Knowing the basics is a fine place to start. But what about dealing with all those curves kids tend to throw you? What about those sticky situations—which is how we started to think of them—that leave you floundering? What *do* you do if your beautiful new baby spends most of his waking hours—and there are plenty of those— crying inconsolably? What do you do if your two-year-old plays out a scene from *The Exorcist* every time you hit the supermarket checkout line with its treasure trove of candy? What do you do when your four-year-old stumbles into your bedroom while you and your partner are making love? What do you do when that most natural of motherly duties—breast-feeding—isn't coming naturally? How do you handle these problems in reasonable, positive ways without damaging your child's psyche or becoming a looney tune yourself?

At the time, we weren't planning to write a book. We were just trying to provide our readers at *Children* with the best possible child-rearing information available. But we couldn't help playing around with the idea of a "wish" book—the kind of book you wish you had when faced with one of those situations that confound your reason and challenge your common sense. We knew it would contain the advice of the top professional experts in the country. But what would set it apart would be the reassuring comfort of other parents who would share their in-the-trenches experience.

And that's what this book is. In it, you'll find the results of years of research—explained by more than fifty of the country's leading experts—on the best ways to handle everything from your child's tantrums to school phobia to a death in the family. And more than one hundred parents will tell you what *really* worked for them. (Since I'm the parent of a preschooler, I child-tested many of their suggestions during the writing of this book.)

One thing this book is not is a cookbook. We're not offering parenting recipes that, if they're followed to the letter, will result in perfect children and family relationships. What you'll hear us say over and over again is that all children are different, even children in the same family. What works with one may not work with another. That's why we've offered a variety of alternatives, sometimes contradictory.

There's no absolutely "right" way to be a parent, no surefire formula that will turn out perfect children like identical loaves of bread. Each child is born with a distinct temperament that will dictate what parenting techniques you'll find successful. You know your child better than anyone else does. We hope this book will give you some guidance that, combined with your own instincts, will make the wondrous and sometimes frustrating job of raising someone from scratch a little easier.

—Denise Foley

# PART · ONE
# BODY WORKS

# CHAPTER 1

# AGES AND STAGES
# ▪ The Way Kids Grow

## THE SITUATION ▪ Your Child Is a Late Walker

My daughter is sixteen months old and still not walking. In fact, she doesn't even seem very interested in it, especially since she covers plenty of territory on her hands and knees. We've even tried "walking practice"—walking her around ourselves while holding on to her hands—but she doesn't take the hint. Is this cause for concern?

## WHAT THE EXPERTS SAY

Not likely. Most kids become upright and mobile between nine and eighteen months. About 5 percent of them aren't walking by the time they're sixteen months old.

If your daughter is twenty months old and still not walking, you should see your pediatrician, suggests Barry Zuckerman, M.D., director of the Division of Developmental and Behavioral Pediatrics at Boston City Hospital and professor of pediatrics at Boston University School of Medicine. Your pediatrician will want to check your daughter's muscle tone. Poor muscle tone can be a symptom of a serious condition, but it could also be normal, says Dr. Zuckerman. Some children are born "loose limbed" and they usually don't walk until they're fifteen or sixteen months old. They usually have been slow to turn over as well. Your pediatrician may review with you when your child reached her other milestones, such as standing, crawling, and talking, to determine if she's having developmental problems. It's rare, says Dr. Zuckerman, to find a child who is a late walker who doesn't have some other developmental delays.

Remember that two major factors affect a child's walking: motor maturation and activity level, which is linked to her temperament. "Active children are going to be on the move more," says Dr. Zuckerman. "Also, some children who are slow to adapt to new things may be capable of walking but won't do it right away. They take things slowly. Usually parents have that sense about their children whether it takes them a little while to get used to things or they just go for it."

As for your walking practice, that's fine so long as both you and your daughter are having a good time. But, says Dr. Zuckerman, it probably won't make your daughter walk faster or better. She'll do that in her own good time, and you're better off not trying to pressure her.

## WHAT PARENTS SAY

*Our daughter didn't walk until she was past sixteen months. Of course, there were the inevitable questions from the grandmothers: "Why isn't she walking?" We really didn't worry about it. Then we went on vacation with friends who had a child two weeks younger than ours who was walking. The kids hung around together all week. I don't know if this had anything to do with it, but a week later our daughter was walking. She must have thought, "Hey, look where you can go. Look at all the neat things you can get into." We don't worry if she's a little slower picking up physical abilities. She's really more interested in verbal things than activities. She loves learning numbers and letters. When it comes to play, she loves to sit on the floor and play with Legos and blocks. We think it's hereditary. My wife and I aren't physical people, either.*

*Jeff M.*
*Virginia*

■

*Our daughter is eighteen months old, and other than a step or two when prompted, she hasn't shown any interest in walking at all. We know there isn't any medical problem. The real problem behind a late walker is the people who comment on it in a negative way. My husband and I tell them there is nothing wrong with our daughter and we trust her to make the decision to walk in her own time. We find that those same people change their opinion once they've seen our bundle of energy crawl across the room as quickly as a walker!*

*Rena L.*
*Canada*

## THE SITUATION ▪ Your Child Is Shorter or Taller Than Other Kids

My fourteen-month-old daughter is very small for her age. Everyone treats her like an infant, although she's walking and talking. This really concerns me. My husband's family is on the small side and mine is small to average. My mother-in-law says I'm worrying about nothing, that my daughter's "petite," which is very cute in a little girl. Am I right to be concerned?

## WHAT THE EXPERTS SAY

You might be. While short parents tend to have short children, you shouldn't allow that fact to reassure you too much, warns Joseph Zanga, M.D., professor of pediatrics at Children's Medical Center at the Medical College of Virginia. "It may be that everybody in the family had some potentially correctable problem, and this child may not be destined to be short," says the physician, who is also the medical spokesman for the Human Growth Foundation.

Also, there's some evidence that treatable growth problems in girls are vastly underdiagnosed. Only half as many girls as boys are evaluated by doctors for short stature, although most experts believe there should be no difference in the number of boys and girls identified as short. "When it comes to concerns about height, we don't have equality of the sexes yet," says Dr. Zanga. "We have different expectations for boys and girls. The boy is a runt, a pipsqueak, ridiculed and excluded from activities; the girl is petite, dainty, cute, and lovable. So for many of these girls, their growth problems are ignored, and their treatment delayed. Once these children reach puberty and the growing ends of the bones have begun to close, it is very difficult to get them much more height."

A recent study showed that children who were unusually short for their age scored lower on tests of self-esteem, social popularity, happiness, and self-satisfaction. These children often fall victim to bullies or to deflect the teasing, become the class clown. Frequently their school performances suffer.

You should be going to your pediatrician for regular preventive health-care visits where your child's height and weight are measured and plotted on a growth curve. She'll be ranked by how she compares to other children her age. It's usually of no concern if a child is at the lower or upper end of the curve. You may have cause for worry, however, if she drops off the curve. For example, if she starts out at the sixtieth percentile, falls to twenty, then to five, then drops off the chart entirely, it's clear she's failing to grow.

Your child should have her biggest growth spurt in her first year of life, adding an extra seven to ten inches to her birth length (which for most kids is nineteen to twenty-one inches, although slightly higher and lower are also normal). In the next year, she should grow another four to five inches. (Most premature babies will have caught up to normal growth by this time, although some may take a little longer, and some, if they had other birth problems, may never catch up.) From two years of age to puberty, she should put on two to two and a half inches a year and then, in the pubertal growth spurt, should put on another two and a half to four and a half inches (three to five inches for boys).

Your child's height, of course, is genetically determined. If you and your spouse are both small, the probability is great that your child will also be small (the same holds true for tallness). It doesn't matter if she's consistently at the twentieth percentile or below, as long as she's *still growing* at a regular rate. You need to ask yourself some important questions:

■ Is my child so much shorter or taller than children her age that it's painfully obvious to everybody?

■ Is my child treated as if she were younger than her age because she looks so young?

■ Is my child still wearing last year's clothes or outgrowing clothes faster than usual?

■ Is my child unable to keep up with children the same age in normal activities?

■ Is my child between the ages of two to fourteen growing less than 2 inches or more than three inches a year?

■ Is my child showing any signs of early sexual development (before seven in girls, nine in boys)?

If your answers disturb you, it's time to see your pediatrician. Though for most kids the cause will turn out to be heredity, about 20 percent may have an illness that is stunting their growth. It could be a disease of the digestive tract, kidneys, heart, or lungs, a nutritional deficiency, diabetes, even severe stress. Cystic fibrosis, a genetic ailment, also causes short stature because of malabsorption problems. Some children may be short because of a hormone imbalance, such as lack of thyroid hormone (hypothyroidism); too much cortisol, or stress hormone (Cushing's syndrome); or lack of growth hormone (GH deficiency). Other causes of short stature include intrauterine growth retardation, slow growth before birth caused by maternal smoking, alcohol use, or hypertension during pregnancy; chromosome abnormalities such as Turner's syndrome, which affects females; or other genetic syndromes and bone diseases.

An X ray of your child's wrist bones will tell the doctor whether her "bone age" is normal, and hormone tests will determine whether her problem is an endocrine imbalance. About ten thousand to fifteen thousand kids in the United States are too short because they have a pituitary growth hormone deficiency. Today, with the availability of biosynthetic human growth hormone, children with this diagnosis can receive daily injections of growth hormone throughout their entire growth period (for girls, to age sixteen, for boys, eighteen).

If it turns out that your child has a condition that is not correctable or is short by virtue of heredity, your main focus will become his or her emotional well-being. "Parents need to be very attentive to working with their children to emphasize their strengths and de-emphasize their weaknesses," says Dr. Zanga. "The story of the Ugly Duckling still has importance and impact. The short-statured little girl or little boy may not be a basketball player, but he or she could be a swimmer or a gymnast or a brilliant scholar. Tall is usually less of a problem than short. Tallness is a plus—unless you're a thirteen-year-old girl. That tall thirteen-year-old will often become a fairly average sixteen- or eighteen-year-old, but in the meantime, you need to talk to her about basketball and modeling careers, things she can do to use her height to good advantage."

## WHAT PARENTS SAY

*My daughter is at the top of the charts for height and is a head taller than her same-age playmates. A few times kids have told her she is huge or "too tall," and I have had to explain to her that her daddy (whom she adores) is very tall, as are her favorite auntie and uncles. I tell her that to be tall is good and to be able to reach higher than kids her age is a treat. She can also reach the monkey bars at the park, get the milk out of the fridge, reach her toothbrush, and wash her hands without a step stool. If she gets teased in school, we'll simply have her uncle and her dad, who are both six feet eight inches tall, take her to her classroom and meet the other kids, who, we hope, will see their size as positive.*

*Ena C.*
*Minnesota*

■

*For three years in a row, my son was the smallest in his class. Although my father, my grandfather, and the whole line were small, we were still concerned that perhaps he wasn't growing fast enough. We took him to the doctor, who X-rayed his wrist bones. As it turned out, he was growing fine and was just on the small side. Now, we're working on building his self-confidence. We never say, "When you get bigger." We say, "When you get older." We enrolled him in karate, which has not only helped his coordination but helped him become more outgoing and confident.*

*Kathy B.*
*Pennsylvania*

## THE SITUATION ▪ Your Child Removes His Diaper

If I don't pick up my son (who's almost a year old) as soon as he wakes up from his nap, I can usually count on finding him with his diaper off and if there's anything in it, discovering its contents all over the place. What can I do?

## WHAT THE EXPERTS SAY

"That's called stool smearing and it's really quite common," says Robert Mendelson, M.D., professor of pediatrics at Oregon Health Sciences Center. Although some people recommend putting the child's disposable diapers on backward (with the tapes in the back, where they're harder to reach), the determined child will find some way to accomplish this distasteful task, which the Mendelsons think is usually the result of boredom. "It's like Play-Doh to them," says pediatric nurse practitioner Lottie Mendelson.

Simply clean it up, indicate that you consider the activity "yucky," and go on about your business. Try not to leave your child alone with only his diaper for a plaything. Tuck a few soft toys in the corner of his crib or attach a play box to the railings.

## WHAT PARENTS SAY

*My daughter always took her diaper off when she had a bowel movement. I read that this sometimes meant the child was ready to be toilet trained. I went out and bought her a potty. She very quickly trained.*

*Cynthia P.*
*New York*

▪

*My baby used to remove her onesie and her diaper. After that I put it on backward so that now she does not even know she has snaps.*

*Ena C.*
*Minnesota*

## THE SITUATION ▪ Your Child Is a Late Talker

Katie is fifteen months old and I'm still waiting for my first "Mama." Her older brother said his first word at eleven months. Is there something wrong?

## WHAT THE EXPERTS SAY

If your child is late to talk—and fifteen months isn't so late that it's cause for worry—the first question you need to answer is, can she hear? Most speech delays are related to hearing loss, which can be associated with frequent ear infections. If she's always reacted to the telephone and voices, her hearing is probably fine. Before you take her to the pediatrician, you can test her hearing yourself by talking to her in a normal tone of voice while her back is turned. "If the child doesn't react to mother's voice, that should be a concern," says George Sterne, M.D., professor of pediatrics at Tulane University.

The second question—is she babbling? Up until they're about six months old children all over the world make the same sweet gurgling and cooing noises. At about the six-month point they begin to babble in what speech expert Barry Guitar, Ph.D., calls "the music of the language" they will eventually speak. In other words, their meaningless sounds are "spoken" in the intonation patterns that they hear.

The third question you need to answer is, does the child understand the spoken language? When you say to her, "Do you want to go outside?" without reaching for her jacket or the door, does she seem to understand? Does she respond to commands, such as "Stop that"? If she doesn't do any of these things, a hearing problem may be at the root of her speech delay.

For some children, a speech delay or other speech problem is the earliest symptom of an undiagnosed developmental problem. There may also be a physical problem, such as a cleft palate.

In general, most children begin vocalizing by the time they're seven or eight months old and have said one or two meaningful words by the time they're ten to twelve months old. By the time they're fourteen months old they usually have four to six words at their command, though it's not until they're about nineteen

months old that they put two words together, something that's
not officially a sentence until it contains a noun or pronoun and a
verb. Those pronouns are indiscriminate, by the way. "Me go" is
a perfectly normal sentence to be uttered by a two-year-old. By
the time most kids are three, they have a vocabulary of 250 words
and can use plurals and form three-word sentences. Some kids
are a little slower; others are advanced and still fall within the
normal range.

Plenty of quite normal things can occur to keep a child from
speaking. One of them, oddly enough, is walking. "As a general
rule," says Dr. Guitar, professor of speech pathology in the Department of Communication Science and Disorders at the University of Vermont, "kids don't simultaneously work on both things.
They don't have the available neural circuitry. You can imagine
from your own experience trying to do two hard things at the
same time. You're better off just doing one of them."

Also, and we offer this purely as our own and Dr. Sterne's ob-
servations, sometimes second children (and presumably the third
and fourth and on down the line) don't utter their first word early
on because, frankly, they can't get it in edgewise. Big brother or
big sister is always talking for them. A recent study at the University of New Hampshire also found that mothers tend to talk in
less complex ways to second children. Where a mother might say
to her firstborn, "Would you like to go outside?" she's likely to
abbreviate it to, "Outside?" with her second child.

If your child is inhibited because someone else is always speaking for her, Dr. Sterne recommends that you avoid anticipating
her every need and responding to the sibling acting as her simul-
taneous translator. "Suddenly become a little bit dense, unable
to understand all the pointing and grunting," he suggests. "Try
not to be so helpful. Sometimes we're so quick to anticipate and
respond to children's needs that we don't give them a chance to
ask."

And talk with your children. A number of recent studies have
found that children whose parents talk with and not at them
develop language skills much earlier than other children. Talking
with a child means pausing occasionally to listen, too.

With older children, who understand what you're saying, stick
to topics that interest them: what they're eating, the pictures in a
book, ducks at a pond.

A speech delay is not necessarily a sign of impaired intelligence, just as precocious speech doesn't guarantee your child will become a National Merit Scholarship winner. "I have a niece who's quite bright, but she didn't say a word until she was two and a half," says Dr. Guitar. "Suddenly, she came out with a fully formed sentence. Some kids are just more verbal than others."

## WHAT PARENTS SAY

*My second child was a late talker. He was born with a cleft lip and cleft palate. The speech pathologist gave us several ideas of things to do at home. When my son wanted something, he would just point and make a sound. He would get frustrated very easily about not being able to communicate with anyone. We were taught not to give in to him so easily when he wanted something. We slowly pronounced the word to him and urged him to try to say it. We'd praise him for trying. A speech teacher from our local school district came into our home once a week and worked with him. When he turned three, he was tested again and accepted into a special preschool at the local elementary school, where he received speech therapy and got to be around other children in a learning environment. Today he is five, and his speech is where it should be for his age. It's hard to imagine that just a few years ago he wasn't talking yet, and now he won't be quiet!*

*Kathy H.*
*Nebraska*

∎

*My oldest child spoke early. She and I spent a lot of time alone together and I talked to her all the time. I even read the paper to her. When we had our son, she was twenty-one months old and I guess I just took care of him, rather than carrying on conversations with him. As he got to be sixteen or seventeen months old, we realized he wasn't saying anything. He would point at the sink and squeak and our daughter would pipe up, "He wants water." If I offered her a piece of cake, she would say, "The baby wants one, too." Then it dawned on me. She was doing all the talking for both of them. I made a big deal out of talking to him more and asking him questions.*

*He's an adult now and has a very high IQ, so his late talking had nothing to do with his intellect.*

*Pat W.*
*Pennsylvania*


**THE SITUATION ▪ Your Child Won't Potty Train**

**What do you do for a child past the age of three who still is not potty trained? This has become an ugly battle between us and our son.**

## WHAT THE EXPERTS SAY

Have the bugler sound retreat. You and your child need to take a potty-training break. You aren't going to make any progress unless you put some distance between yourselves and the unpleasant experience you're now going through.

Take a month, even six weeks, off. And during that time, suggests Martin Stein, M.D., professor of pediatrics at the University of California at San Diego, take a long look at recent family history. A number of things could be going wrong.

Has your child been through any major life events? Is there a new baby in the house? Have you moved, changed caregivers, been sick? All of those things can interfere with potty training— and in fact, can cause a potty-trained child to regress.

If you've been sick, started a new job, or in some way have been emotionally unavailable to your child, he could be using his resistance to secure a little more nurturing. Potty training is an autonomy issue, a rite of passage, if you will, from baby to big boy (or girl). For a toddler, accustomed to voiding at will, using the potty is a big responsibility. While it may offer him a sense of control over his life (something all kids want and need), he may also be a little hesitant. After all, he's got it pretty good now. He goes in his pants and you clean him up. For a kid, it's a little like giving up the maid when you've never cleaned house in your life.

The first time Denise and her husband attempted to potty train their son, he followed one successful day with a day of clinging and crying and begging to be diapered. "We thought he needed a little more time to get used to the idea of being one of the big guys, so we put his diaper back on and decided to postpone 'Potty Training Part Two' for at least a month," she says. It worked. Patrick was potty trained on the second attempt, during the writing of this book, just a couple of months short of his third birthday.

How has your child handled the other developmental milestones? If you had trouble weaning him from his bottle or pacifier, he may be one of those children who have trouble with change. Does he throw a tantrum when he doesn't get what he wants? Do you have battles over meals, too? Maybe he's a child with a strong sense of independence who is going to involve you in a power struggle over whatever he can control.

A child who gets anxious about change may need a little more time to get used to the idea of giving up diapers for the potty. A strong-willed child needs to believe it's as much his decision as yours for him to use the potty.

How have you handled potty training so far? Nagging and cajoling tend to backfire. Overpraising can be intimidating to a child, particularly a perfectionistic one who might give up after his first little accident. "Certainly give praise if they have a bowel movement, but don't put on the *1812 Overture*," says Dr. Stein. "You can give a mild reward, a little toy or a special dessert, something big enough so the child gets the idea that mommy and daddy are really happy about this."

Something that has worked for several parents we know is a "surprise bag," which contains all sorts of small prizes the child can select if he's had a dry morning or used the potty. Others use charts on which the child is allowed to place stickers for each success.

Have you and your spouse and your child's caregiver been consistent in your potty instructions? "Inconsistency in potty training, as in any other newfound skill, can create ambivalence and frustrate the child," says Dr. Stein. Have you inadvertently been discouraging the child because you still want him to remain dependent on you? Examine your actions.

Are you feeling pressure from society—the nursery school that won't take a three-year-old in diapers, the neighbor who claims that her child was trained at ten months—and passing that anxiety on to the child? If so, you need to "detoxify the situation," suggests Michael Jellinek, M.D., chief of child psychiatry at Massachusetts General Hospital and associate professor of psychiatry at Harvard Medical School. "There is a lot of community pressure to be the first, the youngest, the most perfect, the least dependent. This is not the time to succumb to those pressures. If the child is ready to move on to the next stage, the main thing is to avoid a power struggle. Say, 'Hey, okay, you don't want to be trained? No sweat.' Then take at least a month off—which is a pretty long time for a three-year-old—and depowerize the whole thing," he says.

In fact, says Dr. Jellinek, you might even want to involve a neutral third party—a grandparent or a caregiver—who can restart the process for you. We know one woman who sent her strong-willed almost-three-year-old to grandma's for the weekend and he came back without diapers. "For many parents," Dr. Jellinek says, "the daycare provider has become the point person for the first parental effort."

An older sibling or potty-trained friend can also help. With little encouragement, another child is usually willing to tutor anyone in something he recently learned. In any case, the other child can be an effective role model.

Take a deep breath, *relax*, and start over. Buy a new potty. "Put the child's name on it, make it bright colors. If the child is attached to his old potty, make it look new by putting stickers all over it," suggests Dr. Stein.

Give him a chance to get comfortable on it. Spend some time in the bathroom with him—with you sitting on the toilet—and read or talk. If you can catch him about to have a bowel movement, actively encourage him to use the potty. Dr. Stein also advises that the same-sex parent role-model toileting behavior. One thing that worked for Denise was to enlist one of Patrick's bath toys as a role model. Once wet, his terry-cloth Ernie doll "peed" quite effectively, so she had Patrick help Ernie use a pretend potty and praise him for being such a "big boy." "For Patrick this was a chance to act out through play. It was like a rehearsal for the real thing," she says. "He loved the game, potty trained fairly quickly after that, and still likes to have Ernie 'pee' in the bathtub."

It might also help to take a diaper with a bowel movement in it and empty it into the potty. "Clearly by the time they're three they know that's where it's supposed to go, but you are reinforcing it this way," says Dr. Stein. "Do this several times."

Something that worked for several mothers we know—and which Denise used effectively—was to stop using diapers altogether except for bedtime. It's a lot easier for a child to remember to use the potty while wearing those brand-new big-kid pants instead of that familiar old diaper. It's also a way of making your message to the child clear: that using the potty is something you *expect* him to do. Parents who sidle into potty training, who seem to have mixed feelings about it themselves, can leave the child with the idea that he doesn't have to go at it seriously. Keeping a training kid in diapers may spare your furniture, but it could prolong the process. Good training pants, with a thick, padded crotch, will help.

One fairly common side effect you may experience when you have a child who is resistant to potty training is that he may begin withholding bowel movements. Sometimes this occurs if the child has been constipated or has had a painful bowel movement. To avoid the pain he now associates with elimination, he may withhold bowel movements for days. That in itself is painful. That's why it's important to have a medical examination if you're having problems potty training your child. Usually, says Dr. Stein, putting the child on a high-fiber diet as directed by your child's doctor—lots of grains and fresh fruit—and giving him fruit juices in place of milk (which can be binding) will solve this problem.

The most important thing is to have a good attitude. If you never said a word about toilet training, sooner or later your child would do it on his own. No kid ever carted a diaper bag off to college. Think of potty training as what it is: a skill that, once your child masters it, will make him so pleased with himself you're not going to be sure which of you is happier.

## WHAT PARENTS SAY

*Our son was almost three when we trained him. He understood immediately about urinating in the potty, but he didn't like having a* bowel movement on it. He had stomachaches from holding back, and eventually, he had accidents. Our doctor said that some kids develop a fear of having bowel movements on the potty after one painful experience or just watching "part of them" get flushed away. He said to put him on the potty every day after breakfast because often the body naturally has to go at that time. He said to leave him on for ten or fifteen minutes and then praise him for trying, even if he didn't go. We tried it and within a week our son had settled down to a regular routine and was no longer afraid.

Jennifer B.
Pennsylvania

■

My son was two when I learned I was pregnant again. The pressure was on. I didn't want two in diapers, and I wanted him to start nursery school in the fall. My first approach was to buy books. The basic theory behind all of these books is that if your child can understand what he's supposed to do, he'll be able to do it. Our son already appeared physiologically ready because he had been waking up dry for weeks.

Well, my son liked wearing underpants, so for one day he was pretty successful. I praised him and called him a "big boy," just like the books said. The next day he had a dozen accidents. But he didn't want to go back into diapers. I got a big barrel and filled it with brightly gift-wrapped presents and told him he could have a gift for each day that he kept his underpants clean.

I decided that maybe he didn't like the potty chair, so I invested in a seat with a squeaking horsie's head that fit directly onto our toilet seat. I read more books. Next, I tried bribery. Then one day I overheard him constantly saying to his Fisher-Price dolls, "Do you have to make?" I decided to give up.

The next time he had an accident I said to him, "Okay, I give up. I can't make you do this. When you are ready, you let me know." Keep in mind that six months had passed, and he was wearing (and I was washing) underpants!

The next day, while I was in my kitchen, I heard a toilet flush. I asked my son what he was doing. He said he had "made," wiped, and flushed by himself. He's been clean and dry ever since.

In conclusion, I'm convinced that you can't toilet "train" your *child. My new son will have to ask me for underpants when* he's *ready, not when I'm ready.*

*Amy B.*
*Pennsylvania*

# CHAPTER 2

# BREAST OR BOTTLE
■
# The First Supper

**THE SITUATION** ■ **You Have Trouble Breast-feeding at First**

I had no end of trouble trying to breast-feed my first child. Initially she had trouble latching on; then my breasts hurt so badly even wearing a blouse caused me pain. I finally gave up after only six weeks. I felt like a total failure. I'm expecting my second child and I'd like some advice on how to make my second attempt more successful.

## WHAT THE EXPERTS SAY

"Breast-feeding is all natural," says Marsha Walker, R.N., IBCLC, a lactation consultant and president of Lactation Associates in Weston, Massachusetts. "But it's also an art and a skill that a mother needs to learn how to do. If she's never seen it done, how is she supposed to know what to do?"

Her suggestions: Take a prenatal breast-feeding course. Many hospitals, childbirth education programs, or breast-feeding support groups give them. Read everything you can. The more you know about breast-feeding, the more confident you'll be. Perhaps most important, get help. Contact your local breast-feeding support group, such as La Leche League or Nursing Mothers Councils, or call a lactation consultant (whose services may not be free).

"What a baby needs is to be put to the breast frequently with a nurse or lactation consultant or an expert there observing the feeding," says Walker, who has helped mothers of neurologically damaged infants successfully breast-feed. "Most problems are fixable—if you get help. Otherwise you'll just quit and regret it."

Check out the breast-feeding policies and the lactation support provided at the hospital where you're going to deliver. (If you're going to a birthing center where you won't have an overnight stay, ask if there's a breast-feeding counselor available.) Many programs offer a home visit by a nurse practitioner. Choose a hospital that encourages "rooming in," where the baby is with you all the time, not kept for long periods in the nursery. "A baby needs early and frequent breast-feeding and lots of contact with the mother," says Walker.

You need to start your baby at the breast soon after delivery. You can even begin breast-feeding in the recovery or birthing room. This is true even if you have had a cesarean section. If your baby spends much of his time in the nursery, you can lose the opportunity to learn his early feeding cues. When he is with you, you can put him to breast frequently, before he cries and becomes overhungry. A screaming baby has been asked to wait longer than he can for a feeding and will often reject the breast or go to sleep as his behavior deteriorates.

When the nurse brings your baby to you from the nursery, you may notice that his little cart contains a supply of sugar water or formula. Tell them to take it away! "Babies don't need tons of food," says Walker. "If the baby isn't put to the breast enough, or is not breast-feeding correctly, a nurse needs to help you with positioning. Normal, full-term healthy babies do not need supplements if they are feeding correctly or often. When you introduce an artificial nipple, you're asking the baby to configure his mouth and suck in a way that is directly opposite the way he needs to configure his mouth to suck the human nipple."

To control the fast flow of water or formula out of a nipple, the baby has to thrust his tongue forward over the nipple hole. If he tries that on a breast, he'll spit out the nipple. Also, an artificial nipple just slides right into the baby's mouth. To keep the human nipple in his mouth, the baby has to draw it in himself. Also, the baby is likely to get more out of a bottle than the breast, which, in the beginning, contains colostrum, a highly nutritive food that doesn't flow like formula. A baby who is bottle-fed early on may have trouble switching to the breast later. Not only doesn't it work the same way, but the payoff in food isn't as great. And the less he nurses, the less milk you'll produce.

Getting off to a good start is important. Denise's experience is a case in point. She delivered her son at a high-risk pregnancy center. The nurses were busy and no one offered any breast-feeding advice. Because of pregnancy complications, Denise had been unable to attend breast-feeding classes (not to mention childbirth classes), and the hospital provided a lactation consultant only during the week. Patrick was born on a Friday night. To top it off, after Patrick was born, the pediatrician whisked him off to the nursery because the baby's blood sugar was low. There he was given bottles of sugar water to stabilize him. When a nurse finally wheeled him into Denise's room the next morning, she found that her new son came equipped with diapers, pins, and eight bottles of formula—but no instruction booklet.

"I fed Patrick alternately at my breast and with the bottles of formula, and it was clear from the start which he preferred," Denise says. "He greedily gulped down the formula and cried every time I tried to feed him at the breast. Although I saw the lactation consultant in the hospital, had the head of the local breast-feeding support group come to my house along with my cousin's wife (who was successfully breast-feeding her new baby), and had the help of my pediatrician, I never successfully breast-fed Patrick and gave up after a few weeks. To get some breast milk into my son, I rented an electric pump—in addition to buying a hand pump—and fed Patrick breast milk in a bottle. I had to give that up, too, because I found myself pumping milk when I should have been sleeping. I truly believe that all of this misery— and I *was* miserable—would have been eliminated if I'd had better guidance at the hospital."

To avoid potential problems, make your wishes clearly known before you go to the hospital or birthing center. "Negotiate," suggests Walker. "Find a friend: your pediatrician, a nurse, somebody who will support you in your decision." Discuss breast-feeding with the pediatricians you interview prenatally to determine if you are on the same wavelength. Deputize your partner to speak on your behalf if necessary. If the hospital doesn't have a lactation consultant, arrange beforehand to have your own come in. While books are helpful, few if any have the detailed how-to pictures you need to breast-feed successfully, especially if you encounter problems.

Remember, most women can breast-feed successfully—*with help*. You may even be able to breast-feed your adoptive baby, thanks to a new device that allows the baby to feed at the breast, receive milk, and stimulate the breasts all at the same time. However, do not attempt this without the help of a lactation consultant or a physician to make sure the child is being properly nourished.

Here are a few of the more common breast-feeding problems you might encounter:

■ A baby who sucks but doesn't feed. Babies are born with a sucking reflex, but that doesn't mean they know how to breast-feed. "Some babies are very good at mimicking breast-feeding," says Walker. "Their little jaws go up and down at ninety miles an hour, but they're not taking in milk. That's nonnutritive sucking."

These children need to be trained to suck correctly. A lactation consultant can help you. One of the techniques (and there are many) Marsha Walker uses is a dropper filled with breast milk. Instead of squeezing the milk into the baby's mouth, a finger is placed in the baby's mouth with the dropper next to it. Every correct suck is rewarded as it draws the milk out of the dropper. Most babies figure this out after some practice. This same technique and others help babies who have been bottle-fed, too.

"What you want to see is the baby sucking rapidly about twice per second and then slowing down to about once per second with a drawing motion on the areola, followed by a swallow," says Walker. "If the baby is taking in colostrum or milk, you're going to see a few sucks followed by a swallow. If the baby isn't swallowing, you know he's not getting colostrum or milk."

Babies who have trouble breast-feeding need lots of practice, so you're going to want to feed yours ten to twelve times in a twenty-four hour period, even if you have to wake him up. "Most babies cry enough times to be well fed, but some newborns are very sleepy," says Walker. "Their hunger signals are very different. Some babies don't wake up and cry when they're hungry. They shut down and go back to sleep instead."

■ Your nipples are flat or inverted. This can make it difficult for a baby to latch on. To find out if you have this problem, Marsha Walker recommends you do a "pinch" test. Grasp the areola—the pigmented ring around the nipple—with your thumb and forefinger and squeeze *gently*. If the nipple doesn't protrude but goes flat or actually inverts, you may need to do some nipple preparation before you breast-feed. You can roll the nipple between your fingers, use cold stimulation to make the nipple erect, use a breast pump, or wear breast shells between feedings.

■ Your letdown reflex isn't engaged. Many successful nursing mothers will tell you that the merest peep from a baby—anyone's baby—will trigger their letdown reflex, which is the body's way of pushing fat-rich milk to the nipple to be available for the baby. You know when you've engaged the letdown reflex because you'll probably see or feel milk dripping from your breast or feel a fullness or tingling. Many things can inhibit the letdown reflex—fatigue, stress, fear, interruptions, pain, all things that are common to the postpartum experience. Breast-feeding should always be done in a relaxing atmosphere. Pick a spot in your home—an easy chair, a comfortable bed—and do all your breast-feeding there. Play soft music if it relaxes you. Keep distractions to a minimum. You can even use your Lamaze breathing to help relax you (some women even say it helps ease the initial soreness that often accompanies early breast-feeding).

■ Your nipples are sore. For most women this is unavoidable, says Marsha Walker. What most women experience in the early days is normal early tenderness when the baby first latches on. The baby is sucking hard, and before the milk starts to flow there's a vacuum. Once that vacuum is interrupted by the baby's swallowing milk, the pain should disappear. If it doesn't, Walker says, you may have a positioning problem.

Correctly positioned, the baby's body is on its side level with the nipples. His head is up quite high on the breast, his mouth wide open and symmetrically attached to the nipple, taking in about one-quarter to one-half inch of the areola. You should not be leaning over the baby. One way to help you position your baby is to place a pillow on your lap, which will allow you to draw the baby closer to your breast. Place the baby on his side, with his legs curled around your waist. You can also lie side by side with the baby. Some women find the football hold helpful: place a pillow to your side and sit the baby facing the breast with his mouth at the level of the nipple.

Support the weight of your breast with your four fingers cupped under the breast and your thumb just beyond the areola. If your baby is hungry, he'll begin rooting. Just lift the breast slightly to guide the nipple into his mouth. You may need to pull his chin down with your index finger if he is not opening his mouth wide enough to take in the nipple and part of the areola. You will have to try this several times before you get it right. It will help to have a knowledgeable observer, a lactation counselor, a nurse, or a successful nursing mom on hand.

To help care for your nipples, express a little milk and rub it on the nipples and air-dry them for about ten minutes after nursing. Though some women swear by creams and tea bags, Marsha Walker says these rarely work (and forget rubbing your breasts with a rough towel—that *never* works). Avoid nipple shields, any drying agents such as alcohol or soap, and remove any wet nursing pads promptly.

■ Your breasts are engorged. Engorgement can also make your breasts sore. It can even cause a low-grade fever, and because your breasts grow full and hard, the nipples may flatten out, making it difficult for the baby to latch on. The best way to deal with engorgement is to prevent it. Nurse your baby frequently —every two to three hours. If your baby doesn't take in much milk during the feeding, express your milk. Your baby should be nursing between seven to ten minutes on each breast. Don't try to cut down on that time, thinking it will help prevent soreness. It does just the opposite. If your baby doesn't wake up for feedings, wake him up.

If your breasts are engorged, increase feedings to every ninety minutes to two hours, making the feedings of short duration (five to seven minutes). Moist heat also helps, especially if followed by breast massage. If your breasts are so full that your baby can't latch on, express some milk before putting the baby to the breast.

■ You have plugged milk ducts. Your breasts may hurt if your milk ducts become plugged, a condition that may often materialize as a sore lump in the breast. Hot compresses or showers or soaking the breast in a bowl of hot water may help, as may more frequent feeding or pumping the breasts to keep milk flowing. Massage over the lump and around the entire breast during the soaking and feeding sessions. Constrictive clothing, such as underwire bras, can also contribute to the problem.

■ You have an infection. Mastitis, a breast infection, also makes breasts sore. It is often accompanied by a fever and flulike symptoms. If this occurs, see your physician. He or she may prescribe antibiotics. You will need to rest, drink plenty of fluids, and nurse frequently. Massage any lumps or hard areas during each feeding.

■ You're fatigued. If you find you can't cope with the sleep deprivation that normally accompanies new parenthood, you aren't alone. Most experts recommend that nursing mothers nap in between feedings while the baby sleeps, a fine solution if it's your first baby, but not so practical if you have a toddler in the house. So you may need help.

A helpful friend and a supportive partner always helps, as does a cleaning person or a high threshold for dust. Put off most housekeeping chores until you're feeling a little better. You don't need a spotless house, just a sanitary one.

Though it sounds as if there's a solution to every breastfeeding problem, there isn't. Even if you do everything right, you may still not be able to breast-feed successfully. Nevertheless, you can still have a happy, healthy child. Bottle-feeding allows daddy to get closer to his baby—and you to get more sleep, so you're not too fatigued to enjoy your new family. If your child suffers slow weight gain because of breast-feeding problems, a formula-supplemented diet will cause the baby to start gaining weight. (But don't diagnose and treat this problem yourself! See your doctor for an accurate diagnosis of the problem, which can be caused by a variety of factors.) One study done at the University of Maryland found that breast-fed infants were crankier than bottle-fed babies (although they were physically healthier).

Don't feel like a failure, and above all, don't feel guilty if you can't breast-feed. Just get on with the job of being a good and loving mom. You don't need to breast-feed to do that.

## WHAT PARENTS SAY

*Be thoroughly prepared before you start. Before starting to nurse my two children I read as much as I could about the mechanisms of breast-feeding. When the problems arose (and in most cases they will), I knew basically what caused them and what could be done to alleviate them. This is especially important if you have no one around to ask.*

*Remember that your state of mind is extremely important. Be positive toward the experience. Avoid, at least for a while, people who are critical of nursing. Be convinced that what you are doing is the absolute best for your child and that you can do it.*

*Keep in mind that nursing is nature's best example of the law of supply and demand. The more you let your baby suck, the more you produce. When he goes through growth spurts and seems always hungry for a day or two, don't think your milk is not rich enough or that you do not have enough. Just let him suck and suck, as often as he wants, and soon you'll be up to par again.*

*It is not magical. Nor mystical. Only natural. But just like most natural things (such as pregnancy, childbirth, and mothering) you will benefit from a healthy dose of knowledge.*

*Heidi C.*
*Alabama*

■

*Successful early weeks of nursing begins with a formula-free home. I found this the number one rule and threw away the "emergency" dry formula the hospital sent me home with. Three friends of mine failed to stick with it during those somewhat difficult weeks because they turned to that stash of formula. Their own milk soon dried up. They had no choice but to give up.*

*The number two rule: seek out reassuring people. Your husband will probably be your best bet. Mine was there to give me round-the-clock reassurances that nursing is natural but the art of nursing takes time. Call other supportive people such as La Leche League members. I called several times and they were so friendly and gave great advice. They actually talked me out of quitting when I had an especially bad day of sore nipples.*

*Number three: keep reminding yourself of the benefits of nursing. They always outweigh the reasons for giving up. As my baby is getting older, my concern is how sad I will be to end one of the most rewarding experiences I've shared with my baby.*

*Carolyn H.*
*Georgia*

■

*My mother, who nursed all seven of us, gave me the best advice on breast-feeding: relax. Find a quiet, comfortable spot and put up your feet. Forget all your problems and enjoy being close to your baby. If the baby is fussing, sit back and let him vent his frustration, then try again. I used this relaxation method when nursing both of my children and had great success.*

*Rena L.*
*Canada*

## THE SITUATION ■ You Want to Breast-feed Twins

**We've just been informed by our doctor that our first baby, due in seven months, is going to be twins! Am I going to be able to breast-feed both of my babies—and if so, how?**

### WHAT THE EXPERTS SAY

Yes, you'll be able to breast-feed your twins, though it's going to take a lot of motivation and in the beginning, some logistical help. You might want to get a head start by setting up your support system now, says lactation consultant Marsha Walker. If you know a mother of twins, contact her and find out how she did it. Otherwise, you can turn to the Mothers of Twins Clubs, the Visiting Nurse Association, or your local breast-feeding support group.

Take a breast-feeding class through your hospital, a lactation clinic, or childbirth education programs. Read as much as you can, even if you have to order books through interlibrary loan. It's important that you know as much as possible in advance, not only to help you breast-feed your twins successfully, but to hold at bay those well-meaning friends and relatives who may try to talk you out of it.

Contact the hospital where you'll be delivering and ask them about their breast-feeding policies and lactation support. Too often hospitals take the path of least resistance, not allowing the mother and children to work out their nursing techniques in the hospital room. Rather, the babies are whisked in and out of the nursery at scheduled times and may even be bottle-fed overnight. Make your wishes clear. (See "You Have Trouble Breast-feeding at First" earlier in this chapter.)

While you're visiting the hospital, take a look at the special-care nursery. If your babies are born prematurely or are small at birth, they may be spending some time there. Ask what provisions are made for breast-feeding infants under special care. If your babies are going to have a prolonged stay in the hospital, chances are you will need to pump your breast milk. Find out where you can rent an electric pump.

According to Marsha Walker, you can count on pumping your milk eight or more times a day simply to maintain a good milk supply. You won't have your babies there to help stimulate the letdown reflex, and an electric pump is as mechanical as a cow-milking machine, so you'll need to work a little harder at "setting the mood." Find a relaxing, comfortable place, turn on some music, read a book, or talk to your husband or a friend, and massage your breasts for a few minutes before pumping. This will help stimulate letdown.

You'll need to alternate sides about every five minutes at first. In the beginning, you may feel a little nipple tenderness, which is normal. You may also feel a little crampy, which is also normal. That's your uterus returning to prepregnancy size, something that's hastened by nursing. You'll want to pump fifteen minutes on each breast, building up pumping time gradually. Air-dry your nipples for five to ten minutes after each pumping session.

Expressed breast milk can be frozen, but check with the hospital. Some prefer fresh milk, which you'll have to take to the hospital nursery daily.

It may happen that one baby will be able to come home before the other. Simply breast-feed the one and pump milk for the hospitalized sibling. You may also be able to breast-feed the infant in the hospital. When the hospitalized baby comes home, you may find he needs more frequent nursing or supplementary bottles.

If your babies need to be bottle-fed in the hospital, even if it is with breast milk, you may have some trouble getting them to take the breast. This is why it is absolutely vital for you to have the help of a breast-feeding counselor or lactation consultant, who can come into your home and teach you and your babies the proper breast-feeding techniques. Your infants may need suck training, since bottle-feeding configures the mouth in a far different way from breast-feeding, says Marsha Walker. Some babies may also go directly from gavage (tube) feeding to breast with the help of a supplemental nutrition device. And you will certainly need the support.

Even identical twins don't always have identical sleep-wake schedules and appetites. You may find you have one baby who needs to nurse every ninety minutes to two hours and another who's content to feed every three hours. Make sure both infants feed at least eight times in a twenty-four-hour period, waking up a sleepyhead who isn't nursing enough. They're getting enough to eat of you're changing diapers eight to ten times a day (that's for each!) and they're gaining four to eight ounces a week. The hold positions for twins is the same for a single infant, but you may need help at first in positioning two across your lap or in the football hold.

Try to keep a chart of who got fed when. This is particularly helpful with identical twins, whom you may not be able to tell apart right away. A chart also helps for changings and even for keeping track of which baby fed at which breast. The reason the latter is important, says Walker, is that you may have one strong baby and one weak one. The stronger baby exerts greater sucking pressure and stimulates more milk supply. That's why you'll want to be sure you alternate breasts with each child. Later on, your babies may come to prefer one side to the other. If so, they'll stimulate the breasts to produce the amount of milk they need. In the beginning, however, you'll want to keep switching them so you're assured of an adequate milk supply.

If possible—and try to make it possible—have someone stay

with you for the first few weeks as you adjust to having two babies. Family and friends can take over all the rest of your duties so you can devote full attention to your babies, who are going to take up all of your time anyway. Make sure your free help doesn't take over the care of the babies and leave you with the household duties.

If you can't get free help, ask your breast-feeding counselor or childbirth educator if any doulas are in your area. Doulas are literally mother's helpers, women who come into your home and take care of you so you can take care of your baby. An ancient occupation, it is just now making a comeback—and not a moment too soon.

Accept any and all help, even if it's offers of frozen tuna casserole or a couple of hours of baby-sitting from someone who doesn't know what she's getting into. Give yourself every break you can.

Once you and your babies have settled into a good nursing routine, try giving them a bottle once a day. This will allow your partner to take over a feeding, giving you a needed rest and him a chance to get to know his children and play a larger role in their nurturing.

## WHAT PARENTS SAY

*I had my twin girls at thirty-five weeks and they were in intensive care for a while, one longer than the other. I used a breast pump in the hospital, and as soon as I was allowed, I breast-fed them in the nursery—but I didn't breast-feed exclusively. While I breast-fed one, I'd bottle-feed the other. The next time I'd switch them. In the hospital, the nurse made me a couple of safety pins with the girls' names on them and I attached them to my bra strap so I always knew who had what last. When I got home, I continued to alternately nurse one and bottle-feed the other. Fortunately, the nurses encouraged me. I was overwhelmed by the thought of nursing all the time. I also had a son who was just a few days short of turning two. It was definitely exciting! Fortunately, my twins took to breast- and bottle-feeding right away. At night, we kept them in two cradles at the foot of our bed. The one on the right was mine, the one on the left was my husband's. When they would wake up, we would feed them with whatever means we had available! It really worked very well. If you were lucky, yours slept right through!*

*Dru Ann K.*
*New Mexico*

■

*Once you make your choice to breast-feed your twins, you should start right in the hospital, even if your babies are in intensive care. When I was in the hospital, the nurse told me I needed a good night's sleep, so they were going to give the babies sugar water the first night. I said, "No way!" We women have to be our own advocates. I started nursing my twins right away, each one five minutes on each side, building it up to ten minutes because I wanted to get my milk in as soon as possible. I nursed them individually the first couple of weeks.*

*Once I got braver, I tried nursing them simultaneously. It worked okay, but it got better once they got more control of their heads and necks. In the beginning, I'd get one on, and while I was fumbling to get the other to latch on, the first one would fall off. I needed help to get them into position. I found it helpful to prop them in place with a folded blanket rather than a pillow, since pillows tend to settle. Though some mothers nurse simultaneously by placing both infants in the football hold, I find it easier to get one in the traditional hold position, lying across my body, and hold the second one in the football hold, with his head propped across the tummy of the first baby. Otherwise, I have baby limbs flailing from either hip. Now I usually only nurse simultaneously the first thing in the morning, because both babies are hungry at the same time. Nursing individually has helped me focus in on one baby at a time.*

*I kept careful track of how many times each one ate, for how long, who went first, and so on. At the next feeding, the one who went second went first, so I was always sure they each got a chance to get the milk with the high-fat content. I also kept track of wet and dirty diapers, just for my peace of mind that they were doing well.*

*When they were about four weeks old, and I knew they were sucking and nursing well and I had a good milk supply, my husband and I decided to go out. I pumped some milk and got two baby-sitters, who gave them bottles. The babies weren't crazy about it, but it was something I wanted to introduce so I could get away sometimes. Like any mother you can get overwhelmed.*

*The other thing I should mention is that I'm eating 3,500 calories a day to establish a good milk supply. This is a key thing a mom has to do. Life has pretty much come to a standstill so I can successfully nurse. They each take eight feedings a day, not at the same time. In between, I eat and drink. I've just started swimming laps and getting out with my older son. That's pretty much my life. But my babies are thriving, and that's helped me counter the response of people who find out that I'm nursing twins and say, "You're kidding?" It can be done!*

*Martha F.*
*New Mexico*

## THE SITUATION ▪ Your Breasts Leak in Public

There's nothing like standing in front of your boss and coworkers wearing a silk blouse with breast-milk stains. What do I do for leaking?

## WHAT THE EXPERTS SAY

You're actually lucky. It sounds as if your letdown reflex is working like a charm. But leaking breasts are annoying. Breast shells encourage leaking, says Marsha Walker, so try a folded handkerchief, cut-up cloth diapers, or cloth or disposable breast pads.

However, you must change the pads or whatever you use frequently! Rubbing against a wet pad or cloth can make nipples quite sore.

One thing you might try when milk lets down at an inappropriate time is to press the heel of your hand against the nipple or cross your arms over your breasts and press back toward your chest. That should stop the milk flow.

If you find one breast leaking as you're nursing, try catching the milk in a bottle or pump it. You'll then have some extra milk on hand so daddy can handle a feeding, and at the same time, you'll increase your milk supply.

## WHAT PARENTS SAY

*This recalls a personal experience. I was my sister's matron of honor, and at the reception I glanced down and noticed an expanding wet spot on my silk suit. Hoping no one else would notice, I ran to the bathroom, replaced wet with dry nursing pads, and turned on the bathroom hand drier, which did the job in less than a minute. Luckily there was no stain.*

*Lois S.*
*New York*

## THE SITUATION ▪ You Are Being Pressured to Breast-feed (Or Not to Breast-feed)

I've had some trouble breast-feeding and my mom is pressuring me to quit. I really want to continue, but it's so hard! How do I handle this?

I'm going to be having my baby in about four months, and I've decided I don't want to breast-feed. When I tell people my decision, they look at me as if I have the maternal instinct of Ma Barker. But I know myself: I don't handle sleep deprivation well, and if I bottle-feed, my husband can handle some of the night feedings. How do I answer those looks I get when I say I don't want to breast-feed? After all, it's my life, right?

## WHAT THE EXPERTS SAY

There will always be someone who thinks she knows more about how to take care of your child than you do. "I call them the 'buttinskis,' " says lactation consultant Marsha Walker.

It's really not unusual for moms and grandmoms to subtly discourage a new mom, particularly if she's having trouble. "Many of these women discourage breast-feeding because they are trying to validate that what they did for their children was correct," says Marsha Walker. "In all fairness, many of these women didn't breast-feed because breast-feeding was mishandled by professionals. They were told they didn't have enough milk, or that they were too high-strung, which is all a bunch of nonsense. Nevertheless, your mom is watching you pouring forth milk and thinking to herself, 'Maybe what I did with my children was not right.' It becomes a direct challenge to her own parenting."

Your response requires some charity and tact, says family therapist Marcia Lasswell, Ph.D., professor of psychology at California State University in Pomona. "They are doing it out of good intentions ninety-nine percent of the time. So you need to respond that way. Just say, 'Thanks for your help. I'll think about that,' or, 'I'll ask my doctor about that.' "

In fact, says Marsha Walker, have your response at the ready. Don't wait for the postpartum assault. "It's very difficult for the postpartum mother to be empowered," she says. "The postpartum time is different from other times. She may be chief executive officer of the Bank of Boston, but a woman can't make decisions on the spur of the moment at that point in her life."

Tell the buttinskis—in the nicest possible way—that you have decided to breast-feed because:

■ "There are allergies in the family and breast-feeding helps cut down on allergies."

■ "It's something I've dreamed about doing and it makes me happy."

■ "I think this is the best nutrition for my baby. Recent studies show breast-fed infants are healthier in the long run than bottle-fed babies. They have fewer respiratory infections and ear infections."

Pick your own one- or two-line explanation that will follow your heartfelt thank-yous for their concern.

If you *don't* want to breast-feed—even in light of all this information—you need to have the courage of your convictions. It is your life, and it should be your decision. Denise's experience might help. "I was, for a variety of reasons, unable to breast-feed my son," she explains. "I had a lot of friends who had babies within weeks of me, and they were all breast-feeding like earth mothers. On the other hand, I also had friends and relatives pressuring me to quit. When I finally did, I felt like a failure. But the bottom line is that my decision turned out to be for the best. Bottle-fed, my son was as healthy as my friends' breast-fed babies, and I was a better mother to him once I started getting enough sleep. Knowing how difficult it is for me to handle sleep deprivation, I might make the same decision again. Nutritionally, I know formula is second best. But emotionally, bottle-feeding was in my best interest and my son's."

It's always been our feeling that the person who has to live with the consequences of a decision is the one who ought to make it. So, unless one of those folks giving you "looks" for deciding not to breast-feed is willing to take over as wet nurse, we'd say it's time to tell the buttinskis to butt out.

(But before you make your final decision, check out the parent advice below for an unusual compromise.)

## WHAT PARENTS SAY

*Breast-feed and bottle-feed the same baby? Ask for advice and La Leche League shudders, doctors blanch, and even best friends think you're crazy. It can be done successfully, however, with a little patience and persistence. I breast/bottle-fed both my sons (for six and nine months respectively) with a minimum of difficulty. That didn't mean I could disappear from baby for eight hours, but I could be gone for two or three hours and leave a contented husband with baby and a bottle. Like anything new, it took a bit of practice to learn how my body would react with a different situation. My first son didn't care where the milk came from and would have guzzled it out of a wooden bucket. My second son preferred me, but learned to be flexible. He weighed ten pounds at birth and exclusively breast-feeding him would have consumed most of my waking and sleeping hours.*

*Aneeta B.*
*Virginia*

## THE SITUATION ▪ You Want to Wean Your Baby

I've been breast-feeding for nine months. Although it's been wonderful, I'm starting to think of it as a burden. My daughter has four teeth already, and she bites me occasionally. Besides, I'm starting to feel trapped by feeding duty. When is the best time to wean?

## WHAT THE EXPERTS SAY

"The time to wean is when the mother or baby loses interest," says lactation consultant Marsha Walker.

Although the American Academy of Pediatrics recommends that babies be breast-fed for their first year of life, how long you breast-feed is really a personal matter. For some mothers, the baby is the one to quit first. "They're highly distractible when they get older," says Walker. "When they get up and start to cruise, they may only come back to the breast to 'touch base' with you. You might find them reaching for your fork, which is their way of saying it's time for solid food."

Unfortunately, the major reason most women quit early is because of a "real or perceived low milk supply," says Walker. And it's more often perceived or caused by poor management on the part of professionals than real. "Mothers say their child is crying or doesn't sleep, which to me is not necessarily a sign that the mother doesn't have enough milk," Walker says. "Many babies are not content and they're still fully fed. The mothers are simply interpreting this behavior as hunger." True low milk supply has a number of causes and should be checked out by a professional. (See "Your Child Cries All the Time," in Chapter 11.)

If your only reason for weaning was your daughter's biting, you could probably solve that problem and continue breast-feeding. "Babies don't usually bite until they get their uppers, and you'll find they usually bite toward the end of a feeding, when not too much milk is coming out," Walker says. "They like to try those new teeth out."

To cut down on this painful teething, you can give your child something cold to teethe on before nursing her. The cold will numb her gums. If she bites at the end of a feeding, simply take her off the breast or switch her to the other side if she's still hungry.

If you're beginning to think of breast-feeding as a burden, it's probably time to stop even if your daughter doesn't seem ready. Though her readiness might make it easier, you can probably still wean her in a week or two, says Walker. "How long it takes depends on the child's age. It goes quicker if the child is older because older babies don't have as many feedings, so you don't have as many to drop. If you're trying to wean a younger infant, who now has ten feedings a day, naturally it's going to take longer, because you can only eliminate one feeding at a time."

To start the weaning process, drop one feeding. "But weaning is a process of substitution, so you need to give the child a bottle of formula, a cup of milk, or some attention, depending on her age," Walker says. "When you're weaning, you're taking away two things: food and attention. You can't withhold both. If you give the baby a bottle or a cup, don't walk away. Stay with her and hold her as you did for breast-feeding. With an older child, take her for a walk or play with her." The attention may also help cut down on the baby's protest at having lost the pleasures of on-demand breast-feeding.

Wait a few days before dropping a second feeding "until your breasts get the idea of what you're doing," Walker suggests. "Judge when to drop the next feeding on how your breasts feel." Once you start dropping feedings, your milk supply will decrease. However, before it does, you may experience soreness from engorged breasts.

If you need to wean before going back to work, give yourself some extra time for the process so you and your baby don't feel rushed.

## WHAT PARENTS SAY

*I had to wean two at once since I have twins. I just gave them a bottle once a day in place of nursing. When I got too uncomfortable, I would nurse. I gradually dropped the nursing, substituting more and more bottles. It only took me a couple of weeks to wean the twins.*

*Dru Ann K.*
*New Mexico*

## THE SITUATION ▪ Your Older Child Tries to Interfere With Breast-feeding

My three-year-old son has been asking to breast-feed since we brought his baby sister home. Is this normal? I've been refusing him in the gentlest way possible, but he continues to try to interfere when I'm nursing. How can I handle this without making him feel excluded from this special time I have with his sister?

## WHAT THE EXPERTS SAY

Your son is manifesting a common symptom of sibling rivalry. (For more help dealing with sibling rivalry, see Chapter 14.) He may be jealous of the newcomer, who obviously makes you feel so happy and who shares a bond with you that he thinks he doesn't. After all, you have this "special" touching time together. Naturally, he'd like to be part of it.

Pediatric nurse practitioner Lottie Mendelson suggests that you need to give your older child some extra attention just for him.

You may not be able to include your son in your breast-feeding sessions. You're going to need some peace and quiet to nurse and get to know your new baby. Explain that you need some time alone with his baby sister, after which you want to spend some time alone with him. If possible, arrange for someone else—his dad or a grandparent—to do something with him while you breast-feed, at least in the early days.

If the child will be quiet while you're breast-feeding the new baby, allow him to sit nearby and watch. Since you have one hand free, you may be able to read to or snuggle with him. Explain to him what you are doing. Then do something with him afterward —take a walk, read him a story, play a favorite game. He needs to have a special touching time together with you.

To help him feel that this baby is his, too, allow him to participate in her care. He can help you bathe her, pick out her clothes, entertain her.

"Point out to him all the things that he can do that the baby can't," says Mrs. Mendelson, who has raised four children. " 'Mom's going to the store and the baby can't, but *you* can, because you're a big boy. The baby has to go to bed now but *you* don't, because you're a big boy.' He needs to find out that there's something good about being a big brother."

It's very helpful if friends and relatives don't stumble over him on their way to get a look at his baby sister. Denise always brings a "big brother" or "big sister" gift for older siblings when a new baby arrives. Ask visitors to talk to your son first, before they see his baby sister. He'll probably have much more to say, anyway.

If your older child gets enough individual attention, he should give up his interference in a short time.

## WHAT PARENTS SAY

*I did two things to prevent my two-and-a-half-year-old from feeling left out when I nursed his new sister. For one, I milked a few drops into a cup, just so he could see that, tastewise, this was nothing to envy. Then, I let him "nurse" his Cabbage Patch doll while I nursed the baby. I gave him a pad like the one I used over my arm to prevent leaks and spills from the other breast. Then I helped him into position. It was a game he could get back to a few times and that we captured on a photograph he is very proud of, but after that it was no longer terribly interesting.*

*Heidi C.*
*Alabama*

■

*When my new baby needs to breast-feed, I bring out a "busy box" for the older child. This box contains approximately twenty individually wrapped gifts such as coloring books, wind-up toys, small dolls, or puzzles appropriate for her age group. I keep the busy box hidden so she can't get to it, but at feeding times she gets to select one gift. While I feed the baby, our older daughter opens up her surprise, and because it's the first time she sees it, she plays with it for about twenty minutes—which gives me time for an uninterrupted feeding.*

*Ena C.*
*Minnesota*

■

*Our first son was twenty-one months old when his brother was born. While he never asked to breast-feed, he initially got in the way when I was nursing the baby. He quit after his dad and I began offering him time to act like a baby again, which he eagerly agreed to. We would lovingly cradle him in our arms or put him in the crib —with never a hint of shaming. We also pointed out how he could do lots of things the baby was incapable of doing, such as play with toys and eat crackers and cheese. He soon decided he preferred toddlerhood.*

*Kellen D.*
*Washington*

## THE SITUATION ▪ You Want to Breast-feed in Public

**Is there some modest way to breast-feed in public?**

## WHAT THE EXPERTS SAY

It's really a shame that a beautiful, natural act such as breast-feeding has become so unnecessarily fraught with sexual overtones. We personally believe that mothers should be able to breast-feed anywhere without fear of shocking others. The act of having a baby shouldn't carry with it a sentence of temporary imprisonment. However, we understand that many people don't have such liberal views and that many breast-feeding mothers are embarrassed to expose themselves in public, even to feed a hungry baby.

Yes, it is possible to breast-feed discreetly in public. Most mothers wear roomy overblouses and carry a cloth or blanket that covers what the blouse and the baby do not. But for more ingenious ideas, we turned to the experts: nursing mothers.

## WHAT PARENTS SAY

*While I never felt comfortable breast-feeding in the park or in a public plaza, I have done it in the car. But the best place to breast-feed is in a dressing room of a department store. It's quiet, fairly clean, usually roomy enough, has a comfortable chair, and no one bothers or interrupts you. (This is in contrast to a public rest room, which can be smoky, dirty, crowded, cramped, and full of people in a hurry.) The lady in charge of the dressing room is usually sympathetic, too.*

Lois S.
New York

■

*When breast-feeding while shopping, I made attempts to find a women's lounge in the malls and even asked to use the employee's lounge in a major department store.*

Dyanne F.
New Jersey

■

*When I was breast-feeding, I found it helpful to carry a colorful shawl or large scarf for privacy in public. I would get my son latched on and then just drape the shawl over him and over my shoulder. It also came in handy for leaky breasts, and since it was a Peruvian Indian shawl, I felt pretty stylish.*

Sheila E.
New Hampshire

■

*When my daughter was a nursing infant, I went with my mother to a large discount children's store. There are benches near the check-out area for tired shoppers to sit on, and I sat on one and (I thought discreetly) nursed Rachel. On the bench next to me was an elderly woman, who was watching me with some interest. I thought,"Uh-oh, she's going to make some remark about how bad it is to nurse a baby in public." Instead, she smiled and said it made her remember* nursing her own children when they were little. She admired my daughter's rosy cheeks and said that mother's milk makes the most beautiful babies. What could have been a disaster instead became one of my most treasured memories.

Ginny P.
Massachusetts

■

When I nurse my twins in public, I do it one at a time, since if you do it simultaneously, you're exposed belly button to neck, and I'm not comfortable with that.

Martha F.
New Mexico

# CHAPTER 3

# DIET AND EATING
∎
# The Food Wars

**THE SITUATION ∎ Your Child Doesn't Eat Enough**

My two-year-old son doesn't eat enough to keep a flea alive. He seems to be healthy, but I worry that he's not getting proper nourishment. Should I try to get him to eat more?

## WHAT THE EXPERTS SAY

No. Force-feeding your child can only result in unpleasant scenes at the dinner table (not to mention the potential for long-term lingering problems with eating and food). The fact that your son appears healthy and energetic is the best sign you could have that he is indeed eating enough.

You probably recall seeing your child gobble up platefuls of food when he was younger. He was growing a lot faster then—most likely about fifteen pounds his first year, says Quentin Van Meter, M.D., chairman of pediatrics at the Naval Office in Oakland, California, whose special interest is kids' metabolism and growth. Starting at age one (and for the next seven or so years) a child's rate of growth slows noticeably to about four or five pounds a year. He simply requires less food.

"Toddlers may eat dinner one night, and then not eat dinner for the next three days," says Dr. Van Meter. Or they'll eat a hearty lunch one day, a huge breakfast the next, and very little else. "I always ask the parents, 'Does your child have at least one meal a day that he seems to love and eat a lot of?' They usually answer yes."

These "noneaters" should be perking along beautifully when their height and weight gains are plotted on the growth curve. That won't happen if something's amiss with a child's calorie intake, Dr. Van Meter points out.

Meanwhile, here are a few tips to help you live through your child's poor-appetite periods:

- Let your child decide how much he wants to eat. Ask him if he'd like a half a hamburger or a whole one or four french fries or six, for example. At this age, your child's appetite center is telling him when he is *truly* hungry, unlike an adult, whose appetite is stimulated by habit or emotional hunger as often as it is by physical hunger. Skipping a meal or two won't hurt him. More than likely, it will increase his appetite for the next one.

- Ignore how much your child is eating—or not eating. It should not be a topic for discussion at the table.

- Limit between-meal snacks and make sure the ones you do serve are nutritious.

- Don't let your child drink more than sixteen ounces of milk a day, and even less juice. This volume of fluid, with its fats and sugars, can shut off the appetite just enough to keep your child active and happy, but he won't be getting a balanced meal.

- Put *less* food on your child's plate than you think he'll eat. Nothing turns a kid's appetite off faster than an impossibly large amount of food.

- Have your pediatrician review your child's growth charts with you for reassurance.

- Ask your pediatrician about giving your child a daily multivitamin if you are still worried about his total nutrition, although actual vitamin deficiencies are rare. The doctor may want to do a simple blood test to determine if the child is anemic—a condition that would require nutrient supplementation.

## WHAT PARENTS SAY

*When my child went through this stage, it was frustrating until I began to empathize with her. I enlisted her help by introducing her to the entire process: making a list, clipping coupons with safety scissors, grocery shopping, and even preparing (or watching me prepare) the meals.*

*Deborah M.*
*Ohio*

∎

*We have a rule in our house: if you don't eat what you have on your plate, that's okay. There will be no issue made of it. But don't ask for dessert later in the evening.*

*Susan S.*
*Pennsylvania*

∎

*Since my son's intake of food during the day barely reassures me that he's not starving, snack time is as important as any mealtime could be. I'm not comfortable giving him boxed cookies or crackers. Instead, we play "The Ingredients Game." I'll rattle off a number of choices and he'll pick and choose for his tummy's delight. We'll begin with either a pear, apple, or banana, for example, and then he'll choose a topping such as peanut butter, applesauce, cinnamon, wheat germ, or chopped walnuts. Together, we then assemble his choices in his favorite bowl or dish.*

*Dyanne F.*
*New Jersey*

## THE SITUATION ∎ Your Child is a Picky Eater

Our four-year-old daughter is an extremely finicky eater. Just when I think it's safe to serve a particular food (she's eaten it before and liked it), this same food suddenly turns her

stomach. How can I keep dinnertime from turning into World
War III?

## WHAT THE EXPERTS SAY

You can't if your expectations don't change. Nobody really
knows why a child's food preferences shift from one week to the
next—or one day to the next. But as pediatrician Quentin Van
Meter points out, "if you ever want to put yourself in a position of
total frustration, it's going to be by trying to get the picky child
to eat."

Try these tactics (no tricks!) for mealtime harmony:

- Make mealtime as positive as you can. Even if your child
doesn't want to eat, she needs to socialize at the dinner table,
says Dr. Van Meter. Most meals take fifteen to twenty minutes,
and that's how long you can expect your child to sit at the table
and join the discussion—which, by the way, should never be
about how much or how little your child is eating.

- Keep a selection of your child's favorite foods on hand. Even
picky eaters have a few that you could consider nutritious, such
as peanut butter, cereal (whole-grain, low-sugar varieties),
cheese, and fresh fruit. Make one or more of them available for
the times when she is sure to reject what you're serving.

- Don't insist that your child sit at the table until her plate is
empty. You'd gag on a piece of cold, limp broccoli, too.

- Follow the "no dinner, no dessert" rule, but don't use it as a
punitive measure. Simply state it to your child in a pleasant,
matter-of-fact way. Dr. Van Meter says it's not wise to give your
kids calories that are not balanced, if that's all they're going to
take in.

- Invite kids over who eat the foods your child won't touch.
One study of two- to five-year-olds showed that you could reverse a child's hatred of a particular food by seating her with a
few children who liked that same food.

- Don't insist that your child try new foods. If she sees them
often enough on the table, she will try them when *she's* ready.

Ask her if she'd like to taste a new food, but don't give her a hard time if her answer is no.

■ Try plain foods. Kids often don't like stews or casseroles because they can't identify the ingredients. Set aside some plain rice or pasta before you top the rest with a sauce your kids may reject.

■ See if your kids might eat their vegetables raw rather than cooked. Eileen's stepson, Sacha, won't touch a cooked carrot or string bean, but he does like them raw—and has even been known to ask for seconds.

## WHAT PARENTS SAY

*My son used to protest any new food even before trying it, but I found a way around this. I say, "We've never had this food before and I want everyone's opinion on it." Since he doesn't want to be left out, he'll usually try it so he can offer his opinion. I also found that letting the picky eater choose a food for that night's dinner helps. He is then more likely to eat it since it was his choice. I always call it to the attention of the rest of the family, too. Saying, "Drew picked tonight's vegetable," makes him feel so proud.*

*Laurie S.*
*Ohio*

■

*We have a game at our house based on healthy food. Mommy says, "What should we have for dinner? Let's see, something that's not healthy, so my kids will stay little forever. How about (cupcakes/ cookies/potato chips)?" They say, "No, we want carrots!" (Or salad or celery or whatever is healthy.) Begrudgingly, I give in—"Oh, all right." And then my son says something like, "Come on, Mom, you want us to grow up big and strong." And of course, I do, I do!*
*Weeknight dinners consist of a rotating selection of the seven or eight things I know they will eat of the macaroni-and-cheese, spaghetti, hamburger, or chicken variety. Sunday is family-dinner night: a real occasion with a formal table, candles, and some kind of elaborate entrée usually cooked by Daddy. They'll eat just*

*about anything on Sunday nights because it is our special "Family Dinner." Kids love ceremony.*

*Nicole W.*
*Connecticut*

■

*If you're worried that your picky eater will not eat what's served at a relative's house, try this. Ask your relatives to share favorite recipes with you, then prepare them routinely for your family. Before you visit a relative, ask her if she would make a recipe that your family especially likes. She will be genuinely flattered, and your child will be more inclined to eat it because you can say this is "just like the chicken I make."*

*Susan B.*
*Washington*

■

*My daughter isn't a picky eater except for vegetables. She really doesn't eat them unless I hide them—as I've learned to do—in pizza or spaghetti.*

*Jeff M.*
*Virginia*

■

*First, always have more than one nutritious food to offer. Then you know that whatever is picked will still be good for them. Second, don't try to teach the principles of good nutrition to preschoolers. Instead, talk to them about where the food comes from, how it is grown, and how it is cooked. Kids seem to be fascinated by these tidbits.*

*Sheila A.*
*Louisiana*

## THE SITUATION ▪ Your Child Won't Drink Milk

**Even as an infant, my daughter wasn't a big fan of milk. Now that she's a toddler, I worry that the cup or so a day she does drink isn't enough to build strong bones. How much milk does a child need for optimum health?**

### WHAT THE EXPERTS SAY

It depends on the age of the child. According to Joel Steinberg, M.D., director of the Weight Guidance Program for children at Children's Medical Center of Dallas, an infant's cool reception to milk could be caused by feeding her solids or juice too soon. When babies are given solid foods or sweet juice too early, they tend to fill up on those to the detriment of milk, which probably comes second in the meal. To encourage babies to drink more milk, there should be no competition from other foods.

Babies need milk more than anything else. It's the most "calorie dense" of any food—which is important when you consider an infant's relatively *small* stomach capacity and the relatively *large* amount of calories she needs for normal growth. Babies also need the high fat content in milk for the normal development of brain cells and enzyme systems. That's why low-fat or skim milk should never be used for children under two years of age.

After the first year, it's okay if other foods compete with milk for a child's attention, but a child should still drink about a pint (sixteen ounces) of milk a day, Dr. Steinberg says. It's the calcium in milk (more than the fat) that kids need at this age, and so if less milk is consumed, it's important to make up the difference with other calcium-rich foods, such as cheese, yogurt, or other milk-based foods.

If your child still isn't getting enough milk, or if he can't tolerate milk or milk products for one reason or another (allergy, lactose intolerance), consult your pediatrician. He may suggest a calcium supplement for your child.

## WHAT PARENTS SAY

*Many kids who won't drink white milk will drink chocolate milk. Start with the milk very chocolaty, then slowly reduce the amount of chocolate you add. Soon they'll be back to white milk again.*

*Debbie V.*
*Pennsylvania*

■

*My seventeen-month-old daughter wouldn't drink milk from her bottle, and trying to give it to her in a cup was even more difficult. However, she does love bananas. So now I make her banana milk, which she loves. I put eight ounces of milk and one-half banana in the blender, add about three ice cubes, and blend for about twenty seconds. My banana milk is equal to a serving of fruit and milk and contains no added sugar.*

*Gail M.*
*New York*

### THE SITUATION ■ Your Child Wants to Eat the Same Foods Every Day

My five-year-old daughter goes on food jags—wanting only one particular dish at dinner, for example, for weeks or months on end. Her latest passion is for canned spaghetti. Is there any health danger to this practice?

### WHAT THE EXPERTS SAY

Probably not, as long as her diet remains relatively balanced. Look at her overall dietary picture, says pediatrician Quentin Van Meter. Over a period of several days, is she getting a reasonable amount of protein, fiber, complex carbohydrates, vitamins, and minerals (such as calcium and iron) from the foods she is eating? Is she taking in enough calories to ensure a steady increase in her height and weight? If so, then you must ask yourself what is behind these food preferences.

Perhaps your daughter simply loves the taste of a particular food. (Are grown-ups much different? How many of us eat the same breakfast or lunch foods day in and day out?)

If that's the case, the ball is in your court. How do *you* feel about preparing a separate meal for your child? Are you grumbling under your breath while you're stirring Velveeta and pasta shells for the umpteenth time?

We have a friend who says that when she was a child, she ate a hamburger for dinner nearly every night for more than six months. Her mom used to buy the meat, make it into patties, and freeze them in individual packages. It amounted to a five-minute prep time at dinner, so she didn't mind doing it.

On the other hand, your child's refusal to eat what the rest of the family is eating could be an attempt to control and manipulate you. Dr. Joel Steinberg of Dallas Children's Medical Center says that that's a pattern you want to interrupt as soon as possible. "After the age of three or four children learn how to control certain situations—particularly mealtimes. The child might refuse to eat what's served, and the parents, fearing she will starve herself, will make the dish she says she wants. And so it begins."

But you don't have to give in, Dr. Steinberg insists. If you feel that it's time to challenge your child's food jag in a constructive way, try these tactics.

For breakfast and lunch offer your child a choice of two things you know she likes. Just two. For dinner, serve her what the rest of the family is eating and say, "This is what we're offering," explains Dr. Steinberg. "Obviously I wouldn't offer brussels sprouts for dinner, but I would try the normal foods kids usually eat. Tell her she doesn't have to eat it, but that that's all there is. Usually within a week, most young children will begin playing around with the food offering and taste it. As long as she knows she's not being forced, she'll start eating, especially if eating doesn't become an issue."

It's very rare that a child's food preferences are so limited that there is cause for nutritional concern—although Dr. Van Meter has known kids who've lived on what he calls the "thin air and Kool-Aid diet," licking the jelly off a peanut butter and jelly sandwich and drinking a glass of fruit punch, for example. Which, by the way, is severe enough to warrant a call to your pediatrician, he says. When a child's diet is consistently that deficient in all nutrients, doctor and parents need to work together to move this child back toward a more balanced diet.

## WHAT PARENTS SAY

*My daughter is currently on a bread and butter food jag. I tell her that she can have some if she eats the food in front of her first. The bread and butter serves as a treat and then she's too full to want sweets.*

*Kelly T.*
*Florida*

## THE SITUATION ▪ Your Child Is Too Skinny

**Although my son was a hearty eight pounds at birth, he's grown into a very skinny five-year-old. I noticed when he was undressing that I could even see some of his ribs. My mother is constantly pressuring me to fatten him up, but I'm not so sure that that's the wise thing to do. His appetite is on the small side, but it's generally well balanced. How can I tell if his skinniness is cause for worry?**

## WHAT THE EXPERTS SAY

The boniness you describe is not necessarily a sign that your child is too skinny for his own good. In fact, he could be one of the lucky ones: someone who will never have a weight problem.

To find out if your son is such a person or if his thinness is indeed a sign of trouble, you need to examine his growth patterns. Take a look at the number of inches he is growing each year and at the number of pounds he is gaining. Pediatrician Quentin Van Meter says that from age three to twelve, kids gain an average of four to eight pounds per year and grow about two to three inches.

It's when there's a marked deviation from one or both of these averages that pediatricians begin to worry.

Your doctor probably has a record of your child's height and weight gains over the years plotted on special growth charts. These graphs compare your child's growth with what the body does naturally in a healthy state. A child who appears very lean might be growing in height at the seventy-fifth percentile but only in the tenth percentile for weight and still be perfectly healthy, Dr. Van Meter explains. (In this example, the percentiles mean that 75 percent of kids the same age are shorter than the patient, while only 10 percent are lighter.) But here's the key: as long as each year's gain in weight and height are enough to keep your child in the percentiles *he has established*, it's a positive sign. And he'll probably remain on the lean side, growing at a rate that's appropriate for his particular metabolism—whether it suits grandma's idea of what's healthy or not.

"Steady gains are what we look for," Dr. Van Meter stresses, "and when we don't see them, that's a red flag to the pediatrician." In other words, a child who is growing two inches a year but whose weight gain has dropped off or stopped is obviously going to start looking skinnier and skinnier. If that occurs, your pediatrician will want to explore the situation, looking for a dietary or metabolic reason. He won't be concerned by a stomach virus or a flu that knocks off a few pounds. That's a water loss and will be regained quickly after recovery. It's a flat line on the growth curve—no weight gain for six to twelve months—that will cause him to look for a diagnosis and treatment.

## WHAT PARENTS SAY

*My son is slender like I was as a child (and still am as an adult). I just let him be. He is healthy and gets regular checkups; it's just hereditary. I do make sure that he is offered three meals a day and snacks, and I watch his food groups. I do not call attention to his slenderness, nor do we ritualize eating at our house (eating all of the food on your plate, desserts as rewards, specific behavior at the dinner table, etc.). We keep mealtimes informal and relaxed.*

*Angela W.*
*California*

## THE SITUATION ▪ Your Child Is Overweight

Ever since my daughter was an infant she's been chubby. I don't think there's a food she doesn't like. Now at age four, however, her chubbiness is starting to look unattractive, and I'm concerned that her weight problem will only get worse as she gets older. I want to spare her the insults from other kids that are bound to happen if she continues on this path. Can a child her age be put on a diet?

### WHAT THE EXPERTS SAY

You're wise to be concerned about your child's potential for gaining weight. It's not something that's likely to go away on its own, says Dr. Joel Steinberg, director of the Weight Guidance Program at the Children's Medical Center of Dallas. Once eating patterns develop, they tend to persist, and so the sooner you and your child learn what a healthy diet is, the easier and more lasting the adjustment will be.

Obviously we can't cover all you need to know about weight control for children in this short space. Volumes have been written about the problem; it's that important. But we can give you the general principles, plus a few tips to help you get started toward healthier weight-control habits not only for your chubby daughter but for your whole family.

The first thing to remember is that genetics play an important role in whether or not your child will have a weight problem. Research has shown that if one or both parents are overweight, their child is more likely to have that tendency as well. That doesn't mean the situation is hopeless, however. It just means that you have to do what you can with your child's environment —the one place where you do have some control.

Kids with big appetites will eat what's put in front of them, so it's important for you to know what and how much that should be. A consultation with a pediatrician is in order because unlike an adult weight-reduction diet, food should not be restricted to such a level that your child actually loses weight, Dr. Steinberg points out. The fact that your child is growing, and will be for many years, must be taken into consideration. The object is to give your child enough calories to develop normally and maintain her present weight—an amount that should be determined by your pediatrician or a nutrition specialist. Then, as she grows, she will naturally slim down. Eventually, your child's weight will be appropriate for her increased height.

If you're concerned that the volume of food you offer may not be enough to fill up your child's ample appetite, Dr. Steinberg recommends a diet that provides 50 to 60 percent of its calories from carbohydrates (complex carbohydrates are best), 20 percent from protein, and only 20 to 30 percent from fat. Here's why. A pound of fat has twice as many calories as a pound of carbohydrates. "That means your daughter can eat twice the volume of carbohydrate foods [fruits, vegetables, grains, cereal] than fatty foods [most cakes, cookies, cheeses, anything fried]," he explains. She could feast on a skinless, broiled chicken breast, baked potato, and some angel food cake, for example, and still have eaten fewer calories than if she had had one piece of *fried* chicken. The fact is, this is a diet that the whole family would be wise to follow. Besides the benefit to your waistline, a lower-fat diet can help prevent heart disease and cancer later in life.

Try these additional suggestions from the experts:

■ Invest in a book that gives the nutritional breakdown of foods (including brand-name packaged items) to help you figure out what to serve.

■ Read the labels on foods before you purchase them. It's a revelation to discover not only the total calories per serving, but the percent of these calories that comes from fat.

■ Substitute for high-fat foods their new low-fat counterparts. Mayonnaise, yogurt, ice cream, milk, cheese, bread, margarine, and other foods come in low-, lower-, or no-fat varieties with practically no difference in taste.

■ Encourage your child to get exercise (walking and cycling are good). It's even better if you join her.

■ Limit the number of hours your child spends in front of the TV, especially if that's a popular place for her (and you!) to snack.

■ Don't use food as a pacifier. It's easy to give your child food when she's bored, tired, or in need of attention. Instead, try to interest her in another activity, preferably one that's action oriented.

■ Help build your child's self-esteem by pointing out her strong points. Is she a good reader? Does she show a flair for math, art, or humor? Overweight kids need to feel that there's more to them than excess pounds.

■ Participate in your child's nutrition program with words *and* actions. It's not enough to tell her that fatty foods are bad for her, for example. Show her how important this is by limiting the fat in your diet as well.

■ Don't ban high-calorie foods altogether. There's nothing wrong with birthday cake and ice cream or with the whole family's going out once in a while for hot fudge sundaes, says Dr. Steinberg. As long as it's just that—once in a while.

## WHAT PARENTS SAY

*The tendency to be overweight runs rampant in my family. So when my daughter was born, I was determined to save her from the agonies of being chubby. My husband and I made a pact: we would never, ever make her clean her plate; we would never say, "You can have your Rocky Road pie with hot chocolate sauce only if you finish everything on your plate." We just tried not to make a big deal out of food. She finished what she finished, and if there was dessert to be had, she could have some. We also never used food as a reward or for consolation. So far, at age thirteen, she's long and lean and never gorges herself with food. I'm green with envy.*

*Mary N.*
*Pennsylvania*

# CHAPTER 4

# SEXUALITY
▪
# Discovering Their Bodies and Yours

**THE SITUATION ▪ Your Child Asks Where Babies Come From**

Recently my good friend visited us with her newborn infant. My three-year-old daughter was fascinated by this tiny baby, which probably explains her question to me later that day. "Where do babies come from?" I guess I was rather surprised by her question, since she's so young, and I wasn't sure what I should tell her. I want to answer all her sexuality questions openly and honestly, unlike my own mother, who was clearly uncomfortable with any mention of the subject. What exactly is the right way to answer this question?

## WHAT THE EXPERTS SAY

Starting at about age three, most kids become quite interested in the subject of where babies come from, as your daughter has demonstrated. And now you have the opportunity to do what your own parents couldn't—give her the information she seeks in a manner that will make it easy for her to come to you again with other, more difficult, questions.

You're fortunate that your child started asking sex questions so young. Even parents with a high embarrassment quotient should have little trouble fielding the questions that a three-year-old might ask. That's because at this age a simple answer is all that's needed—in fact, all that would be understood, says Lynn Embry, Ph.D., a child and family psychologist in Tucson, Arizona. As your child gets older, your answers should become more detailed. But for now, you might start by saying, "Babies grow in a special place inside the mommy called a uterus." And that might be enough to satisfy her at this time. On the other hand, she may want to know more. Typical questions of three- to five-year-olds are:

■ How does the baby get in there? Answer: The daddy plants a tiny seed (called a sperm) inside the mommy, where it meets with the mommy's tiny egg (called an ovum). And that's how a baby gets started.

■ How does the baby get out? Answer: When the baby is ready to be born, it comes out of the mommy's vagina. (Your child might want to know where the vagina is, so consider having a simple picture book on hand to help you out, advises Dr. Embry. It's probably not a good idea to use a doll, since they are almost never anatomically correct.)

■ How does the daddy's sperm get inside the mommy? Answer: When a mommy and a daddy want to make a baby, they get very close and hug and kiss. Then the daddy puts his penis inside the mommy's vagina. The sperm comes out of the daddy's penis to meet with the mommy's egg.

Granted, this last is the question that parents have the most trouble with. They just can't bring themselves to tell their child who puts what where without dying of embarrassment. If you fall into this category, let your child know. You could say, "I feel a bit shy when I talk about this subject with you, probably because my own mother was, too. I'm glad that you're more comfortable with it." Then to make it more comfortable for you, too, get a children's picture book that explains where babies come from and go through it together.

According to Dr. Embry, even when kids do ask tough questions, they may not fully understand the answers. (Let's face it, some of it does sound preposterous!) "Children will absorb only what they understand," she says. "If something is too difficult for them, or doesn't seem to make sense, they'll blank it out. Then sometime in the future they'll ask you the same question again, at which time they may be able to grasp the concept."

If your child never asks you questions about where babies come from, she should be helped to ask. It could be that she has gotten the message from you that the subject embarrasses you or is taboo for some reason. You could introduce the subject the next time you see a pregnant person or someone who just had a baby. The point is, you want to be the kind of parent your child can approach with *any* questions, no matter how much the answers make you blush.

## WHAT PARENTS SAY

*When I was pregnant, my two older daughters were starting to ask a lot of questions. At that time the Lifetime channel was airing a show on childbirth, and we decided to let the girls watch. They were really excited about seeing the developing baby and the subsequent birth. Now no more questions.*

*Beverly C.*
*Virginia*

■

*When my five-year-old nephew asked about where babies come from, his mom and I told him the truth. We showed him a diagram with anatomies of men and women, and one of a baby inside a uterus. It was hard to answer when he asked, "How does the baby get out of the tummy?" Then when I had to have a cesarean section, he was kind of confused.*

*Amy V.*
*California*

■

*I told my kids that when a mom and dad love each other, it causes a baby to grow inside mommy's womb. Then, if they ask, I say that God created a special way for babies to come out. I answer the specific question and any more that follow. As they grow older, I've gotten more detailed and technical in my answers.*

*Mr. and Mrs. Stephen W.*
*Oregon*

**THE SITUATION ▪ Your Child Catches You and Your Partner Making Love**

Recently, my five-year-old daughter walked in on my husband and me when we were making love and wanted to know what we were doing. I'm sure I must have mumbled something, but I was so startled I can't remember what I said. Now I'm worried that this experience might have long-lasting harmful effects on my little girl. What *is* the right way to handle this situation?

## WHAT THE EXPERTS SAY

There's hardly a couple alive who hasn't been "caught in the act" at least once by their kids. And while it can certainly put a damper on sex, it's unlikely to cause any lasting effects on the little witness.

To your child, it's just another event in her life, says Shirley Zussman, Ed.D., a sex therapist in New York City, and it's important for you as parents to treat it that way. "At the moment it happens, try not to react with any degree of shock or anger or yelling," she says.

In most cases you'll need to throw on a robe and escort your child back to her room so she doesn't get the feeling she's being rejected or thrown out for coming in at the wrong time, says Dr. Zussman. Sit with her for a few minutes until she is more relaxed (and you are, too), and let her know you'll talk more about it the next day. Then do it. Explain to her in simple words what it was she saw. "Mommy and Daddy love each other and we sometimes want to feel close and hold and touch each other." There's no need to go into any more detail unless your daughter asks another question or she seems upset in some way, says Dr. Zussman.

Sometimes children get frightened because they hear groaning or moaning noises that they don't understand. To them it may sound as if you're fighting, not playing. Again, reassure your child that this is a way that Mommy and Daddy express their love for each other.

Dr. Zussman advises putting a lock on your bedroom door for those intimate moments when you absolutely do not want company. But be prepared to explain to your curious kids why that door is only locked *sometimes!* It can be as simple as telling your child that there are times when Mommy and Daddy need privacy. Then explain to her that she is entitled to privacy, too.

## WHAT PARENTS SAY

*When my daughter was three years old, she caught us making love. The next morning, she wanted to know why Daddy was squashing me. I told her as simply as possible that when two people love each other very much as her father and I do, we show each other by getting very close and hugging and kissing. She must have been satisfied with the answer because she never asked again.*

*Cerene C.*
*New York*

## THE SITUATION ▪ Your Child Holds His Genitals

I noticed recently that my three-year-old son puts his hand in his pants and holds his penis. He doesn't do it all the time but often enough for me to be concerned. Sometimes I notice him holding it while he's watching TV, and other times he does it in the bathtub. Why does he masturbate, and what should I do about it?

## WHAT THE EXPERTS SAY

Most likely he holds his penis because it's there. If you observe your son over time, you will probably find that he holds his ear, his chin, and his foot, too, points out Edward Christophersen, Ph.D., professor of pediatrics at Children's Mercy Hospital in Kansas City, Missouri. It's only when he grabs his penis that grown-ups start to squirm.

The fact is, masturbation is perfectly normal and occurs just as frequently among little girls as it does among little boys. Even small infants sometimes reach down and touch their genitals, a practice that should not be discouraged. It's a way for children to gain a sense of their body image and gender identity, adds sex therapist Shirley Zussman. "It's also a preparation for adult sexual life, as children learn their bodies can be a source of pleasure," she says.

For the most part, it's best to be tolerant of this behavior and just ignore it, say the experts, especially if it's occurring at times of relaxation, such as bedtime or in the bath, as it is with your son. The last thing you want to do is have a long discussion with your child about it, says Dr. Christophersen. That will simply draw his attention to it and guarantee its continuation, usually for purposes of what Dr. Christophersen calls "secondary gain." In other words, your child might think, "If I put my hand in my pants, watch this lady jump. Then I can interrupt Mom's little bridge party in two seconds."

Suggesting that your child masturbate in private is perfectly appropriate, but the suggestion needs to be made without giving the impression that it's wrong, Dr. Zussman advises.

- Wrong way: "If you're going to do that, I don't want to see it —go into your room."

- Right way: "I know it feels good to touch yourself, but it's one of the things people do in private."

When is masturbation at this age a matter for concern? Both Drs. Zussman and Christophersen agree that the situation needs to be explored further if masturbation is so excessive that:

- your child resorts to masturbation rather than join other children at play

- your child spends much of his free time masturbating in front of the television

- your child withdraws when he is hurt or angry to be alone in his bed to masturbate

## WHAT PARENTS SAY

*I have explained that it is not polite to explore one's body in front of other people, just as it isn't polite to pick your nose in public either.*

*Basically, we ignore it when it's done in private. Both my husband and I have told our son that he is a wonderful little person with all kinds of different parts to him.*

*Angela W.*
*California*

■

*When my daughter was two and a half years old, she would masturbate by rubbing herself against a person's leg while sitting on his or her lap. We kept reminding her that this is a private activity that should be engaged in when alone, preferably in her bedroom or the bathroom. This problem resolved itself by the time she was three and a half.*

*Wanda R.*
*Illinois*

## THE SITUATION ■ Your Child Likes to Play Doctor

I found my five-year-old daughter playing doctor with the little boy who lives down the street. They were half-undressed at the time, and although the play seemed innocent enough, it made me uneasy. I don't want to inflict my hang-ups on my child, but I'm not really sure this kind of play is okay. If playing doctor is wrong, what's the best way to tell her to stop?

## WHAT THE EXPERTS SAY

Playing doctor isn't inherently wrong any more than playing teacher, detective, or fireman is. You'd probably have no concern at all if you saw your child pretending to bandage a hurt or take the pulse of her friend. It's when the play has sexual implications —pulling down pants and peeking at genitals—that it makes us uncomfortable.

Sex therapist Dr. Shirley Zussman says that children usually play doctor this way because they are curious about the human body and about sexual differences. Examining each other's body is one way for kids to get answers to some of their questions. "As a therapist," says Dr. Zussman, "I frequently ask about childhood memories. Almost everybody recalls playing doctor, even though it occurs so early in life. It appears to be an almost universal experience."

But regardless of how *your* parents handled it, doctors today agree that at no time should your child be punished or shamed for playing doctor. Instead, say to her in a very matter-of-fact tone that you would prefer she didn't play that game. Then explain to her about respecting the private parts of her body. Make it clear, too, Dr. Zussman stresses, that she should *never* put anything into any body opening, and that includes the rectum, vagina, ears, nose, even the mouth.

This is also a good time to encourage your daughter to ask questions that might be of concern to her, which often center around sex, birth, and reproduction. (See "Your Child Asks Where Babies Come From," earlier in this chapter.)

### WHAT PARENTS SAY

*I encourage doctor-playing, but set a limit—clothes have to stay on, no instruments in any places that aren't safe, and no touching someone else's bottom, because it is a special place that can easily be hurt.*

*Helene M.*
*Maine*

### THE SITUATION ▪ Your Child Stares When You Undress

When my child was a baby, I thought nothing of undressing in front of him. But now that he's four I'm beginning to feel uncomfortable. He's noticed that I look different from him, and sometimes he giggles about it. When should parents cover up?

## WHAT THE EXPERTS SAY

From the sound of it, neither of you is comfortable with your nudity anymore, and that's the best indication that it's time to cover up. Here's why. Kids around this age become more aware of sexual differences and more interested in exploring them, says Anne Bernstein, Ph.D., professor of psychology at the Wright Institute in Berkeley, California, and a practicing psychologist. But your child's curiosity does not need to be satisfied by seeing you nude.

On the contrary, adds sex therapist Dr. Shirley Zussman, nudity may intensify this curiosity to the point of anxiety and may be too stimulating for children to handle. That's particularly true when it's mother-son or father-daughter exposure, since it's between the ages of three and five that children are commonly drawn to the parent of the opposite sex.

The context in which the nudity occurs needs to be taken into consideration, too, says Dr. Zussman. It's one thing for your son to see you naked in the process of undressing. It's quite another if you walk around the house nude or hug your child while naked, she says. These activities might be regarded as too provocative and overstimulating for your child.

Look for signs that your child is sexualizing the experience, says Dr. Bernstein. Ask yourself these questions:

- Does your child try to touch you in places that you don't feel comfortable being touched?

- Does your child giggle a lot or blush when he sees you nude?

- Does he make comments about your naked body?

Nudity can also make a child feel uncomfortable when it occurs with the parent of the same sex, Dr. Zussman points out. "Some little boys are made anxious by the size of their father's genitals as compared to their own, for example. And a little girl may feel inadequate in comparison to her mother's body." In general, though, discussing these differences can be part of healthy sex education.

And so can introducing the idea of privacy. You might say to your son, "I prefer the door closed when I'm in the bathroom or getting undressed. Perhaps you would like to be more private at those times, too."

On those occasions when your child happens to walk in while you're undressing (as you know he will), there's no need to cover yourself in a panic. Casual nudity is just that—casual.

## WHAT PARENTS SAY

*When my child stares at me while I'm undressing, I do absolutely nothing. I answer any and all questions as truthfully as I can and continue to undress as usual.*

*Mary R.*
*Puerto Rico*

■

*Now that my daughter is five years old, she loves to question everything. When I get undressed, I always notice that she stares at my body. My belief has always been never to be ashamed of your body and to call body parts by their right names. When we undress, she asks what each part is for and I tell her. Then I ask if she understands. As she gets older, the questions will get deeper. If you don't answer your children's questions, they will find out the answers in other places. Better you tell them than someone else.*

*Cerene C.*
*New York*

■

*As long as the child is comfortable being naked and around naked parents (just in passing, not while playing), it's okay. However, once the child expresses modesty and asks for privacy (such as going to the bathroom alone or dressing alone), the parent should honor that and show some modesty with him or herself.*

*Ena C.*
*Minnesota*

# CHAPTER 5

# ILLNESS
■
# Sick Days

**THE SITUATION** ■ **Your Child Is Exposed to Infectious Conditions at Daycare or School**

I know kids are exposed to germs all the time, especially at daycare. And while I'm concerned about all the infections and viruses that run through the center, I now have a new worry. Recently a friend of mine told me that a classmate of her daughter's came down with meningitis. Now I'm afraid that something like that can happen to my child, and I want to be prepared. What should I do if my child is exposed to a serious disease such as meningitis?

## WHAT THE EXPERTS SAY

To put this in perspective, be aware that kids are exposed to germs virtually every day, not only in daycare, but at school, camp, the movies, anywhere groups of people congregate. And they catch much of what's going around. According to the American Academy of Pediatrics (AAP), children up to age two have six to ten illnesses every year; three- to five-year-olds only slightly fewer.

Little kids haven't had a chance to build up their immunity to the common bugs, says New Orleans pediatrician George Sterne, M.D., cochairman of the AAP/American Public Health Association National Health and Safety Standards for Child Care Project. What's more, babies and toddlers have little control over their bodily secretions and are constantly crawling all over each other, a combination, says Dr. Sterne, that puts them at even more risk of infection. "Little kids get sick more often because they haven't built up their immunity, but to build up an immunity they have to get the illnesses." Kind of a catch-22.

Dr. Sterne is not suggesting that you keep your child away from other kids. Most of the germs kids pick up are trivial—colds, coughs, stomach viruses. Others are not quite so trivial, but still easily managed—chicken pox, ear infections, bronchitis, diarrhea, flu, strep throat. None of these is preventable; you just have to field them as they come.

Your specific concern about meningitis, however, is indeed warranted. There's nothing trivial about this disease—it can kill. Bacterial meningitis is an infection of the lining of the brain and spinal cord, explains Raymond Karasic, M.D., staff pediatrician, division of infectious diseases at Children's Hospital of Pittsburgh. It can be caused by a variety of bacteria, but in kids the bug most often responsible is *Hemophilus influenzae* type B, or H. flu, for short.

Until recently, only children over eighteen months of age could be vaccinated against H. flu meningitis, and even then it wasn't 100 percent effective. But now a new vaccine is available that can be given to children at two months of age. It's imperative that all kids receive it, says Dr. Sterne. The peak age for contracting H. flu meningitis is around nine months, so if kids can be inoculated under six months of age, this disease can essentially be eradicated.

Whether your child has received the H. flu vaccine or not, however, exposure to this germ requires further action, and it must be handled by public health authorities rather than private physicians, Dr. Sterne stresses. "Individual doctors may not be trained in the epidemiological approach that is needed to ensure that everyone in a community is protected." And the community can be at risk because even though most kids won't come down with the infection, those who are exposed to meningitis will harbor the germ in their noses and throats, making them little Typhoid Marys, with the potential to spread disease wherever they go. Public health authorities will insist that everyone exposed be treated simultaneously with a medication called rifampin. And they mean everybody—kids, daycare center staff, and parents. Rifampin kills the H. flu bugs where they live, so they cannot infect your child or anyone else who comes in contact with him.

Aside from meningitis, another potential problem disease is hepatitis A, an inflammation of the liver caused mostly by viruses. Also known as infectious hepatitis, this disease is usually very mild in young children, involving a little vomiting and a low-grade fever. It may be completely missed—that is, until the child's parents or older siblings come down with it and get very sick indeed.

In a daycare setting hepatitis can spread like wildfire, says Dr. Karasic. If there has been exposure, the public health authorities will take over, much the same way they do for an outbreak of meningitis. They will recommend that all those exposed be given a shot of immunoglobulin within two weeks of exposure to prevent the spread of the disease.

A disease called cytomegalovirus (CMV) is commonly found in daycare centers, too, with potentially catastrophic consequences. Kids will not become sick from this virus, and most likely neither will their parents, explains Dr. Sterne. But if a pregnant woman picks up CMV from her toddler (it's excreted in the baby's urine and saliva), she may deliver a severely damaged child, much like German measles produces.

Daycare centers can do much to help prevent the spread of infection, Dr. Karasic emphasizes. The AAP agrees, stating that washing hands scrupulously after changing diapers and before preparing food or handling another child can dramatically decrease the risk of any infection, especially those that are transmitted by the fecal-oral route.

Dr. Sterne adds that parents of children still in diapers must be practically obsessive about washing their hands after changing diapers. And they should make sure that the staff at the daycare center feels the same way. To further minimize the chances for infection, examine the center for overall cleanliness, Dr. Sterne says, and make sure your children are up-to-date on the vaccines that are available.

## WHAT PARENTS SAY

*Waiting for the last of those chicken pox to finally dry seems to take forever to a youngster. Days of being cooped up in the house away from friends, outings, and school activities only adds to any discomfort. Once the fever and any ill effects have passed, why not* have a chicken pox party? The guest list can be limited to just family or even a few "immune" friends. But it must definitely be highlighted with a big white cake covered with red dots!

Karin M.
Iowa

∎

When ill, my six-year-old son seems comforted with a story of a similar experience that I or his father had when we were children. I think this sharing helps him realize he's not alone in what he's feeling.

Linda H.
Rhode Island

∎

(Note: The ideas below were written with bumps, scrapes, and bruises in mind, but they can be applied (literally) to an arm that's sore from a recent immunization, as well.)

I keep a package of blueberries in a doubled Baggies bag in the freezer for small hurts, strawberries for bigger ones. Whenever someone gets hurt, we go to the freezer to get the "berry bag." They usually stop crying before we even place the bags on the hurt since they are excited about getting their bag out of the freezer themselves.

Colleen A.
Illinois

∎

My mother-in-law gave my son a wonderful little item called a Boo-boo Bunny. It's a washcloth knotted and tied in the shape of a bunny that holds an ice cube, and it's applied to any and all boo-boos. The sight of this silly creature perched on his knee and the creative games that ensue quickly take his mind off the pain, while the ice helps with any swelling or bleeding.

Mr. and Mrs. Gary C.
Maryland

# IMMUNIZATIONS

The American Academy of Pediatrics recommends the following schedule of immunizations for all children:

■ **DTP** (diphtheria, tetanus, pertussis): two months, four months, six months, fifteen to eighteen months, and at four to six years. Tetanus and diphtheria at fourteen to sixteen years.

■ **Polio:** two months, four months, fifteen to eighteen months, and at four to six years.

■ **Measles:** fifteen months and at eleven to twelve years.*

■ **Mumps:** fifteen months and at eleven to twelve years.*

■ **Rubella:** fifteen months and at eleven to twelve years.*

■ **Hib-Conjugate (*Hemophilus influenzae* meningitis):** started at two months, repeated at four months, and then given again at either six and fifteen months or at twelve months depending on which vaccine for *Hemophilus influenzae* infections was previously given.**

* Except where public health authorities require otherwise.
** As of March 1991, two vaccines for *Hemophilus influenzae* infections have been approved for use in children younger than fifteen months of age.

## THE SITUATION ■ Your Child Gets Sick at Daycare

Yesterday, the head of my child's daycare center called me at work to say I'd better come and pick up my son (age two) because he was running a fever of 101.5. I had to cancel an important meeting that had taken weeks to arrange, but of course my son comes first. When I got to the daycare center, my son was playing quietly with some toys, and although he still had a fever, he didn't appear deathly ill. When is it safe to leave a sick child in daycare until the end of the day, and when is it truly a medical necessity to take him home immediately?

## WHAT THE EXPERTS SAY

From your description it would probably have been okay to leave your mildly sick son in daycare until the end of the day, as long as the state you live in or the daycare center doesn't have a regulation against it. From the center's point of view, however, they may not be equipped to deal with a sick child—perhaps they can't spare a staff member to give one-on-one care, or they don't have room set aside for him to rest quietly. But the most likely reason daycare providers want parents to take a sick child home is that he may be a risk to the other kids.

The key sign of a serious illness? It's not necessarily the fever, says pediatrician Raymond Karasic. Fever is part of many relatively trivial infections, including colds and other upper-respiratory infections—not reason enough to prohibit a child from attending daycare or school, in Dr. Karasic's opinion. The exception is a very high fever. Remember, for kids, a fever of 102 degrees F. or less is considered low grade. A fever of 104 degrees or 105 degrees F. is considered very high.

The best indication of severe illness is whether your son looks sick. Kids don't hide it when they are feeling really bad, so ask your caregiver to describe your son's appearance. Symptoms that may justify taking your child home include:

- too sick to interact with others

- too sick to play with toys

- frequent vomiting

- profuse (explosive) diarrhea

- certain types of rashes

- trouble breathing (not just from a stuffy nose, but rapid breathing or needing to work hard to breathe)

- fever above 102 (*any* fever in an infant)

Although a high fever may not be any more significant than a low-grade fever, sometimes it is a marker of more serious infection and should be treated that way, adds Dr. Karasic. (See "Your Child Is Exposed to Infectious Conditions at Daycare or School" earlier in this chapter.)

## WHAT PARENTS SAY

*When my one-year-old is sick, I invite a favorite person over to spend time with her (usually a grandparent). The novelty of a new person with a fresh approach at the end of the day relaxes her and gives me a much needed break to shower, do dishes or wash, glance through a magazine, or call a friend. When I'm refreshed, I can be a better nurse.*

*Sue R.*
*Pennsylvania*

## THE SITUATION ▪ Your Child Has a Nursery School Classmate With AIDS

**I've been told that a child in my son's nursery school class has AIDS. I don't really want to send my child to another school, since the teachers and the program are both excellent. But I would if I thought there was any reason to be concerned for his health. Is there?**

## WHAT THE EXPERTS SAY

All the evidence says no, and there's quite a lot of research to go on, according to the Centers for Disease Control (CDC) in Atlanta.

The AIDS virus is actually quite difficult to transmit, and kids aren't exposed to the usual routes—sharing intravenous needles with an infected drug user, having sexual intercourse with an infected person, or receiving contaminated intravenous blood products.

Parents' concerns usually center on the fear that their child will become infected if he is bitten by a child with AIDS. In all the years of recordkeeping, no one has ever contracted AIDS that way, says pediatrician Raymond Karasic. The CDC agrees. What's more, after following over twelve thousand AIDS victims and their families, the CDC says that not one family member has been infected by regular, everyday contact. And there have been no cases of a child's contracting AIDS in a school setting.

So far, the statistics are clearly in your favor—this disease plays hard to get. Of course, no one wants her child to be the first exception, either. If you still feel uneasy about keeping your son in a classroom with an AIDS-infected child, then your only recourse is to remove him and send him elsewhere.

## WHAT PARENTS SAY

*Although my two sons have never had a classmate with AIDS, we have discussed this terrible disease more than once. My husband, a doctor, has treated many people with AIDS, and we wanted to be sure that our sons had the correct information and could ask us any questions they might have.*

*We started out when they were very young explaining that they were not at risk for AIDS now and wouldn't be until they were older and sexually active. We stressed that the possibility of getting AIDS when they were older made it important that they always be responsible in the way they thought about sex.*

*We also told them that most children who have AIDS either contracted it before birth from an infected mother or are hemophiliacs who got the disease from contaminated blood. (Now, of course, that's much less of a concern because blood and blood products are tested for the disease.) We also stressed that it was not possible for them to get AIDS in the bathroom or by just playing with someone who has it.*

*We also wanted to alleviate any concerns our kids might have for their dad's safety since he was dealing with AIDS patients every day. My husband would take the boys to the hospital quite a bit and show them how he goes through putting on rubber gloves and other protective garments before examining an AIDS patient. We think our explanations did a lot to relieve all their worries.*

*Susan B.*
*Wisconsin*

**THE SITUATION ▪ Your Child Gets Carsick**

**Is there anything we can do to keep our three-year-old daughter from throwing up every time we take a trip that lasts longer than thirty minutes?**

## WHAT THE EXPERTS SAY

A few possibilities are worth mentioning, although none is a cure. Susceptibility to motion sickness is one of those conditions that never completely goes away, but people do learn to live with it eventually.

Nobody really knows when the problem of motion sickness (road, sea, or air travel) actually begins, since babies often throw up, says Patricia Keener, M.D., a neonatologist and professor of pediatrics at Indiana University School of Medicine in Indianapolis. But if your daughter has been a fussy car traveler since she was very little, motion sickness may be at the root of the problem, since most babies are actually comforted by riding in a car.

Motion sickness, for the record, is caused by any constant pronounced movement on the part of the inner ear that regulates balance, according to the *American Medical Association Encyclopedia of Medicine* (Random House, 1989). It doesn't always result in extreme nausea and vomiting (that's the worst). In its mildest form you may only feel a bit queasy or have a headache.

Here are a few dos and don'ts for car travel with a susceptible child:

▪ Don't smoke in the car when your child is present. That goes for cigarettes, cigars, or pipes. A fume-laden atmosphere aggravates an already queasy stomach.

▪ Avoid irritating foods. Dr. Keener says that orange juice, in particular, seems to be hard to handle. You might want to avoid spicy or greasy foods as well.

▪ Don't feed your child a full meal before heading out. And remember, once she's carsick, just the sight of food can make your child feel worse.

■ Seat your susceptible child in the front for long trips, since backseats seem to sway more. It may not be the most pleasant for the parents, says Dr. Keener, but it's better for the child.

■ Make sure your child can see out the window. Car sickness is known to occur when your ears and eyes are getting different messages, that is, if the eyes don't see anything moving, but the ears tell you you're in motion. Front, by the way, is better than side, and side is better than not being able to see anything.

■ Tell your child to look at a point on the horizon. Looking out of side windows usually makes it worse since your eyes must keep readjusting to the constantly moving scenery.

■ Don't focus on close work. That means reading is out if car sickness is in. Books with larger pictures and fewer words, however, may be okay. Or try a tape player with music or prerecorded stories and a set of personal headphones.

■ Talk to your doctor about recommending an antinausea medication. Even an over-the-counter preparation such as Dramamine should be discussed with your pediatrician first, says Dr. Keener. Moreover, if your child is already taking medicine for another ailment (an ear infection, upper-respiratory infection, etc.), there could be an adverse effect when the drugs are combined.

If it's any consolation, most people who have problems with motion sickness learn to adjust as they get older.

## WHAT PARENTS SAY

*I keep saltines in the glove compartment of the car for anyone feeling a little carsick.*

*Jerry S.*
*Pennsylvania*

## THE SITUATION ▪ Your Child Gets Sick While Away From Home

What should be included in a medical kit for trips away from home? And what other precautions should we take to protect our child in case of a minor or major mishap?

### WHAT THE EXPERTS SAY

With kids, it's practically inevitable that at least some medical provisions you take on a trip will be needed. Most problems will be minor—a slight fever, a stuffy nose, a scraped elbow—things you can easily handle yourself, just as you would if you were home, as long as you have a few supplies with you.

The American Academy of Pediatrics recommends taking a first aid kit that contains:

- acetaminophen
- thermometer
- antibiotic ointment
- alcohol
- calamine lotion
- cotton balls
- gauze pads
- bandages
- antihistamine if your child has allergies

Bring medication for motion sickness if that is likely to be a problem, and #15 (or higher) sunscreen if you'll be out in the sun a lot.

If your child should come down with a more serious illness such as an earache, persistent vomiting, or severe diarrhea—the most common ailments you might encounter while you're away on a trip—you should take your child to see a doctor and not self-medicate, says Michael K. Levine, M.D., a practicing pediatrician in Atlanta, Georgia, for twenty-five years.

You could visit a local hospital, he says, or ask the hotel you're staying at to recommend a pediatrician. If that doesn't bring immediate comfort, call your own pediatrician back home. He can refer you to a doctor no matter where you are in the United States. "Every pediatrician has a book called *The Fellowship Directory of the American Academy of Pediatrics*," says Dr. Levine. It lists every board-certified pediatrician in this country and gives phone numbers and addresses as well. When you call the doctor you've been referred to, simply explain the circumstances.

Dr. Levine says he sees many patients coming through Atlanta on their way back and forth to Florida referred to him by hometown pediatricians.

## WHAT PARENTS SAY

*My two-year-old daughter and I were in the children's section of the public library when she announced her tummy was "icky." She'd been fine all day and had no trace of a fever. I thought I'd just distract her by reading aloud. Never underestimate a child's diagnostic skill when it comes to the status of her stomach.*

*Before I knew it my daughter was spewing lunch all over herself, me, the chair, and the floor. When she stopped retching, I rushed Kay toward the ladies' room, leaving my purse and books behind. Thank goodness there was no line! Another mother rushed in with wet paper towels and comforting words.*

*I will never again doubt my child's assessment of the situation. If she says she's going to throw up, she's going to throw up, now. Next time, I will grab my belongings and take them with me to the ladies' room. That way you don't have to face the cleanup crew and the people whose dinners you've ruined. I'm going to add several paper towels to my cornucopia of purse paraphernalia. A tissue just doesn't cut it when it comes to major action.*

*Kirsten N.*
*Washington*

## THE SITUATION ▪ Your Child Seems Depressed

**Is it possible that my five-year-old daughter can actually be depressed? Sometimes she seems so sad that I want to try to cheer her up. How can I tell if her sadness is a normal part of growing up or if she needs to be seen by a specialist?**

### WHAT THE EXPERTS SAY

Kids, even babies, can indeed suffer from depression, a fact that surprises most people. But doctors estimate that 10 percent of children in the United States suffer from some form of depression before age twelve. Not all depressions need the help of a specialist, however. Some degree of sadness is normal in children, up to a point, says Henri Parens, M.D., director of infant psychiatry at the Medical College of Pennsylvania in Philadelphia.

The normal depressions are the reactions to the losses we all experience in life, he explains. For a child, that can range from the loss of a favorite toy to the loss of a parent—anyone or anything the child values. There could even be a feeling of loss on the arrival of a new sibling. "The child views this as the loss of exclusivity with the parent," says Dr. Parens.

You should never assume that your child is sad for no reason. No child is ever sad without just cause, he says. And even though it breaks your heart to witness this unhappiness in your child, resist the temptation to try to cheer her up, says Dr. Parens. You don't want your child to mask her real feelings, which is what you are asking her to do if you say, "Don't be sad. Please smile. I can't stand to see you so sad."

"The fact is, your child needs to be able to feel sad at times. If you deny her that, you take away the opportunity to help your child truly feel better," Dr. Parens says. "She needs to talk to you about what is making her feel sad, and you need to encourage her to do it. Only then can she work through her pain and truly feel better."

A normal depression can last anywhere from six weeks to three months. Dr. Parens recalls that a patient of his who had lost his father was depressed for about three months. "His whole development stopped. In other words, behaviors that were age appropriate and evident before the father's death suddenly ceased," he explains. "The boy moped, was depressed, clung to his mother, but finally was able to work through it and recover." (See Chapter 10, "Death—Coping With Loss.")

When does normal depression cross the line to abnormal? Dr. Parens says that even though a depression may be normal for up to three months, if your child displays any of the following symptoms for even a few *weeks*, she should be evaluated by a professional:

- Sad look. Kids with moderate to severe depression look distinctly unhappy, with smiles that are fleeting at best.

- Tuning out the world. It's typical for depressed kids to be preoccupied with their own worries to the exclusion of the outside world.

- Loss of appetite or overeating. Either one can be a sign of depression.

- Trouble sleeping, or sleeping too much. Again, extremes are indicative of trouble.

- Emotions slowed down. Kids may sit slumped over and stare at the floor.

- Weeping or wanting to cry.

- Declining to play with other kids.

- Poor school performance. This usually stems from a lack of interest or from difficulty in concentrating.

- Physical symptoms such as headaches, stomachaches, or leg pains.

Don't assume that your child will "grow out of it," Dr. Parens stresses. Childhood depression should never be taken lightly because if left untreated, the effects may eventually lead to drug abuse, aggressiveness, suicide, or violent acts against others.

# PART · TWO

# MIND MATTERS

# CHAPTER 6

# EMOTIONAL DEVELOPMENT
## •
## At Their Own Pace

**THE SITUATION • Your Child Won't Give Up His Blanket or Pacifier**

My son, who is three, has "bonded" to a ratty old receiving blanket that he not only sleeps with but likes to carry around, especially when he's tired. I've tried to get it away from him, but he cries inconsolably without it. What can I do?

## WHAT THE EXPERTS SAY

Do what pediatrician George Sterne did. Relax. "My daughter went off to college with *her* baby blanket, although she could certainly function well without it," says Dr. Sterne, laughing. "The truth is she wore it as a muffler. She still has it, and she's very well adjusted."

Transitional objects, as these beloved items are known, aren't anything to be concerned about. In fact, says Dr. Sterne, "they're necessary and they're wonderful! We all need to learn to care for something other than ourselves." Most kids establish a love relationship with something soft, warm, and furry around the time they begin to realize they are not the universe—at about six months or so. They may become attached to a blanket or a stuffed animal—whatever they find in their cribs—which serves to help them adjust to the absence of their primary security object, mom. Despite popular belief, it doesn't mean they're insecure.

Of course, at times blankies or teddies really aren't appropriate companions—at nursery school, for instance, where they can become potential health hazards—so you may have to do some delicate negotiations to wrest them away temporarily.

The one security object most parents hate is the pacifier, and that, too, calls for a relaxed attitude. Most kids, if they use one at all, abandon it by the time they're a year old. If they persist, usually peer pressure will make them give it up. "Kids tend to turn to their pacifiers when they're upset and under stress, and if you oppose them directly on it, you put them under more stress and it makes matters worse," says Dr. Sterne. You can try giving the child something else to occupy his hands (though not necessarily his mouth) or distracting him with some enjoyable activity, even a hug, which he'll probably prefer.

## WHAT PARENTS SAY

*My two boys had pacifiers when they were babies and I dreaded taking them away. Quite by accident one day, while visiting friends, my oldest boy, who was almost two at the time, lost his pacifier. We looked everywhere, but it was nowhere to be found. To our surprise, he wasn't too upset. He cried a little that night and that was it. He accepted it. When my second boy was two, the same thing happened. My third baby is only seven months old, but when she's a little older, we're going to lose her pacifier, too!*

*Kim M.*
*Texas*

■

*The rule in our house is that the pacifier and blankie stay in the child's bed. He can have it anytime in his bed, but that's where it stays.*

*Debbie V.*
*Pennsylvania*

■

*I still have my blanket. The more my mother took my blanket away, the closer I grew to it. I took it with me on each of my births. It's just a part of me. It comes out now once in a blue moon. The more parents pull, yank, or hide a piece of the child's security, the closer the child becomes to it and the harder it will be to give up. They'll give it up when they're ready.*

*Cerene C.*
*New York*

## THE SITUATION ▪ Your Child Sucks Her Thumb

**My five-year-old daughter sucks her thumb. My mother tells me it's going to ruin her teeth, but my pediatrician tells me not to worry. Who's right?**

### WHAT THE EXPERTS SAY

Unless you can actually *hear* your child sucking her thumb, or if it seems to be her favorite activity to the exclusion of playing with her friends, we're on the side of your pediatrician. "The only kids who are damaged by thumb-sucking are the aggressive ones, the ones who are really pulling hard," says pediatrician Robert Mendelson, M.D. In fact, studies have shown that dental and facial malformations occur most often if the child continues to suck her thumb vigorously after she's lost her baby teeth and is beginning to sprout her grown-up teeth, usually sometime after the age of six. About one in ten kids continue to suck their thumbs between the ages of six and twelve.

Most kids who suck their thumbs do so for security and comfort, and it's perfectly normal and harmless. In infants, that's an excellent selling point for thumb-sucking—no more wailing for a lost pacifier when the source of relief is firmly attached. It also gives them a sense of control over an important aspect of their lives: comfort seeking. Many kids use thumb-sucking as a way to fall asleep, after which their thumbs will slip out of their mouths. Even some adults use this soporific technique.

"Almost always, social pressures will terminate public thumb-sucking," says Dr. Mendelson. But very rarely will parental opposition do any good. In fact, he says, if a parent focuses too much attention on thumb-sucking, it then becomes an attention-getting device. If you need to do something, provide the child with an array of activities, especially if you notice that she sucks her thumb when she's bored. You might want to spend a little more time alone with her. She may need more attention from you, especially if she has an archrival for your affection, such as a sibling. Never punish a child for thumb-sucking, and make it clear that you realize that it's a habit that's hard to break. (How hard? Just stand at the door of any college classroom at exam time and you'll see all sorts of thumb-sucking-like behaviors, from pencil gnawing to nail chewing.)

Thumb-sucking is one of those childhood problems that usually goes away when you ignore it. If it doesn't, or if you think your child's thumb-sucking is excessive or is causing a dental problem, see your pediatrician or pediatric dentist. Sometimes thumb-sucking can indicate an emotional problem that needs extra help.

Your doctor might recommend an intraoral device that keeps the child from getting any sensation from the thumb-sucking. Or he or she might suggest some behavioral methods. Those may include teaching the child to recognize the behaviors or situations that precede her thumb-sucking and to substitute alternative comforts or a system of rewards for going longer and longer periods without putting her thumb in her mouth. None of these measures guarantees overnight results, however, so be patient.

## WHAT PARENTS SAY

*My five-year-old sucks his thumb when he gets upset or when he gets tired. My husband and I try not to nag him because he will just suck his thumb more. I have noticed that when we don't say anything, he won't do it. But as soon as we say something, he'll start sucking again.*

*Brenda H.*
*North Carolina*

■

*I do not worry about thumb-sucking. A thumb-sucker knows how to comfort himself. If the child is still sucking his thumb by pre-school, I explain that this habit must be left at home. I would not deny a child his thumb in the privacy of his room, but like mastur-bating and nose-picking, it should be kept private. You can explain that big boys and girls don't suck their thumbs in school, which the child will become aware of on his own.*

*Linda U.*
*Pennsylvania*

■

*My daughter sucked her thumb between the ages of three and six. Nothing, nothing, nothing worked! We tried Tabasco sauce, Band-Aids, humiliation, screaming, threatening, bribing, everything. Nothing, nothing, nothing worked! She stopped after going to first grade.*

*Susan S.*
*Pennsylvania*

## THE SITUATION ■ Your Child Clings

**Why do I feel like a magnet? Whenever we're in the same room, my nineteen-month-old son attaches himself to me. And when we're not in the same room, he wanders around looking for me. He's been this way on and off since his first experience with sep-aration anxiety at around nine months. How much longer is this going to go on?**

## WHAT THE EXPERTS SAY

It's not at all unusual for a child your son's age to be clingy. Clinging behavior can stretch to three and in some kids, beyond, especially when they're anxious. Rather than being a sign of de-pendence, it's actually a good sign that your child is getting ready to separate from you. "From eighteen months to about three years, all kids go through periods of clinging, periods of 'leave me alone,' periods of 'don't touch me but I want you within eyesight,' which is a kind of visual clinging," says William Sobesky, Ph.D., clinical assistant professor of psychiatry at the University of Colorado Health Sciences Center. Why? At this point in your child's mental development he has realized that you and he are both separate individuals who can choose to be apart from one another. He's walking, probably talking, and exploring his world. On the one hand, this independence is exhilarating. But it's also scary.

What you need to do is somewhat tricky. "You need to be supportive and available to the child while at the same time encouraging an appropriate kind of separation," says Dr. Sobesky. "You want to give the child the message that 'I'm there for you when you need me,' but you don't want to do that so much that the child starts to feel it's not safe to be away from you."

Don't push your son away when he clings—that will probably only make him cling more. Give him reassurance, but also seek out opportunities for him to learn that he can do just fine without you. If you haven't done this already, leave him with a baby-sitter or another family member for an hour or so. Don't overreact to the screaming and carrying on that will probably precede your exit. Just acknowledge the child's feelings—"I know you feel bad" —and assure him that you'll be back. (See "Your Child Cries When Left With a Sitter" in Chapter 16.)

Denise's pediatrician, Dr. Jeff Fogel, gave her some sage advice when she asked about how to cure her son of what appeared to be terminal separation anxiety. "If you never go away," he said, "how is he ever going to learn that you come back?"

The only time clinging might be the sign of a deeper problem is when it's excessive—the child is inconsolable when you are out of reach and sight—or if the behavior incapacitates the child, particularly if that child is over four, says Dr. Sobesky. Then you might went to seek professional help.

## WHAT PARENTS SAY

*My son has a real separation problem. When he was about two, he got hysterical if I had to go someplace. I found a solution with the help of my neighbor. I told him Mommy would be back and I left him with my neighbor for fifteen minutes the first day. The second day, I did it again. After a few days, I left him for an hour. It got him used to my coming back.*

*Pat W.*
*Pennsylvania*

## THE SITUATION ▪ Your Child Wants to Play Outside Unsupervised

**My daughter is four and I don't like to let her out to play if I can't be there with her. She gets angry with me when all of her other friends are outside without their mothers. Am I being overprotective?**

### WHAT THE EXPERTS SAY

It all depends on where you live and where the children are playing, says Dr. Bob Mendelson and his wife, Lottie, a nurse practitioner. If your daughter wants to play with her friends in a fenced-in backyard where they can be seen from a window (and someone is watching), she can probably go out without you. If they roam the neighborhood beyond your sight, or if you live on a busy street, you're right to want to accompany your daughter outside. In fact, say the Mendelsons, until kids are about seven to ten, they really aren't completely trustworthy outside alone and need you to check up on them frequently. "Children don't know that they're destructible," says Dr. Mendelson. "If a ball rolls out into the street, they're likely to run into the street after it, ignoring traffic." (See "Your Child Runs Into the Street" in Chapter 12.)

At four, your child's ability to judge what—and who—poses a danger to her is immature. At her age, it's too much to expect her to be mindful of everything you've taught her about traffic and talking to strangers when she's focused on play. "You need to protect a child. They just don't know to be afraid," says Lottie Mendelson.

## WHAT PARENTS SAY

*"Mom, I want to go outside and play by myself," said my young daughter one day. I wanted to encourage her to be independent, but stay attuned to just what degree of independence she could really handle. When she started calling me every six seconds for something, I explained to her that it was she who had insisted on being outside by herself, and besides, I was busy inside. Suddenly she didn't feel comfortable. So we sat and talked about rules, and we set a limit on how far she was allowed to go (to the edge of the lawn, to the sidewalk, not beyond the big bush, etc.). It gave her a sense of security when I explained that I could see her within our boundaries, but once she crossed outside of that area I could no longer see or hear her. I was firm and consistent, yet warm and loving. She ignored the rules a couple of times and she had to come in. Now she will ask me about going farther because she realizes it means being able to stay outside. We have also talked about talking to strangers and not going into the street for any reason. The rules and boundaries will change as she gets older and I get more confident.*

*Dore D.*
*California*

# CHAPTER 7

# SELF-ESTEEM
■
# The Big Buildup

**THE SITUATION ▪ Your Child Puts Herself Down**

My daughter is a very bright four-year-old whose favorite phrase is "I can't." She's gotten to the point where she won't try something new if she thinks she can't do it right the first time. When we praise her for doing something well, she insists she *doesn't* do it well. What can we do to help boost her self-esteem?

**WHAT THE EXPERTS SAY**

First, you can ask yourself if she's following in your footsteps. Are you a perfectionist? Does she hear you put yourself down for making mistakes? Have you somehow transferred the notion to her that unless she does something right the first time she's a failure?

Studies have shown that kids with high self-esteem usually have parents with high self-esteem, and it's not hard to understand why. We're our kids' first role models. Without knowing it, you may be teaching your daughter that anything short of perfection is not acceptable *because you cannot accept it in yourself.* You may unwittingly be telling her that anyone who fails is unlovable *because you can't love yourself when you fail.*

"If we are perfectionistic, our children will be," says parenting counselor Joanna Lerman, M.S.W. "So the best way to teach your child is to model the behavior yourself."

Look for opportunities to show your child that you can lose and still be worthy of love. Did you miss out on a job promotion? Tell her about it and explain that what was important was that you tried your best and that you're going to try again. You can do the same thing with a deflated soufflé, crooked wallpaper, or a dropped stitch. What's critical is that she see you bounce back from failure with your self-esteem intact. "Parents should show their children as many times as they can that they can make mistakes and that making mistakes is okay," says Lerman.

Failing, after all, is part of the learning process known as experience. In fact, you might want to change your language so that failure seems like a positive, rather than a negative. If your daughter has trouble learning to draw a tree, for instance, stress the fact that with each attempt she's learning more and more what *not* to do. "That branch doesn't look quite right, does it? Well, now you know that's not the way to do it. Maybe you could try it another way. Trees are hard to draw."

If she has a hard time coping with a failure, you need to help her learn to think of herself as being disappointed in what she did, not in who she is. If she misbehaves, stress that what she did was bad, but that she herself is not. Her lovableness doesn't rise and fall with every little thing she does. It's a given. Don't burden her with a label—*klutz, slob, naughty girl*—because labels tend to become self-fulfilling prophecies, a psychological trap for kids.

If she puts herself down, avoid the temptation to dismiss her feelings with a well-meaning "Oh, you shouldn't feel that way," a subtle way of telling her that she's wrong to feel the way she does, which she may simply interpret as further proof of her stupidity. Acknowledge how your child feels, but help her focus on how difficult the task is rather than on her belief that she can't do it.

"It's very important to change their language," says Linda Dunlap, Ph.D., assistant professor of psychology at Marist College in Poughkeepsie, New York, who is also a consultant to a program for speech-delayed youngsters. "When a child says, 'I can't,' reinterpret it for her. Tell her, 'You probably think that's going to be hard. It's probably going to take a lot of work. You're right. So let's go to it.' "

While some praise for a job well done is perfectly acceptable—necessary, in fact—try to avoid overpraising a child. Most children realize on some level that their little drawings are not museum quality and that they are not "the smartest little girl in the world." Not only do you come off as insincere—a serious breach of parent-child trust—the child may interpret your praise as expectation: "I expect you to paint perfect pictures. I expect you to be the smartest little girl in the world."

Some of the most credible praise a child can receive is praise given behind her back, suggests Lerman. If your daughter brings home a particularly nice drawing from nursery school, make sure she's within earshot in another room when you give daddy a call to tell him about it.

And perhaps the best praise you can give a child is respect for her opinion and abilities. Your aim as a parent is to supply your child with what she needs to build her self-esteem, what Joanna Lerman calls the "three Cs": confidence, capability, and control. You can do this by giving the child choices—as simple as allowing her to pick out her clothes or choosing a bedtime routine. You can also set her up for success. For example, buy clothes that are easy to put on and shoes that fasten with Velcro to make it possible for her to get dressed all by herself—which is especially important for a handicapped or developmentally delayed child. Pick a simple recipe and guide her through it (one in which eggs need to be cracked is a sure kid-pleaser). "Anytime you give a child power it makes her feel wonderful," says Lerman. In fact, the four most precious words your child can utter aren't "I love you, Mommy" but "I did it myself."

Toddlers are particularly vulnerable to wounded self-esteem, especially when they reach the stage, around the age of two, when they're struggling to achieve some control over their lives, usually by wielding the ubiquitous word "No!" You can imagine how easy it is to lose self-confidence when you see that all your well-meaning attempts to become a powerful, independent individual are getting on everybody's nerves.

## WHAT PARENTS SAY

*When either of my children puts himself down, I say, "Please don't say that about someone I love so much."*

*Debbie V.*
*Pennsylvania*

∎

*Instead of passively saying "Good boy" to my four-year-old for everything he does well, I comment on the action itself. "Sensational face-washing!" "Excellent coloring job." "I couldn't have cleaned up that room better myself—marvelous work!" He beams and prides himself in every task, not to mention that it's increasing his vocabulary. He's mastered adjectives and the art of praise. He now tells me, "Terrific meal, Ma!" or "You look fantastic in that dress!" Which has boosted* my *self-esteem.*

*Wendy M.*
*Massachusetts*

■

*One thing in particular has been a favorite "esteem-booster" with our four-year-old daughter. When her usual nighttime routine is over, we do Proud Things, as we call it, as she snuggles into bed. I quietly tell her six or ten things she did that day that made me feel proud of her. This could be anything, big or small, that would make her feel good about herself. But no matter what kind of day we had, I don't mention any of the frustrating things that she may have done. Then, at the end, I'll say, "But most of all, I'm proud of you for being the very best you that you can be." She loves hearing it. And both of us feel good, even on those "trying" days.*

*Jeanne P.*
*Washington*

■

*Our two-and-a-half-year-old wanted so much to be able to tie her shoes, and when she couldn't, she would become angry. We explained to her how proud we were that she worked so hard and wanted to, but that most kids needed to be five before they could tie their shoes. It was amazing how much pressure was taken off her when she understood why she couldn't.*

*Vickie R.*
*Missouri*

## THE SITUATION ▪ Your Child Shows Off

My five-year-old son is a show-off. He does all kinds of goofy things for attention. Worse, he brags about himself to his friends, and they can't stand him anymore. We've tried giving him our full attention when he demands it, we've tried talking to him about it, and now we're yelling at him out of impatience and frustration. But we're beginning to think he's doing this because he doesn't feel particularly proud of himself, and that makes us feel as if we've failed him in some way.

## WHAT THE EXPERTS SAY

A child who constantly shows off is looking for positive attention, some confirmation from the outside world that he is worthwhile—something he may not believe. However, if he's seriously attention starved, he'll accept negative attention, too. As long as he can hold on to the spotlight, he can think he's important. In the long run, the negative attention the show-off receives only erodes his wounded self-esteem further. Scolding or punishing a child for bragging or making a spectacle of himself simply feeds his negative self-image.

What psychologist Linda Dunlap, Ph.D., suggests is that you start giving your child positive attention when he's not showing off. In other words, "catch" him being good. Praise him when you see him perfecting a soccer kick, focusing on his effort rather than his results. Encourage him in those skill areas where he shows some ability or where you see him putting a lot of energy. It's helpful to children with self-esteem problems to know you place as high a value on trying as on succeeding.

Give him the confirmation of his worth that he's seeking, but for real accomplishments and effort. As with all children whose self-esteem is diminished, don't use your love as barter for good behavior or superlative accomplishment.

Don't discourage the occasional self-congratulatory announcement. In fact, that's the perfect opportunity to teach your child that not only is it good to be proud of his accomplishments, but that he can pass that proud feeling on to others by paying them compliments when they do something well. "It's a good social skill to be able to compliment others," says parenting counselor Joanna Lerman. "As soon as a child is able to vocalize how proud he is of himself, he can also understand that it's lovely to give someone else a compliment. People who give other people compliments, who find the good in other people, don't seem like they're bragging when they compliment themselves. In fact, it makes it easier for others to accept what's good in them."

## THE SITUATION ▪ Your Child Shows Signs of Racism

**My son, who is five, goes to school with kids of all races. In fact, his best friend in the neighborhood is a black child (we're white). One day, while my son and his friend were playing at our house, my son got angry and told him he wouldn't play with him anymore because he was black and "black is dirty." I was shocked. We're not racist—a miracle, since our parents are quite prejudiced—and I don't want my son to grow up with those attitudes. What can we do?**

### WHAT THE EXPERTS SAY

Unfortunately, research has shown that even preschool children may become prejudiced, not simply as the result of imitating their parents or other loved ones but because they are accurate barometers of prevailing social attitudes. A recent survey indicated that more than half of all Americans think we live in a racist society. How can we protect our children from their world?

One way, suggests Louise Derman-Sparks, Ph.D., who teaches human development at Pacific Oaks College in Pasadena, California, and is an expert on bias in young children, is to use moments such as you experienced as an opportunity to teach your child about racism and tolerance and to pass along your values. "I think that with four- and five-year-olds, the first thing we need to do is make it really clear that we don't like it," says Dr. Derman-Sparks, who has developed a curriculum for teaching young children to resist bias. "Tell them that what they said was hurtful, that it's not okay to say it in your house. This gives them a concept that will trigger empathy, which is something we want four- and five-year-olds to develop."

Remind your child of something hurtful someone said to him and discuss how he felt about it. Ask him to explain to you why he said what he did to his friend. Point out to your son that he was angry with his friend not because of the color of his skin but because he wanted the Matchbox truck or to go first at Uncle Wiggily. That will help him sort out the real issues of their argument from the insult.

It may also be helpful to go to the library and check out some age-appropriate books on black history and culture, or to peek in on the multicultural neighborhood of "Sesame Street" and talk with your child about how people of all races and cultures can live together.

By the time your child is four or five, he has probably already experienced biases directed against aspects of his own identity, says Dr. Derman-Sparks. He probably won't find it difficult to understand why it's wrong to make fun of people because of the color of their skin if someone has poked fun at his red hair or teased him about his skinny legs.

These same suggestions apply if the child's bias is against any other race or culture, or if the child holds sexist attitudes, such as "Boys can't play house" or "Girls can't be doctors." Between the library and television, you can expose your child to the delights of cultural and sexual diversity, even if you don't live in an integrated neighborhood.

Of course, living in an integrated neighborhood is one of the best learning opportunities. But if you don't live in one, look for other ways to expose your child to other cultures, from museums to shopping malls.

Transmit your values to your child now, while you are still the center of his universe. In a short while, the world will lure him away from you, and you want to make sure he's inoculated against the worst of its influences.

## WHAT PARENTS SAY

*One Christmas my mother gave my three-and-a-half-year-old daughter a black Cabbage Patch doll. I was elated and asked if she loved her new baby doll, to which she replied excitedly, "Grandma knows I have to have different color baby dolls because real babies are different colors."*

*Debi S.*
*South Carolina*

■

*We took the kids with us when visiting our black friends. In general, we think it's best to expose them early to people of other races—not at a distance but in as close or familylike a context as possible.*

*Jerry S.*
*Pennsylvania*

■

*When one of my kids first noticed that people come in different shapes and sizes and colors, it gave me the opportunity to get out the globe and tell them of the places their grandparents and great-grandparents were born: Germany, Sweden, Scotland, and Wales. Then we located the places other people's relatives were born: your friend's parents were born in Mexico, etc.*

*Lori A.*
*California*

■

*When my son said he liked the light children in his class better than the dark children, I told him that melanin in your skin determines how light or dark it would be and the child has nothing to do with it. I told him that melanin is also responsible for his freckles and said, "You wouldn't like it if somebody wouldn't play with you because you have freckles, would you?" He said, "Oh, no, I can't help having freckles. They won't come off." He said that his best friend doesn't like dark children. I told him that his best friend is wrong and that sometimes even teachers can be wrong.*

*Kathy C.*
*Delaware*

## THE SITUATION ■ Your Child Is Shy

**My three-year-old daughter is terribly shy. Will she outgrow this?**

## WHAT THE EXPERTS SAY

She may. About 93 percent of the population acknowledges being shy at one time or another. Studies done by Harvard researcher Jerome Kagan, Ph.D., have also shown that about 10 to 15 percent of all children are shy, while about 10 to 15 percent on the other end of the spectrum tend to be quite sociable. About a quarter of the shy kids don't grow up to be shy, and about a quarter of the sociable children become more shy as they get older. Dr. Kagan believes there is a genetic component to shyness —if you are shy, there's a greater chance that your child will be —but the figures suggest there's a lot of room for environmental influence.

In fact, says Lynne Henderson, one of the founders of the Palo Alto Shyness Clinic in Menlo Park, California, temperamentally shy children whose parents nag and pressure them to be outgoing tend to become more inhibited and self-conscious, as do children who are raised in a critical atmosphere, where everything from how they dress to how they speak is scrutinized. Kids who have an older, dominant sibling who bullies them may also become withdrawn.

But you can help your child make the most of her temperament. First, says Henderson, give up the notion that there's something pathological about shyness. It's only a problem if it significantly interferes with a child's life. "When ninety-three percent of the population acknowledges being shy, shyness is actually the norm," she points out.

You should never call attention to a child's shyness. It's natural, too. If she averts her eyes from strangers, don't explain apologetically, "Oh, she's just shy." Don't label your child, and don't let anyone else label her. If she hears that she's shy often enough, she'll think of shyness as being integral to her identity.

Shyness experts have found that a child's shyness tends to diminish the more successful encounters she has with other children. If you're going to enroll your child in school, make sure her teachers know how to handle shy children so that she's encouraged but never pressured to join in when she's hanging back. Many experienced teachers will partner a shy child with an outgoing one in class projects (some shy kids even seek out more outgoing friends to help ease them through social situations). You will probably need to spend more time with your child in her new school than most parents (the same goes for any social setting for these youngsters). "Stay, chat with other parents, hang out a little bit until the child gets comfortable," says Henderson.

If school isn't in the picture, try to organize a play group with other mothers and children so your child can mingle with others with you still in sight.

You can encourage your child to express herself by listening to what she thinks and feels. When you talk to her about school or a play date, ask her, "Did you have fun? What did you enjoy the most?" so she can prolong her good feelings about the experience. Many parents tend to want to know "How did you do?" which forces the child to compare herself with other children, something you want to avoid.

Parents who themselves are or were shy need to work at avoiding being either overprotective or pressuring in their well-meaning effort to spare their child the pain they felt as a childhood wallflower.

And don't underestimate the ingenuity or resilience of shy people, who often overcompensate for their natural introversion, sometimes by hanging on to the coattails of an outgoing friend or by developing a sense of humor. Writer, radio performer, and chief historian of Lake Woebegon, Minnesota, Garrison Keillor, turned his shyness into a career with the help of his fictitious Powdermilk Biscuits ("which help the shy person stand up and be counted").

## WHAT PARENTS SAY

*Give the child a lot of chances to interact with other children. Play groups and preschool are important building blocks. Invite one or two other children to your home and have the shy child pour drinks and pass out cookies. Get the child involved in out-of-school activi-*

*ties they may show an interest in so they will meet other children and become more confident.*

*Linda U.*
*Pennsylvania*

■

*On the morning of kindergarten roundup, I could see my daughter growing more and more nervous as she waited for her appointment time. I suggested that we help pass the time by working together to make a simple gift for her teacher-to-be, who would be at the roundup. The project helped take her mind off her fears, and when roundup time rolled around, she was so excited about presenting the gift to the teacher that she almost forgot to be shy; she did just fine.*

*Mary W.*
*Kansas*

■

*My daughter has no problem leaving me and going to friends' houses or to school, but has trouble talking to anyone outside of our immediate family. I have helped her talk to children from school by inviting them to our house, then playing games with them. I keep a list of "New People I Talk To" where I write down the name of anyone to whom she speaks for the first time. We also have little assignments, such as asking for stamps at the post office and placing her own order at a fast-food place. We keep a chart on which my daughter loves to put stars and have a list of rewards for her to choose from when she earns it.*

*Sandy B.*
*South Carolina*

# CHAPTER 8

# FEARS

**▪**

# Real and Imagined

**THE SITUATION ▪ Your Child Is Terrified of Bugs and Animals**

I can't recall my daughter's having had a bad experience with a bug or an animal, but she is terrified of both. She'll scream at the mere sight of either, leaping into my arms. How can I help her be less afraid of these harmless creatures?

## WHAT THE EXPERTS SAY

Fear of bugs, animals, the dark, loud noises, and storms is extremely common in young children and will appear at various times as kids mature. "A child who hides from the vacuum cleaner at one year of age or dreads the dark at two may be afraid of ghosts at four and worry about nuclear war at twelve," say Donna Wittmer, Ph.D., and Carol S. Crouthamel, M.S.W., in an article from the September 1986 issue of *Contemporary Pediatrics*, a medical journal for pediatricians.

For most children, adds Cynthia G. Last, Ph.D., professor of psychology at Nova University in Fort Lauderdale, Florida, 80 to 90 percent of those fears are transitory, disappearing as the kids get older. That's a reassuring thought for parents caught up in their child's current bugaboo.

About 50 percent of children who have a fear of animals will have had an actual traumatizing experience, says Dr. Last, such as having been nipped by a dog, for example, or scratched by a cat. Whether the fear is real or imagined, it is handled the same way—exposure to the feared object a little at a time.

Depending on how frightened your daughter is, you may need to start the exposure with a picture of the feared object, advises Dr. Last. Look for books with lots of illustrations or photos that also teach kids something about the bug or animal in question. You could also try using a cute stuffed replica and then move on to a movie featuring the animal or bug in the starring role.

Next graduate to the real thing, but at a distance, Dr. Last cautions. You could stand on the sidewalk and point out the friendly neighborhood collie from two blocks away. A few days later, go out to see the collie from one block away. Slowly decrease the distance between your child and the feared animal. Eventually, your child may even become friends with the dog, says Dr. Last, but don't be disappointed if she doesn't. Something once feared may never be loved, but simply tolerated.

If your child's fears continue or worsen—that is, she now refuses to go out in the street for fear of meeting up with an animal or bug—it may be time for a consultation with a psychologist. Fears are normal, but not when they cause so much distress that they encroach on normal functioning.

## WHAT PARENTS SAY

*My daughter had an intense fear of spiders. I rented the video* Charlotte's Web *and explained how spiders are very nice and friendly. Now when she goes outside, she actually looks for spiders so she can talk to Charlotte.*

*Cheri M.*
*New Jersey*

■

*When my kids showed a fear of animals, I took them to a petting zoo, but we didn't go inside right away. We stood outside and watched while others went in. Eventually, we went inside, too, when my children said they were ready.*

*Jerry S.*
*Pennsylvania*

## THE SITUATION ▪ Your Child Is Afraid of Monsters

My three-year-old daughter insists there's a monster under her bed and another one in her closet. Bedtime has become a nightmare. How can I make the "monsters" go away?

## WHAT THE EXPERTS SAY

There are two ways to approach this problem—acknowledge that the monsters are there and give your child ammunition to fight them with, or reassure your child that there are no such things as monsters. The method you use depends on which you think will work for your child, says Michael K. Levine, M.D., a pediatrician in Atlanta, Georgia.

Fear of monsters most commonly occurs in kids between the ages of three and five. At that age kids have developed a rich imagination, generally a source of pride to parents, but not when little Sarah fantasizes about horrific creatures lurking under her bed or in the corners of her room. Movies and television shows may encourage her already overactive imagination.

Young children believe that those magical creatures exist because they haven't quite learned to distinguish between fantasy and reality, say Donna Wittmer, Ph.D., and Carol S. Crouthamel, M.S.W., in *Contemporary Pediatrics*. Which leads to the first of the possible solutions stated above. Since these monsters are your child's magical creations, give her some magic of her own to protect herself with. Dr. Wittmer and Carol Crouthamel suggest the following:

▪ Let your child keep a flashlight under the pillow. It can be used to examine every corner of her room and reassure her that no monsters are there.

▪ Give your child a spray bottle with "pretend water" in it. She can make the creature disappear by pretending to spray it.

▪ Have your child tell the monster, "I'm the boss here, and I know you're not real!"

▪ Encourage your child to draw a picture of the monster and say to it, "I'm mad at you." Then have her tear up the picture and throw it away.

■ Give your child a list of other things she can do if she should become frightened, such as turning on the radio, playing favorite music on her cassette player, or turning on the light.

Dr. Levine adds that a stuffed animal such as a teddy bear can also act as protection against the monster.

What if you have a child who doesn't buy these routines? It can happen, says Dr. Levine. All of these methods for removing the monster may merely confirm its existence, thus frightening your child even more. In that case, you might try the second method— the truth. Reassure her that there are no such things as monsters. You might say to her, "Mommy and Daddy love you so much that we would never let anything hurt you." Talk to her about imagination, and how that's the only place where monsters live. Therefore, if she has the power to think of them, she also has the power to make them go away.

## WHAT PARENTS SAY

*I placed a lighted fish aquarium in my children's bedroom in lieu of a night-light, leaving their self-esteem intact. I also remind them of how creative they are that their imaginations can think of these things. They often suggest drawing or painting their "monsters," sometimes making them look humorous.*

*Deborah M.*
*Ohio*

■

*Our living room has several teddy bears I have collected. They have become part of our family, and some have become our children's friends. Whenever a problem arose, our son would ask if we could talk to his friends. Playing the role of one of the friends, I was able to respond by pretending to know the incident and help him work through the event. Listening to small talk with teddy bears has helped us understand and grow and dispel tiny tears and fears.*

*Martha F.*
*Indiana*

**THE SITUATION ▪ Your Child Is Afraid of the Doctor or Dentist**

At age two, my son has suddenly grown fearful of his pediatrician. As we arrive, he starts to whimper, which escalates to a full howl by the time we get inside. What can I do? Is this what I can look forward to when I take him to see the dentist?

## WHAT THE EXPERTS SAY

You can't blame your child for developing a fear of the doctor if he associates a visit there with pain. And let's face it, for the first few years at least, your child will be receiving shots and will be subjected to all kinds of intrusive examinations, experiences that don't exactly foster a desire for a return trip. There are ways, however, to help him (and you) get through these trying times.

Handle a trip to the doctor matter-of-factly, advises Patrick Burke, M.D., Ph.D., interim director of the behavioral sciences division of Children's Hospital of Pittsburgh. In other words, it's just another place we go to now and then. Review with your child exactly what is going to happen at each visit. If it's just weighing, measuring, and a few gentle pokes, than say so. You can even role-play the situations he might encounter there. Use dolls or stuffed animals to show how the doctor might look in his throat or tug at his ears.

If the visit is likely to include a shot, explain what that might be like. If it's going to hurt, tell him so, says Dr. Burke, but don't blow it out of proportion. Explain to him that a needle is a small hurt and the pain ends quickly. Remind him that you will be there to comfort him.

For most little children, a trip to the dentist should be easier than one to the pediatrician—no needles lurking here, for the most part. Kids should have their first visit to a dentist by the time they're fourteen months old, says Heber Simmons, D.D.S., past president of the American Academy of Pediatric Dentistry. That's usually to familiarize the child with going to the dentist and to counsel parents on the proper care of their baby's teeth. A ride on the chair doesn't hurt, either.

A simple explanation for a first-time dentist visit works best: "We're going to the dentist and he's going to count your teeth, brush them, and show you how the chairs work." Let the dentist explain everything else, says Dr. Simmons.

If you have a personal fear of the dentist, keep it to yourself. Many children who develop a fear of the dentist do so because a parent, sibling, or friend has told them a horror story. The fact is, dental techniques have come a long way since those painful drills and novocaine needles of your childhood. Good dental care should prevent most serious tooth problems from developing in the first place.

## WHAT PARENTS SAY

*When my daughter was one and a half years old, she was terribly afraid of the doctor. After her second-year checkup I purchased a child's doctor's kit and the book* Big Bird Goes to the Doctor. *We started to read the book a few times each week, relating it to our own doctor's office. The doctor's kit became one of the most popular toys in our home. At my daughter's next visit to the doctor, the change was unbelievable! She sat quietly for a checkup and even received an immunization without a flinch!*

*Kelly C.*
*New Hampshire*

■

*I drew pictures of the dentist's office equipment and explained what the dentist would do. Then my daughter and I counted her teeth by looking in the bathroom mirror. The first appointment of the day is best—no chance to get nervous while waiting. Afterward I got her a coloring book (rather than food or candy) for her grown-up behavior.*

*Deborah M.*
*Ohio*

■

*On our pediatrician's suggestion, we decided it was best that we all go to the same dentist. This has been very successful for us. I began to take them with me to the dentist when they were two years old. They would sit on my lap while I had my teeth cleaned, and the dentist would talk to them about what he was doing. I took them for their first checkups at three years of age. They simply went up and down in the chair and the dentist looked in their mouths.*

*Melissa M.*
*Oregon*

## THE SITUATION ▪ Your Child Is Frightened by Some Men and Women

My one-year-old daughter is generally outgoing, but a few people seem to frighten her. One of them, unfortunately, is my father. Is there some way to figure out what is scaring her about these folks?

## WHAT THE EXPERTS SAY

Take a look at the nurturing styles of the people whom your daughter fears. Men and women often handle babies quite differently, says neonatologist Patricia Keener. Men tend to be much more intense in their stimulation. When they talk to a baby, their voices are louder. They tend to play games that involve more sudden or stimulating motions.

Women are usually gentler in their touch, tone, and handling of babies. Of course, Dr. Keener says, you will see men and women whose styles are the reverse of the above. The point is, some babies are more sensitive to intense stimulation.

This wariness around unfamiliar people, sometimes called stranger anxiety, can often be seen by the time a baby is six months old, Dr. Keener says, and tapers off as the child gets older. "When words become important to your child, when she can begin to express herself and modify an adult's behavior in some meaningful fashion, when she can fend for herself in some way other than by withdrawing with her body or by crying, then you will see this fearfulness subside."

Until that time (which might not occur until your child is five or six years old) here are some coping strategies to try with your father or anyone else who happens to frighten your daughter:

- Reassure your father that your daughter's behavior is normal and is in no way a judgment against him.

- Help your father to recognize the behaviors that seem to frighten your daughter.

- Have your father not interact directly with your daughter when he first sees her. You could even place her in an infant seat near but not directly facing your father. Then gradually move the seat closer so she can get accustomed to hearing his voice and seeing his face.

- Tell your father not to make eye contact right away. Dr. Keener says that often the people children fear most have a very confrontational style. They want eye contact, a high intensity of emotions. They want the child to be giggling all the time, entranced by the interaction. Although some kids can handle that, many can't, and they respond by looking or turning away, and by crying.

- Suggest your father try behaviors that you know your daughter likes and responds to. See if your daughter is willing just to sit quietly in your father's lap, for example. Your father needs to follow your daughter's lead. Eventually, her curiosity will take over and the anxiety should recede.

One final note: If your daughter sees your father infrequently, he may need to repeat this procedure the next few times he visits.

## WHAT PARENTS SAY

*Obtain up-to-date snapshots of your relatives. Point to each person's face, smile, and say "Uncle Russell," just as you would identify a picture in a book. Store the snapshots on a low shelf so your child can reach them easily. Take them with you when you visit your families so that your child will link them with the real people. If you have photos of the relative together with your child, so much the better.*

*Susan B.*
*Washington*

■

*Neither of my children can handle people who instantly sweep them into their arms kissing, hugging, pinching cheeks. I suggested to their grandpa that he essentially ignore them for the next few visits. In each case, by the third visit they were climbing onto his lap and continue to do so.*

*Jill J.*
*Pennsylvania*


## THE SITUATION ▪ Your Child Screams When Getting a Haircut or Buying Shoes

**The way my three-year-old son carries on when getting a haircut or buying shoes, you would think he was being tortured. What is he afraid of, and what can I do to help him get over it?**

### WHAT THE EXPERTS SAY

Think back. Has your child always had a problem adjusting to new situations? Was he finicky or colicky as an infant? Has the unknown always held a certain amount of fear for him? According to psychology professor Cynthia G. Last, Ph.D., children born with this type of temperament are most likely to be fearful of even innocuous occasions.

It's the novelty of the situation that causes the problem, she explains. Your child needs to be repeatedly exposed to the situation that's frightening him. You could practice putting various shoes on your child and then taking them off in a pretend game of shoe store, suggests Dr. Last. Likewise, you could play barber or beauty parlor. This kind of role-playing helps give your child some feeling of control or mastery over the situation.

It's best not to call your child a crybaby or to belittle his fears or humiliate him in any way, adds psychiatrist Dr. Henri Parens. Instead, comfort your child through his fearfulness, and tell him that you would never let any harm come to him. You might also talk about how handsome he will be after his haircut or how beautiful he'll look in his new shoes.

## WHAT PARENTS SAY

*Buy shoes from a catalog. If the fit is wrong, return shoes and reorder from a catalog again.*

*Jerry S.*
*Pennsylvania*

■

*We let our son sit with Daddy in the barber's chair while Mamma tried to comfort. It did not do much good, however, and he was in hysterics after a few minutes. We decided to quit while we were ahead and both his ears were intact and to try again later.*

*The next time Daddy had his hair cut first, with our son in his lap. Our son followed the proceedings closely. There were still whimpers and fusses, but we got through a whole haircut. Since then we have had no problems, though he was allowed to sit in Daddy's lap for the next few times.*

*Heidi C.*
*Alabama*

■

*We combine the haircut with a trip to the ice cream store, and we focus on the cones.*

*Kathy C.*
*Delaware*

■

*My son, age four and a half, has received haircuts from me only— with a bribe of candy for cooperation. He is afraid of the barber for reasons unknown. I plan to cut his hair until he can face the barber, and I predict it will take another year. He will grow into acceptance, and I prefer to give a vote of confidence to his growing maturity rather than force an issue.*

*Sheila E.*
*New Hampshire*

# CHAPTER 9

# LOVE
.
# Puppy and Other Sorts

**THE SITUATION ▪ Your Child Prefers One Parent Over the Other**

Lately my four-year-old son clearly prefers his father to me. The only time he calls for me is when he's throwing up or has wet the bed. Does his behavior mean he loves his father more, or am I being too sensitive?

## WHAT THE EXPERTS SAY

Almost without a doubt your son's preference will switch again and again as he grows up. That doesn't necessarily mean he loves one of you more, only that his needs at a particular time dictate who gets chosen as "most important parent."

It's partly biological, says Kenneth Gordon, M.D., a child psychiatrist and professor of psychiatry and human development at Thomas Jefferson University in Philadelphia. Most small children, especially if they are being breast-fed, are extremely attached to mom (no pun intended). As they begin to separate, they get interested in dad.

It's quite typical for a four-year-old boy to be intensely attached to his father, says Dr. Gordon. At the same time, he's also quite attached to his mother. He doesn't want to be like her so much as he wants her—wants her whole attention. It's completely normal.

Pediatrician Michael K. Levine adds that although he may not be able to put it into words, your son may be attempting to control or manipulate a situation, i.e., to pit one parent against the other, creating a level of anxiety in the family that gives the child the edge. He becomes the center of the show as the parents worry and fight over their son's attentions.

This is a signal to the parents that they are not working effectively as a team, explains Dr. Levine. The parents have to get their act together and demonstrate that the child is not in charge; the parents are.

Your child may also show a preference for one grandparent over another. This could be a form of manipulation again—the one who brings presents is favored. You need to help the "rejected" grandparent understand what is happening, and that in time the behavior will change, says Dr. Levine.

A child will realize soon enough that he prefers the grandparent who spends *time* with him rather than *money*. Dr. Gordon recalls that the grandfather he enjoyed most was the one who taught him how to milk a cow, rather than the one who gave him a $5 gold piece on the rare occasions they were together.

Remember, says Dr. Gordon, "the real joy in child-rearing is giving a child what he really needs, not what he thinks he needs at the moment. Not something he saw on TV, not a material possession, but our company, our interest, our affection, our care. Sometimes even our discipline."

## WHAT PARENTS SAY

*My three-year-old daughter makes it very clear that she prefers me. When she wakes up in the morning and my wife walks into her room first, our daughter almost always says, "I wanna see my daddy."*

*She's beginning to realize that she can control older, presumably wiser people, and that words are one way to do it. Some words are sweet, and some aren't. Part of the problem is our schedule. I always get her ready in the morning because my wife leaves early for work. At that time of the day my daughter's easy to please. Because I work late, though, my wife almost always gets bedtime duty. No toddler is ever happy about going to bed.*

*We're learning to direct her attention to my wife when she is doing something that my daughter really likes, such as needlework, putting away the dishes, going to the hairdresser with Mommy, or visiting Mommy's work.*

*Jeff M.*
*Virginia*

■

*The best way to handle it may be simply to wait until the child matures enough to equalize affections. In the meantime, look on the bright side. I was disappointed when my son insisted on having his bedtime glass of water delivered by his mother. But I was not so hurt when he later insisted on her cleaning up his vomit.*

*Jerry S.*
*Pennsylvania*

## THE SITUATION ■ Your Son Likes to Kiss and Hug His Same-Sex Best Friend

**My five-year-old son is very affectionate with his family and friends. But when he kisses and hugs his best buddy, my husband gets uncomfortable. Is it normal for him to want to hug and kiss another boy?**

### WHAT THE EXPERTS SAY

It's not at all inappropriate for a child your son's age to be affectionate with another of the same sex—up to a point, says Los Angeles psychologist Renee A. Cohen, Ph.D. If what you're describing is all there is to it, then the problem is with your husband and not with your son.

It's understandable why your husband may feel anxious: Americans simply are not as accepting of closeness between two men as many other cultures are. But it would be a shame to transfer that anxiety onto your son, since at age five it is still considered appropriate behavior, and really quite wonderful, Dr. Cohen says.

Being affectionate does have its limits. A problem may exist if your son's displays of affection become intrusive, explains Dr.

Cohen. Does he grab and hug everyone who's around? Does he lack respect for, or recognition of, another's interpersonal boundaries? Does he put his hands on people's private parts? If affection has gone that far, you may want to consult a psychologist.

A child who is not getting enough affection at home might display this type of excessive behavior, Dr. Cohen points out. On the other hand, it could just be that that's the way affection is displayed in your family. Unless the hugging and kissing is intrusive to others, your son's affectionate nature should be admired, not condemned.

### WHAT PARENTS SAY

*My daughter tends to be overly affectionate (hugging and kissing) with her friends, saying, "I love you," to them. I explain to her that not all people come from a "touchy" family such as ours is, and most people are embarrassed by excessive public displays of affection. I also remind her about germs and how easy it is to catch colds when you're constantly clinging to people and they to you. This seems to have helped, but occasionally she needs a reminder.*

*Wanda P.*
*Illinois*

■

*Intervene if your child's friend seems bothered by his displays of affection and he won't stop on his own. Tell your child that his friend has had enough kisses and hugs for now and distract the children with another activity.*

*Susan B.*
*Washington*

### THE SITUATION ■ Your Child Doesn't Like to Be Hugged and Kissed

**Ever since I can remember, my daughter has not been the cuddly type. She often resists hugs and squirms to break free.**

**She's pleasant and friendly for the most part, but her disinterest in physical affection makes me wonder if I've done something wrong.**

## WHAT THE EXPERTS SAY

For some reason, and nobody really knows why, some kids are born more cuddly than others. Recognize her individuality and work with it, says psychiatrist Henri Parens, M.D. If your daughter has always been very active and driven from within to accomplish tasks, she may find being hugged and kissed restrictive. A child involved in an activity will probably balk at being held, whereas at another time she may welcome a hug and a kiss. You need to read the cues your child is sending you.

If she squirms at being held, try a pat on the head or shoulder when you pass by. If frequent kisses are spurned, reserve them for bedtime only. Wait sometimes for your child to come to you. A little playful wrestling on the floor, or a stint as horsey with your child on your back, can show affection without being restrictive. Watch how she plays with her dolls to get clues about how she'd like to be treated.

It's up to you to adapt your parenting style to fit your child's temperament. Parents are there to meet the child's needs, reminds Dr. Gordon. The child is not there to meet *your* needs.

## WHAT PARENTS SAY

*When children don't want to be hugged or kissed, I use the following ideas: I will throw them a kiss and let them catch it. Sometimes I put a kiss in their pocket and tell them to put it on later. If the children have a favorite doll or stuffed animal, I will kiss the toy and let the toy kiss them. This works for hugs, too.*

*Susan B.*
*Pennsylvania*

■

*We have found that when we show affection to one another the kids just naturally pick up on it and enjoy being affectionate as well.*

*Also, they seem to be more open to affection at bedtime, so that is a good time to respond with affection and even talk about it.*

*Bob H.*
*Michigan*

■

*My son is very affectionate with us but isn't very warm with other adults. It takes him a couple of days to warm up to Grandma and Grandpa when they visit, and that's okay—it's just my son's way. I definitely don't let anyone smother him or make him feel awkward. We do a lot of handshaking in the beginning of visits. It sort of breaks the ice.*

*Angela W.*
*California*

## THE SITUATION ■ Your Child Says She Hates You

**In the heat of an argument with my four-year-old daughter, she told me she hated me. I couldn't believe she had actually said those words, especially to me. I've heard from other mothers that this is not unusual, but I'm worried that she'll continue to harbor ill feelings toward me. Am I right to be concerned about her outburst?**

### WHAT THE EXPERTS SAY

Relax. Your daughter's uninhibited verbal display shows that you already have an open relationship with her. Of course, your daughter wasn't feeling particularly loving toward you at that moment, but then you probably weren't terribly happy with her, either.

Try not to take these flair-ups personally. Your daughter will not "hate" you forever in spite of how it looks in the heat of the moment. The fact is, your child will get mad at you at times because you have to say no when what she really wants to hear is yes, says Nancy Samalin, author of *Love and Anger* (Viking, 1990).

It's your job as a parent to set the limits. That means you won't be able to buy her everything she wants, you'll have to turn off the TV set when she wants to keep watching, you'll have to tell her when to go to bed, remind her to brush her teeth—all those boring things that interfere with her fun.

## WHAT PARENTS SAY

*I try not to take it personally, which is hard. I always say, "You are really mad at me right now, and you are being mean by saying that you hate me. Tell me how you feel instead."*

*Helene M.*
*Maine*

# CHAPTER 10

# DEATH
■
# Coping With Loss

**THE SITUATION** ■ **Your Child Loses a Parent**

We've just recently learned that my wife has a terminal illness. Our daughters are very young, only four years and sixteen months. I'm at a loss as to how to deal with them once my wife dies. I'm not even sure I'll be in any emotional shape to tend to their needs. What can I expect—and what can I do, if anything?

## WHAT THE EXPERTS SAY

The death of a parent is the most significant loss a young child can face. Along with the anxiety and loneliness of having lost the central figure of her life, a young child is left with a sense of bewilderment. Children under the age of five are still in the "magical thinking" stage.

"Children don't see death as final," says Joanna Lerman, M.S.W., a parenting counselor who conducts workshops for parents on helping children cope with death. "They see death as something that is reversible, like the cartoon character who gets squashed and then comes back to life."

When mommy doesn't come back, the child may be angry. She may blame her mother for abandoning her. She may look for causes of her mother's death, asking whether "God did it" or if it was something she said or did that made her mother go away. Young children are vulnerable to guilt feelings after the death of a parent because they believe their thoughts can influence life events, says Darlene McCown, Ph.D., R.N., P.N.P., who has stud-ied children's reactions to death.

Very young children—those two and under—may search for the parent and become clingy and dependent on the remaining parent, exhibiting behaviors associated with separation anxiety.

Immediately following the death of a parent, children may not be able to sleep or may have nightmares. They may have little appetite and may even "act out." Dr. McCown's studies found that children who have faced a death in the family also tend to babble or talk too much. Research also shows that major depres-sion is common in children who have lost a parent. Because they may be sad, or have behavior problems, it's important to tell your child's teachers or daycare provider what is happening at home. A recent study of children between the ages of five and twelve found that children often experience their grief six months to a year after their loss, so don't assume they're over it after the first wave of mourning. (See "Your Child Seems Depressed," in Chap-ter 5.)

On the other hand, notes Dr. McCown, your children may ex-hibit no signs of grief. That's a perfectly normal reaction for a very young child. "They rarely cry because they don't think the death is final," she says. "Parents tend to impose what is socially acceptable grieving on children. You're supposed to cry, you're supposed to be sad, and maybe they aren't. Don't make a decision about what's normal too early. Give the child adequate time. Play it by ear. Pay attention to the child and help her express what she is feeling. Accept it and allow it, whatever it is."

One way to help your children express their sense of loss is through play. "Pretend somebody dies and see what happens," says Dr. McCown. Through play, the child may be better able to tell you how she views her mother's death and give you clues as to how to help her understand and cope with her loss. Also, she may be hesitant to burden you with her problems during your time of grief, and she may see "pretend" games as safe arenas for the airing of her sadness.

Though this may go against your grain, make sure your chil-dren understand now that their mother is very sick. "You want the child to know something is wrong, so they don't think every-thing was perfectly normal and then mommy went away. Being part of the hurting process helps," says Dr. McCown.

If your wife is in a hospital or hospice, allow your children to visit her there. Explain to them what they are going to see. It probably won't be as frightening to the children as you think. Denise's mother died of cancer when Denise was four. Although her mother was in a great deal of pain and had lost a leg, what Denise remembers most is sitting on her mother's hospital bed, and sharing a dish of fruit cocktail with her.

Once their mother dies, tell your children about it as soon as you are able. It won't harm them to see you cry, as long as you remain relatively under control. Count on having to explain her death many times over the course of years. "They may ask you about it again in six months, which might mean they're more ready, developmentally, to handle the answer then," says Joanna Lerman.

Assure your children that although their mother is gone, you are there to take care of them. "The biggest issue for children when you are talking about death is their fear that nobody is going to be there to care for them," says Lerman.

It's also a good idea to talk to your children about their loss "year by year as they grow up," says Dr. McCown. Some parents encourage their children to make a memory book, filled with pictures and mementos of the dead parent. Periodically going through photo albums or watching family movies or videos can be helpful. "You need to keep the parent's memory alive and reinterpret the loss in light of new growth and understanding at different ages and developmental levels," says Dr. McCown.

This not only refreshes the child's memory of the lost parent but shows that you understand she still feels the loss. It also serves as an opening for the child to ask questions about aspects of her mother's death she still does not understand. Remember, the loss of a parent is like a burn scar: it never goes away. There is always something to remind you—from the first day of school to your first baby—that someone important is missing from your life.

If you feel you won't be able to deal with your children at first, ask a family friend or a relative who is close to the children to talk to them. In fact, it might be advisable to pick someone now who can take over for you when your own grief will deprive your children of your comforting presence.

As for funeral attendance, most experts believe that children who want to attend a parent's funeral should be permitted to do so, but that children who don't want to shouldn't be forced to go. Children who attended funerals had more behavior problems afterward than children who didn't, says Dr. McCown, who attended a number of funerals to observe children's behavior. "What goes on at a funeral is not child-oriented. More often than not children are hushed up or ignored. The whole point of a funeral is to give us the opportunity to work out our grief, but children have no idea what it is and it doesn't do that for them."

It is best to allow a child who is old enough to make the decision for herself. "Even if the child makes the wrong decision, it was still her decision and it teaches her that she can act on her preferences," says the researcher.

If your child wants to attend her mother's funeral, make sure you tell her in advance what to expect. You may even want to allow her to play a small part in the ceremony—placing a flower on the coffin or if she is old enough, reading a poem. If you don't feel you are up to caring for her during the ritual, make sure someone else will take the responsibility.

It's also important to resume a normal life quickly. Children need the comfort of mundane, daily rituals to make them feel secure again.

## WHAT PARENTS SAY

*My mother died when I was seven. I now understand that the adults avoided us kids because they were so wrapped up in their own pain and didn't want to feel our grief as well. The person I remember with gratitude and affection was the police officer who knelt in front of my sister and me and answered our questions. I am resolved to respect the strength of children and their right to know what is going on, however painful.*

*Kellen D.*
*Washington*

■

*Keep your explanations concrete and age relevant. Most important, give your child the opportunity to participate in grief rituals. Often adults assume a child is feeling a certain way and try to spare the child the pain of grief. While trying to protect the child, you might be causing some very real problems that will come out as she matures.*

*Melissa M.*
*Oregon*

## THE SITUATION ▪ Your Child Loses a Grandparent

**My parents are getting quite old and I know they have only a few years left. How are my children going to react to the loss of Mom-Mom and Pop-Pop? They love them dearly.**

### WHAT THE EXPERTS SAY

Unless a child was unusually close to a grandparent—having a grandmother living in the home, or a grandfather who became a father figure to the child after his parents divorced or his own father died—the loss of a grandparent doesn't have a major impact on a child's life. Unlike the death of a parent, the death of a grandparent doesn't change day-to-day life in any significant way, unless a parent is too distraught to be there for them. In fact, young children, who often believe death is reversible, tend to associate death with old age.

That doesn't mean that your children won't feel the loss of a grandparent, that wonderful font of unconditional love and approval.

Explaining a grandparent's death to a child should be very much like explaining the death of a parent. (See "Your Child Loses a Parent," earlier in this chapter.)

"Prepare a child before an emotional event," suggests Joanna Lerman. "Help them see death as part of life, something that happens. One of my daughter's grandparents is very ill. We hope he's going to be fine, but if he's not, I can rest assured that she has been prepared over the years. The word *death* has been in her vocabulary ever since she could talk. We have taken every opportunity as we went along to point out things that die: a fish, a bug, a pet, even a leaf. When death is kept a secret, children fear it. They need to know that this is the way of the world."

## WHAT PARENTS SAY

*When it was apparent that my children's grandfather was dying of cancer, I needed a way to prepare the three of them (and myself!). In the weeks leading up to his death, reading* Grandpa Lew, Nana Upstairs, Nana Downstairs, *and* The Tenth Good Thing About Barney *and* The Giving Tree *together gave us time to share our feelings with one another. It also presented me with the opportunity to prepare them for what to expect at the funeral and afterward.*

*Amy B.*
*Pennsylvania*

■

*My kids lost their grandfather on Father's Day and their grand-mother two months afterward. Both deaths were unexpected. The kids didn't understand that they were gone. Everyone told me not to take them to the funeral. My son kept asking me if he should go to his grandfather's funeral, and I told him to go to bed and think about it. In the morning he said he thought he should go.*

*(I remembered when our dog of twelve years died three months before. The kids were upset because we took her away without letting them see her. They felt they needed to say good-bye.)*

*We all went to the funeral home before hours. My son placed a Father's Day picture he had drawn in the casket and my daughter a small lock of her hair (she said he always told her he wanted one of her curls). That was their good-bye. There were a few little tears. I told them it was all right to cry. We left when they were ready.*

*We had a private closed-casket service at the cemetery for Grandma later. It was short and all the children were present.*

*I have no regrets. I'm glad I let my children choose.*

*Carole R.*
*Pennsylvania*

## THE SITUATION ▪ Your Child Loses a Sibling

**Our third child was born prematurely and died in the hospital. We held a memorial service for her, which our two preschool-age children attended, but we don't know what's normal behavior for children who have lost a sibling. Is there something else we should do?**

## WHAT THE EXPERTS SAY

The loss of a sibling can have a profound impact on a child, and the older the children are, and the longer they've had a relationship, the more traumatic the loss will be.

"People usually prepare their children for the fact that a new sibling is coming home, and when all of a sudden there is no baby, they miss it, too," says Anne Armstrong, R.N., B.S.N., cofacilitator of the Neonatal Intensive Care Bereavement Support Group at Massachusetts General Hospital in Boston.

One thing to be on the lookout for are feelings of guilt in the surviving siblings. Oftentimes children don't view a new baby brother or sister as a welcome addition to the family. "They may have thought, 'I don't want to share my room with a baby sister. Well, now I don't have to. She's dead. Did I do that?' " says Armstrong.

Assure them that they had nothing to do with the baby's death. "Tell the children in concrete terms that 'your new baby sister didn't live because her heart wasn't made right' or 'she was too small,' " suggests Armstrong. "Tell them it's very sad, and that nothing like this is ever going to happen to them. That's something they're afraid of. Steer away from euphemisms such as 'God took her away because she was such a beautiful baby.' What does that mean? That God is going to take them away? Avoid phrases such as 'She went to sleep and never woke up.' " You don't want them to connect death with sleep."

Don't hide your grief from your children, but try to remember that seeing you lose control may upset and confuse them. Tell them you are sad and miss the baby, and that you may not be able to play or laugh with them right away, but that you will be fine. Be patient if the child begins to act out. It's not unusual for a child to begin regressing or misbehaving, which is as much a reaction to the loss of your full attention as it is to the loss of the sibling.

It is often helpful, when possible, to allow the surviving siblings to see and touch the baby in the hospital when it is sick or even after it dies, says Armstrong. This is especially important if the dying child is older. "It is very disturbing for children to have, for example, a sibling die in a pediatric ICU and just vanish forever," says Armstrong. "It would be more disturbing than seeing the child ill."

From her experience at Mass General, Armstrong says kids who visit their dying siblings in the hospital "see what they expect to see." She explains, "We are horrified as adults because we know that the wires and the tubes mean something serious, but I've seen so many youngsters come in and just start looking at the baby. 'Look at his hair,' they'll say. Or, 'Look, he's opening his eyes.' They don't get as horrified as we think they might."

Even if the child who died was only a few hours old, try to make her real to your other children. Name her, take pictures, and encourage your children to talk about her. "It's important to incorporate her into your life," Armstrong says.

But even if your children have seen their sibling in the hospital, and you've explained the death to them in simple and concrete terms, don't be surprised if they bring up the subject again and again. "They can ask you something that may seem devastating at the time, and often in an awkward situation, such as in the grocery store," says Armstrong. "They may be doing something that reminds them of the baby and they ask you, 'Where did the baby go?' or 'Is the baby coming back?' You think, oh my God, this is going to be awful, but it's not. Just give them a one-line answer: 'Remember, the baby died and she won't be coming to live with us.' That will satisfy them."

Children who have had longer relationships with siblings who die will probably be more bereaved. They may have nightmares, school problems, periods of crying, clinging, and even depression. They may act out, become aggressive or jealous. Studies have found that many of these children express a feeling of loneliness, not only because they've been separated from a sibling, but because they also feel distanced from their grieving parents. They need some time to adjust to their changed role in the family, particularly if the death of a sibling turns a firstborn into an only child or thrusts a second-born into the firstborn's role. Their period of adjustment could last a year or more.

## WHAT PARENTS SAY

*My three-year-old daughter was very confused when her long-awaited brother was born dead. We included her in the hospital delivery room and let her see him and touch him. She also went to the funeral home to see him again and to the memorial service. The more we involved her, the less confused she became. Then she was able to mourn and get over it in a healthy way.*

*Kelly T.*
*Florida*

## THE SITUATION ▪ Your Child Loses a Pet

**My kids have never known a time without my dog, Allie, who will be seventeen this year. Jessie is four and Melinda is almost six. I know they'll be heartbroken when she dies. So will I. How can I help them deal with it?**

## WHAT THE EXPERTS SAY

"When a pet dies, the temptation is to make light of it, to try to make the child feel better," says parenting counselor Joanna Lerman. "You're tempted to say things like, 'Oh, it's okay, we'll get you another dog.' Or, 'Don't cry, it's all right.' Basically what we end up doing is denying the child's feelings because they're so painful to see."

Allow your children to feel their loss. Talk with them about what the dog meant to them and to you. Remember the good times you had together. *The Tenth Good Thing About Barney* by Judith Viorst is an excellent book for helping kids deal with the death of a pet.

"It's important never to deny a child's feelings because they're important," says Lerman. "If you do, the message you give them is that they're not really important. The kid begins to think, 'I guess I don't know how I feel. I know I am real sad, but Mom and Dad keep telling me not to be sad.' It really confuses them."

It would also not be wise to rush out and try to replace the dead pet right away. "We want to teach children that the things we love are not replaceable," says Lerman.

Children under the age of five may not fully grasp the finality of death. They may expect to see Allie come bounding out to them long after she's gone (and so may you). But it may help them to understand if you can bury your pet together or allow them to be with her when she's put to sleep by the veterinarian. (The process is quick, painless, and very peaceful.) Explain to them that she is very old and that her body doesn't work properly anymore, suggests Lerman. You may not want a child to see an animal who is hurt or killed in an accident, but you can explain that the animal was too injured to live.

Often, the loss of an animal is a child's first experience with death. Use the opportunity to talk to your children about the cycle of life: that everything that is born, dies.

## WHAT PARENTS SAY

*When my husband and I discovered Daisy, the little black cat who belonged to our children, lying by the curb, we wondered, how do we tell our children? Do we let them see her?*

*As it turned out, they showed us what to do. We laid her in our backyard and found they naturally wanted to see her.*

*Our daughter wanted to put one of Daisy's favorite toys in the box she would be buried in. Because she always expressed herself in art and writing, I suggested she make a note for the box. "I love you, Daisy," she wrote. It seemed to give her the chance to give her pet a lasting message. She asked if she could clip off some of the cat's fur to save—something I would never have thought of. We did and put it in an envelope. When the cat was buried, it did seem comforting to have one little piece of her to touch and remember.*

*Our daughter cried off and on the whole day. I told her I always thought that when I missed something very deeply it showed I had really, really loved and appreciated that animal or person or place when it was there for me. We asked her friend Susan because she had just lost a cat, too. Our daughter asked her, "How does it feel without your cat?" Her friend told her, "She is always in your heart."*

*Lori R.*
*New York*

# PART·THREE
# FAMILY AND FRIENDS

# CHAPTER 11

# BEHAVIOR

■

# It's a Good Thing They're Cute

**THE SITUATION ■ Your Child Cries All the Time**

We're going into our second month with a crying baby. I've been told he may have colic and that he'll grow out of it, or that he's just temperamentally "fussy" and there's not much I can do. But it's starting to wear us down. Isn't there *anything* we can do?

### WHAT THE EXPERTS SAY

There certainly is, but don't count on anything more than limited success. Crying is what babies do.

You can start by ruling out any physical causes for your baby's constant crying. Have your pediatrician check him over for any physical ailments, such as an ear infection, which can be quite painful. Chances are there's nothing physically wrong with your infant, but the checkup will reassure you.

Now you need a primer on crying. The average baby cries about an hour a day, most often as a form of communication, a way to let you know when he needs to eat, sleep, or have his diaper changed. Babies also cry when they're tense, angry, or lonely. Naturally, they cry when they're in pain. And most parents report that their children have a predictable "crabby hour" every day, often at dinnertime.

Researchers believe that there's a distinct difference between the sounds a baby makes to communicate the idea "I'm hungry!" and the sounds he makes to communicate the idea "There's something sharp sticking me in the side!" But those sounds may differ from baby to baby. You may be the best judge of what your baby's cries mean.

As a general rule, however, says Charles Schaeffer, Ph.D., director of the Crying Baby Clinic at Fairleigh Dickinson University in Hackensack, New Jersey, a low, monotonous, whiny cry followed by a pause usually signals hungry. "It starts low but it can get pretty shrill in some kids right away. They stop and have to catch their breath." A cry for attention, he says, usually starts low and then escalates to a frenzy until you pick up the baby. Most parents recognize the sound of a pain cry—it must be nature's warning siren—and it usually doesn't subside once you pick up the baby, says Dr. Schaeffer. Sick babies often make very feeble cries.

Chronic criers usually fall into one of two categories—colicky or temperamentally fussy. The distinctions between them blur once you take a closer look.

Many doctors consider a baby colicky if he cries for more than three hours a day over a period of more than three weeks for no apparent reason. He's warm, dry, fed, and cuddled, but inconsolable. Colic is a catch-all phrase for a so-far inexplicable condition that seems to strike infants at about two weeks and usually disappears miraculously at anywhere from three to six months. Some researchers theorize that colic is the result of an immature digestive system, which causes painful gastrointestinal upset. In fact, some colicky babies do sound as if they are in pain.

Lately, however, more attention has been focused on a baby's immature central nervous system, and some research indicates that chronic criers may have a sleep, rather than a digestive, disorder.

Maureen R. Keefe, Ph.D., is associate director for research at the Children's Hospital in Denver, Colorado. She has been studying what she calls "irritable infant syndrome," which she describes as "persistent unexplained fussiness" that seems to be linked to a baby's apparent inability to downshift from the waking to the sleeping state.

"Some of these infants seem to get stuck in the highly aroused state that is crying," she explains. "And it seems that the more tired they get, the more difficulty they have getting to sleep. In fact, as they try to fall asleep, they get crabbier and crankier."

The problem certainly isn't rare. Dr. Keefe estimates that somewhere between 15 and 30 percent of all newborns fall into the "irritable infant" category. They are not necessarily the firstborns of inexperienced, nervous parents either. "It's very important for parents to know that it's not something they're not doing right," says Dr. Keefe. "It's something in the baby. This baby isn't very soothable. This is a challenging baby who doesn't give clear clues as to whether he's tired or hungry."

An element of temperament may be involved as well. Excessive irritability tends to disappear once the child passes through the newborn phase, usually at about three to four months. A child who is temperamentally difficult will continue to exhibit some abrasive traits. He may cry easily, be clingy, moody, a poor sleeper, sensitive to lights and sounds, resistant to changes in his routine and environment, a finicky eater. He's likely to throw tantrums and is difficult to distract once his fit is in full flower. He may be stubborn, contrary, and wild. This is a very tough child to parent, and if your child is difficult, get some professional help.

Fortunately, the same techniques seem to work with most crying babies, whether their problems are caused by immature nervous systems or personality traits. These children need a little more help to adjust to the world. You'll usually see some improvement if you impose some routine and structure on their lives.

Start with a daily diary. Dr. Keefe recommends that you record typical feeding and sleep times and fussy periods, to see if a pattern emerges. Chances are it won't. "For these infants it seems to be chaotic," she says. "One hour or one day doesn't look like the next."

But you might see something that suggests a solution to your baby's fussing. For instance, he may not be feeding enough during the day. If he tends to drift off during a feeding, he may only be getting a small snack rather than a real meal and he could be hungry.

If he cries at the same time every night, he may be trying to tell you that he's tired and wants to go to bed. You may notice he cries when he's not being touched—or when he is. Some children crave sensory stimulation, others are easily overstimulated.

Denise's son was a fussy infant who put on what her husband called "The Bad Baby Show" nightly at eight. "He's tired," their pediatrician, Jeff Fogel, M.D., told them. "He's been trying to tell you but you didn't understand him. He doesn't know how to fall asleep by himself, so you need to establish a bedtime and help him."

Dr. Fogel was right. Once Patrick had a regular bedtime and a ritual—a nighttime bottle and some rocking—his fussiness soon disappeared.

Impose some structure. Instead of feeding him on demand, schedule his mealtimes. In fact, schedule his naptimes and bedtime, too. He probably has trouble falling asleep when he's tired, and his sleep problems will only get worse if he's overtired. "Put a little routine in his day around feeding, playtime, nighttime rituals," suggests Dr. Keefe. "It has to be the exact same thing every day that helps him shift down." Many parents find a warm bath, a cuddle, or some rocking and a nursing are a good bedtime routine for a fussy infant, since they're pleasurable and if repeated, a good cue to the infant that it's time to wind down for bed.

Experiment with soothing techniques for crying spells. "Typically, what helps one night doesn't help the next night," says Dr. Keefe. "So you need an arsenal of things to try to soothe your baby."

To get you started, here's a list of techniques that *may* work. Don't be alarmed by the contradictory advice. All infants are different, and what works with one may not work with another.

■ **Time-in.** This is an interesting conditioning technique developed by Edward Christophersen, Ph.D. (whose description of "time-out" is also in this chapter). Dr. Christophersen suggests that you give your child "love pats"—just a brief, gentle touch fifty to a hundred times a day—when he's engaged in noncrying activities. These small gestures of affection will reinforce the child's self-quieting behavior, Dr. Christophersen says.

For chronic criers, he suggests touching the baby's head when he stops crying and withdrawing it when he starts up again to reinforce the preferred behavior and indicate displeasure with the crying. Pick the baby up at the first signs of crying—that often keeps it from escalating—but don't carry the baby around to head off another crying jag, Dr. Christophersen says. If you're always comforting him, the baby will never learn to comfort himself.

Dr. Christophersen also recommends that parents pick up a baby when he's quiet and happy, not just when he's crying. Otherwise the baby will quickly learn that crying will get him more attention. He needs to know being calm and cheerful will get him just as much attention.

The chief advantage this technique has over many of the others is that it's unlikely to establish bad habits that can lead to problems as your child gets older. For instance, children who are rocked, sung, or lulled to sleep never learn to relax and calm themselves. Most experts agree that once children reach about six months, their crying becomes a way to manipulate parents to do for them what they should be doing for themselves. If your child is crying, reassure yourself that there's nothing seriously wrong—and reassure the child that you're there for him. But don't rush in with the emotional first aid at the first peep. Remind yourself that learning to calm himself is the first of many tasks an infant can learn to master. Mastery boosts self-esteem and diminishes anger and frustration.

■ **Body contact.** Some infants like to be vertical on your shoulder. Others like to be draped over your arm, facing outward, or carried in the football hold, their chest supported by your hand and their body by your forearm, under your arm. Many babies like to be carried on the chest, skin to skin, so they can synchronize with your breathing.

■ **White noise.** Many parents swear by the vacuum cleaner. Others turn on the radio between channels. If you've got the money to spare, you can even buy a special white-noise device. Some babies seem to need something monotonous to cut down on disturbing external stimuli.

■ **Movement.** Almost all infants like body movement. They like you to bounce when you walk or to jiggle them. Many infants love the car because it's movement and white noise rolled into one. We've even heard of parents putting their children on top of a running clothes drier. (However, for safety reasons, sitting them in a baby swing might be preferable.)

■ **Swaddling.** Wrapping the child tightly in a blanket, papoose style, makes him feel secure.

■ **Carrying.** This contradicts Dr. Christophersen's advice, but we're including it because a study done at Canada's McGill University found that infants whose mothers carried them at least three hours a day cried an hour less a day than infants who were not carried as much. You can use a front pack, such as a Snugli, to keep the infant close to your comforting heartbeat.

■ **Sucking.** Though you may feel as though you're "plugging" your child's cries, a pacifier can satisfy a child's sucking needs that go beyond his need to feed. If possible, try to help him find his thumb.

■ **Heat.** A hot-water bottle, a heating pad turned low, or even bedclothes first warmed up in the drier may soothe a child enough to lull him to sleep.

■ **Low-level light.** Create a warm, glowing bedroom environment with a night-light. Some children may need some time in a darkened room to help them unwind.

■ **Talk to someone.** Chances are you know another parent who has dealt with a fussy baby. If not, just talk to someone sympathetic and supportive. You may have feelings of inadequacy and guilt, and you need to feel good about yourself as a parent.

■ **Let the baby cry sometimes.** If you've assured yourself your child isn't wet, tired, hungry, sick, in pain, or lonely, you've pretty much exhausted your repertoire of tricks. "A little crying is not going to harm them," says Dr. Schaeffer. "We have this idea that it's our job to keep the baby from crying all the time. But we forget that that's what babies do."

A little frustration is actually a good thing because it allows the child to learn he can solve his own problems. You may be surprised to find your fussy infant rocking himself, sucking his thumb, or discovering himself in a crib mirror.

## WHAT PARENTS SAY

*Do everything you can possibly think of—check diaper, walk, burp, jiggle, point out interesting things out the window, feed. Then put them to bed, shut their door, and turn up the TV real loud and ignore the crying.*

*Debbie V.*
*Pennsylvania*

■

*Despite the best advice, the situation may get so bad that you can hear the baby's cries in your head even when she's not crying. If that happens, you need to get away from her on a regular basis, no matter how young she is. Find a sitter, a friend, or a relative not living in your home, or enroll the baby in an infant care center for a few hours per week. The caregiver will not be as upset as you are by the crying. Do not think of this time off as a luxury that you cannot afford. Constant crying can wear down even the most loving parent.*

*Susan B.*
*Washington*

## THE SITUATION ■ Your Child Won't Share

**Mark is three and we have a tough time getting the concept of sharing across to him. Sometimes he makes a big show of sharing a toy with a friend, but other times he'll simply snatch it away and shout, "Mine!" When do kids learn to share, and how can we encourage it in our son?**

### WHAT THE EXPERTS SAY

They start as soon as you begin teaching them, but it doesn't become a meaningful concept to them until they're somewhere between six or eight, and even then, they won't (and shouldn't) share everything. Not even adults do that.

According to William Sobesky, Ph.D., clinical assistant professor of psychiatry at the University of Colorado Health Sciences Center in Denver, usually around the age of four children will begin sharing with other children, generally as a way to get a positive response from a nearby parent.

You'll also probably see evidence of some altruistic behavior on the part of your preschooler. Instead of bursting into tears when another child is in distress, he may give the other child a hug or share a toy or a treat with him, indicating he's beginning to develop the rudiments of empathy. That's good. "What we are aiming for is to have our children learn to take the needs of others into consideration," Dr. Sobesky says.

A child is most likely to share with another child with whom he has a good, positive relationship, someone he doesn't regard as competition (such as a sibling). He's also more likely to share toys that don't mean too much to him.

If your child is trying to get in your good graces, you're almost guaranteed to see some well-orchestrated public sharing. And don't be surprised if your child quickly catches on to the advantages of the element of reciprocity in sharing.

With a child under six, you need to scale down your expectations. Certainly, use every opportunity to encourage your child to share, but don't expect him to cooperate every time.

If a fight does break out over toys, stand back and let the kids try to work it out themselves (unless blood flows). Wanting to play peacefully together is a powerful motivator for kids to share.

Beware of too much sharing. Although we want our kids to learn to think of others, they need to think of themselves, too. Sharing everything with everyone may make you a candidate for sainthood, but it's really not healthy behavior. Some kids may even use sharing as a way to bribe another child to "be my friend."

"You need to ask yourself, does my child take this too wholeheartedly? Is he always sharing?" Dr. Sobesky says. "Is it hard for him to stand up for himself when he needs to?"

If you reward a child for sharing (but don't punish him when he doesn't), he'll eventually catch on. You may be able to speed the process by showing the child how you share, even if it's only splitting your last stick of gum with him. A good role model is always worth more than a thousand words.

There are other ways to teach sharing, too, says Dr. Sobesky. One is not to indulge your child, a real temptation for guilt-ridden working parents or parents of chronically ill, handicapped, or only children. "If you have everything you need or could possibly imagine wanting, sharing isn't much of an issue for you," the psychologist points out. And the other way is to allow your child, from the time he is able to understand the spoken word, to share in household duties. "Helping out your parents at home is a form of sharing, and early on, that's why children share," says Dr. Sobesky. "They think to themselves, 'I'm doing this for my mom.'"

## WHAT PARENTS SAY

*Make sharing selective, not universally mandatory. Remember there are things you don't wish to share either. So get a "this is all yours box" and a "this is the share box." When a child does share, reward and reinforce him with praise. (This may pay off in more expensive Christmas gifts for you in the years to come.)*

*Jerry S.*
*Pennsylvania*

■

*Whenever we went to a friend's house where we knew sharing would be a problem, we brought a few toys of our own to share and did so as soon as we got there. This makes the host child feel as if he is getting something back in return for having to share his toys.*

*Ena C.*
*Minnesota*

■

*If something is really special to my daughter, or brand-new, I tell her she doesn't have to share it, but to put it away and get out something she will share. I am also very firm about toys that others didn't want to share, telling her, "That's very special to Emmy and she doesn't want to share it, just like you don't want to share your doll."*

*Vicki W.*
*Oregon*

## THE SITUATION ▪ Your Child is Manipulative or Spoiled

I'm embarrassed to admit this, but I think my four-year-old daughter is spoiled. We waited so long for a child that we've really indulged her—letting her stay up late at night, buying her something every time we go to the store, giving in to her tantrums, which have grown worse by the day. We know she's using all this negative behavior to manipulate us, and it's working. We love her, but she's getting to be uncontrollable. What can we do?

## WHAT THE EXPERTS SAY

It would be too glib to tell you to "just say no," though that's the gist of the experts' advice.

You have to ask yourself why it's so hard to say no to your child. Are you feeling guilty because you're a working parent who isn't sure the time you're giving your daughter is enough? Are you afraid of seeing your child unhappy? Are you trying to avoid her wrath? Are you trying to be a "nicer" parent to your child than your parents were to you?

You can readily see by your daughter's behavior that giving in to her every loudly broadcasted whim isn't doing her any favors. While she may like the immediate gratification, she's eventually going to find the real world a tough and unhappy place. No one else she's going to encounter is going to respond positively to her tantrums and manipulations. In fact, it's one sure way of guaranteeing her rejection. Though that certainly isn't your intention, it's the life to which you're dooming her.

"These are kids whom it seems you never can please. They are always frustrated about something. They are never happy, never content," says psychologist William Sobesky, Ph.D.

How can they be? Try as they might, they can't bend the world to their wishes in the same way they bend their parents.

"What is the point of growing up if you are as powerful as any adult?" asks Dr. Sobesky. "One of the powerful motivators for growing up, for acquiring new skills, is so that you can become as powerful as those adults who seem to rule the world. And think of how frightening that is, to be that little and to think, 'I'm as powerful as they are. Who's in charge here? Who can make it safe?' These children go through life constantly searching for somebody who can provide structure and reassurance."

As a parent, that's your job. Tough as it is, you've got to do it. Though children may engage you courageously in a battle for power, for the most part, they want you to win. Otherwise, they feel insecure.

Let's take a look at the logic behind all those reasons you don't say no.

■ "I don't spend enough time with my child because of my job." Do you really think that buying your child something every time you set foot in a store will replace your loving presence? Forget guilt. It's a waste of the time you should be spending with your child. Do something special together. Allowing her to stay up late at night just so you can have more time together isn't really in her best interest, especially if she's tired and cranky the next day. Rethink your priorities. Are you in a job that is inimical to your family life? Maybe it's time for a change.

■ "I don't want my child to be unhappy or angry with me." Your child is already unhappy. And anger, while not pleasant, is often a totally appropriate response to having your demands quashed. You have to face the fact that you're giving in to your child's demands to make life easier for yourself, not for her. You're trying to wriggle out of the rougher responsibilities of parenting. "One of the not particularly fun parts of being a parent is having to say no," says Nancy Samalin, author of *Love and Anger* (Viking, 1990).

You need to accept and learn to tolerate your child's anger, especially when it's directed at you. "I don't think it's fair to say, 'No, you can't have a candy bar and you also can't be upset about it,' " says Dr. Sobesky. "What are we teaching our kids with such a response? That it's not okay to have feelings? I think some parents genuinely don't understand that being angry and frustrated is a healthy thing."

■ "I don't want to raise my kid the way my parents raised me." Did you really turn out that bad? Maybe you're just trying to fulfill a childhood fantasy: "Our parents were mean and made

us unhappy, and we are not going to be like that to our kids,"
says Nancy Samalin. "Well, who didn't hate their parents some
of the time?"

Take a look at your upbringing through your new adult eyes,
not the eyes of a child. When your parents set reasonable limits
and made reasonable demands, weren't they in your best interest, no matter how angry you felt at the time?

You obviously know the part you've played in creating a spoiled
child. The good news is that, unlike fruit, a "spoiled" child can be
unspoiled. It will take time and will require some introspection
on your part. "It may sound pie-in-the-sky, but I really do believe
strongly that it's never too late," says Nancy Samalin.

Here are a few more tactics to try with a recalcitrant preschooler:

■ Use time-out to control angry outbursts. It's a time-proven
behavior-modification technique (see "Using Time-out for Behavior Problems," later in this chapter) that serves several purposes. It's not a tough punishment, so it's not hard for even the
most indulgent parents to use it consistently. (In fact, don't
think of yourself as punishing your child; you're *teaching* her
how to act in society.) And when unspoiling a child who is used
to the rules changing with every stomp of her foot, consistency
is the only thing that will get the message across to her that
there *are* rules of acceptable behavior and that there are consequences to not obeying them. Time-out removes the child from
the scene, giving both of you breathing space.

■ Don't say no when you mean maybe. Don't say maybe when
you mean no. Children quickly pick up on the little clues that
say, "I can be worn down on this one." And the way kids wear
you down is by whining, nagging, tantrums, and all sorts of
obnoxious behavior that you will do anything to stop.

If you don't want your child to have a second ice-pop before
dinner, say no—firmly. If you really don't mind if she spoils her
dinner, then by all means hand it over. But don't hem and haw
because you're afraid she's going to have a fit or nag you for the
whole hour you're cooking dinner. If you give in, the behavior
you're trying to eliminate will continue. What self-respecting
child is going to abandon a great technique?

■ Be aware of your child's temperament. Kids who are intense, difficult, or otherwise strong reactors are formidable. They may react hotly when their demands are turned down. It's tempting to give in when you're dealing with Attila the Child. Sometimes, children of this ilk may seem spoiled, but they're not, says Dr. Sobesky. "It's just more difficult to get them to adapt to your demands or the limits you've set." You'll need to work around their temperaments, which aren't likely to change quickly or significantly. Choose your battles, and don't sweat the small stuff.

■ Avoid bribery. Oh, an occasional "You can have frozen yogurt if you finish your green beans" won't hurt. But, says Samalin, if this is your typical parenting MO, you're *training* your child to be manipulative. "If a child learns that when he does what he's supposed to do he gets a reward for it, then he starts to expect it," she points out. "Then we get mad at them for saying, 'Well, what will you give me?' Any smart child is eventually going to say, 'What's in it for me?'"

Your rewards for good behavior should be more subtle. A smile and a pat when a child remembers to wash before dinner, a "Good girl!" when she cleans up her toys, a quiet cuddle just because you love her, will go much further than money or treats.

■ Accentuate the positive. It's not enough to tell your child what she's not allowed to do. You need to tell her what she *can* do. While she needs to be denied at times, you don't want to serve up a steady diet of negatives. If a child hears "Don't do this, don't do that" all day long, she will probably develop what Nancy Samalin calls "mommy deafness," a chronic condition in which a child appears unable to hear anything a parent says. You may also inadvertently leave her with the impression that everything she does is wrong, which is a serious blow to a child's self-esteem. Turn some of your don'ts into dos. "Don't scream in the house" becomes "Please speak a little more softly when you're inside. Outside is for screaming." "Don't tease the dog" becomes "Sparky really likes it when you pet him rather than pulling his tail."

## WHAT PARENTS SAY

*My husband and I feel strongly that children with defined limits won't manipulate their parents. We have a word in our house that is not always liked but is respected. The word is NO. We will give the reasons we are saying no, but we try to be consistent and say no when we mean it, not when it is a convenient answer for us. Too many parents say "No" when they really mean "Leave me alone right now." And in the end the parents will say yes out of guilt. The message is mixed for kids, so they learn to use this against their parents.*

*Debbie L.*
*California*

■

*I tell my children, manipulation will get you absolutely nowhere. I say, "If you must throw a tantrum at the store because I won't buy you that gum, perhaps you are not big enough to go with me next time." And I stick to my word!*

*Lori A.*
*California*

■

*I find that when I'm overtired or terribly busy, I give in to my children's demands. I try to get enough rest so that I'm not so tired. When I find myself in a tense situation, I try to count to ten and compose myself, then assess things.*

*Kathy H.*
*Nebraska*

■

*The more I tried to avoid conflict with my three-year-old daughter by giving in to her immature demands, the greater the demands became and the harder it was for me to curb her. I could not always expect her to understand how her behavior was interfering with others. However, I can teach her that discipline will be administered when her conduct infringes on other people's well-being. I first try to distract her with some more appropriate interest. If the behavior continues, I use a firm "No." If this does not work, she is sent to her room to sit in her time-out chair until she can regain control. Temporary isolation is an effective way to enforce limits. Once she has indicated that she wants to change her behavior, then she is accepted back into my good graces without humiliation or shame.*

*Dore D.*
*California*

■

*One thing that used to drive me crazy was when my young children nagged and whined to get me to let them have something that I didn't think was good for them (such as another cookie or a toy at the store). I found it much easier to maintain my resolve not to be manipulated if I repeated over and over to myself, "Pretend he's asking for a knife." Sounds silly, but it really helped.*

*Lerri C.*
*Oklahoma*

## THE SITUATION ▪ Your Child Whines Endlessly

**It seems that ever since my son learned to talk he's been a whiner. He's now five years old and I'm so sick of his complaining and negative attitude. I've tried sending him to his room, taking away privileges, even screaming at him. Nothing seems to help. Isn't there some way to make him stop the whining and speak in a normal tone of voice?**

## WHAT THE EXPERTS SAY

Yes, there is. But first you may need to change your expectations of this child. Whining is an expression of temperament, according to Stanley Turecki, M.D., coauthor of *The Difficult Child* (Bantam, 1989) and authority on temperamental kids. Some kids are naturally sunny and positive, but from your description it sounds as though you have a child whose basic disposition is more serious and sulky. A half-smile from a child like that is the equivalent of a whoop of joy from a more cheerful child.

Right now you're spending all your time focusing on why your child is never happy and why he never shows appreciation. And in return you're getting a child who is whining even more, to the point of exasperation (yours). You're in a vicious circle of whining, criticizing, whining, criticizing.

The key is to deal with the problem behavior away from the situation, says Dr. Turecki. In other words, refrain from screaming at your whining child while he's whining. Then at some other calm time take your son out for a treat. During your wonderful time together, try to find something complimentary to say to him: "I really liked the card you made for my birthday" or "Your teacher told me you're doing very well in reading." Tell him how proud mommy and daddy are of him. *Then* in this warm, positive atmosphere, you can gently bring up the problem.

Dr. Turecki recommends choosing your words carefully. "The point is to be neutral, unemotional," he says. "You're speaking to your child about this problem not as a moral flaw, but simply as a bad habit you'd like him to change, and you're going to help him."

The next time your child whines (and he will; everybody forgets sometimes), you can remind him of his habit without sounding critical because you've laid the groundwork for improvement. Now whatever corrective strategies you use will not come as a surprise attack, but simply as a nonjudgmental means to help him overcome his negative behavior.

## WHAT PARENTS SAY

*Whining was starting to be a problem when our daughter was between two and a half and three, until I realized that my husband and I were actively encouraging her to whine because we would give her what she wanted rather than listen to it. Once I figured this out, we changed our strategy. Rather than get her what she wanted, we calmly explained to her that you don't get what you want by whining, you get what you want by asking nicely, saying please, and smiling. At first she would just escalate her whining, which had been working well. But we just kept telling her calmly that the way you get what you want is by asking nicely, saying please, and smiling. I probably repeated those words hundreds of times over a two-week period, but she finally figured it out. And 99 percent of the time now she asks very politely and smiles when she wants something.*

*Vicki W.*
*Oregon*

■

*We refer to whining as "speaking whinese" and say that Mom and Dad don't understand that language.*

*Stephen W.*
*Oregon*

■

*Because we often would not listen to our son's requests until he turned up the volume, he developed the habit of whining whenever he wanted something. In order to curb his obnoxious, nasal moans, we started listening as soon as he began to speak, and if he whined, we insisted that he speak assertively. Even at three, he now knows what we mean when we say, "No whining. Talk to me."*

*Kellen D.*
*Washington*

## THE SITUATION ■ Your Child Has Tantrums

Is there any surefire way to stop a child's tantrums? My two-year-old has thrown fits at home, in church, at the supermarket, and once in the middle of an intersection. I'm ashamed to admit I've lost *my* cool more than once, and when they happen in public, I've even given in. They're not getting any better. What's the best way to handle this?

## WHAT THE EXPERTS SAY

First of all, for most children tantrums are, to borrow from *Passages* author Gail Sheehy, a predictable passage of life. They're a way for a youngster to assert his independence, a sign that he's confident in his relationship with you. They're also a normal, toddler response to the frustration that, at times, seems to dog his every toddle.

To understand his tantrums, put yourself in his place. Imagine feeling really out of sorts and not knowing why. A two-year-old may not be able to identify the source of his crabbiness as hunger or tiredness, two common tantrum triggers. Even if he could, with his limited vocabulary he might not be able to tell anyone that he'd like to take a nap or could sure use a cup of milk and a cookie. So there he is. He feels lousy, he doesn't know why, and even if he did, he couldn't do anything about it. Faced with this predicament, you might throw a fit in the middle of an intersection, too.

At two, children are just beginning to get a grip on their world. But it's a world that bombards them daily with new sensations and nameless emotions, where all that glitters is a no-no and nearly everything they need or want is beyond their reach. And they can't even talk about it! This is a sorry state that, fortunately for all concerned, passes relatively quickly as a child grows and develops new skills. Of course, the way he develops those skills is by encountering frustration, that wonderful teacher of manners and morals. That is not to say you should encourage tantrums. They're an inappropriate demonstration of anger and frustration that can quickly become manipulative.

Most experts will tell you that tantrums begin around eighteen months and continue to three years. However, you may have your first experience with your fourteen-month-old and not see the last of them until your child is four or older. From our experience, the "terrible twos" *peak* when the child is two, but start before the second birthday and end somewhere beyond it.

In fact, you may be able to get some inkling as to whether your infant is going to mature into a tantrum-thrower, says psychologist James Garbarino, Ph.D., president of the Erickson Institute in Chicago. Some kids will be more "temperamentally inclined" to tantrums, he says. "In infancy, they're the kids who are not easily soothed. Once they get set off, their crying and upset escalates. The child may be very reactive: if you go into the child's room while he's dozing, he awakens instantly."

Children who are easily overstimulated are probably going to have trouble handling life's everyday frustrations. There's also the question of family fit. If you're a couch potato whose child runs minimarathons, or an outgoing person whose child is a leg clinger, your child is likely to face more than a few conflicts resulting from his being "out of step" with you.

■ **Learn what sets him off.** Does your child hate to be rushed? Is he continually attempting to do things that are beyond his current abilities? Does he throw tantrums because he wants a treat at the store? Is he more prone to tantrum behavior when he's hungry or tired? If you know what's likely to trigger his tantrums, you can head them off, says Dr. Garbarino. But you need to be creative.

If, for example, your child hates to be rushed, Dr. Garbarino suggests you invest in an inexpensive kitchen timer. "Tell him, okay, I'm going to set the timer for how long it should take you to put your shoes on or have part of a task accomplished. Then come back and set it again for another task." Your child may find getting ready in the morning more a game than a chore, and you'll avoid the conflicts that anger and frustrate him.

Help your toddler when he's attempting to stack his blocks or get down from his chair, or distract him when he's engaged in a frustrating task that's beyond his capabilities. In fact, direct him to activities in which he can experience success. A child who can't hit a ball with a bat can accurately toss a ball into a bucket full of water, a game that also rewards him with a giggle-invoking splash. Bring your own treats to the supermarket and avoid taking your child out when he's hungry or tired. Having a stable daily routine is also quite helpful, especially for the temperamental child. If possible, prepare the child in advance if his schedule is going to be disrupted.

All children can benefit from being given choices. It gives them a sense of independence that can circumvent the power-struggle tantrums. A child who picks his fights over bedtime should be given the opportunity to choose a bedtime routine when his parents choose the time for bed. A finicky eater may be easier to deal with if he picks his meals from a menu a parent provides. Even making clear to a child the consequences of his naughty behavior gives him a choice. For instance: Stop throwing food or go to your room. The child soon learns that he can control when he goes to his room and how long he stays there just by choosing a certain behavior.

■ Once you recognize the signs of an incipient tantrum, distract the child. If you're in a public place, take the child outside. The change of scene may help the child forget what was upsetting him.

It will also remove *you* from an occasion of potential embarrassment. Oftentimes, when we're embarrassed, we do what seems expedient. In most cases that means giving the screaming child what he wants. And one yes in a moment of weakness will sustain a child's hope through dozens of subsequent noes.

Sometimes you'll find yourself in a moral dilemma: when the tantrum is your fault. For example, you need to rush to the grocery store even though you know your child is tired and hungry, and predictably a tantrum erupts. "The parent thinks, gee, I should have anticipated this, so it's my fault and the moral thing to do is give in," says Dr. Garbarino. "If you failed to prevent it, then the *worst* thing you can do is give in, because you just strengthen that response."

Try to remember that most children have tantrums, and despite what you're sure everyone around you is thinking, they're not necessarily a sign of poor parenting.

■ Do not have a tantrum yourself. Perhaps the most important thing you can do for your child is to model appropriate behavior. This means not losing your cool when he's having a tantrum—and not losing it when you are angry and frustrated yourself.

Rather, allow him to see you handling frustration in a calm, reasonable way. "Uh-oh, I got to the video store too late and now I'm going to owe money on the movie we rented! Next time, I'll be sure to return it earlier in the day."

One family Dr. Garbarino knows keeps what they call the Snap Tin in a prominent place in the house. Anytime a family member "snaps out" or is rude, he or she puts a contribution in the Snap Tin and the money goes to charity.

Some parents have told us they've had some luck mimicking the child's tantrum. Often, the children stop and laugh. Others stop and look. But they *stop*. And, the parents say, the tantrums disappear, possibly because the child realizes his only payoff is seeing mom or dad acting like a fool.

■ Time-out. It's more likely that you'll have the best luck if you remove the screaming youngster from polite society. Time-out is an effective technique for calming a tantrum. You can send the child to his room, to an appointed time-out chair or corner, or simply leave the room yourself.

A time-out is more than a breather for you and your child. It's another choice you're giving him, a way to allow him some control over the situation. Implicitly he understands that if he screams, he'll be isolated, but if he calms down, he'll be back in society. (See "Using Time-out for Behavior Problems," later in this chapter.)

With younger children who may not stay in a chair or in their room, you can hold them in a way that's gentle and soothing but not affectionate, unless you find restraint, however kindly intended, makes the tantrum escalate (it can!). One family we know made a time-out corner for their toddler using a small chair that they penned in with two child-safety gates strung together.

Child psychologist Lynn Embry, Ph.D., suggests that time-out be portable. "If your child has a tantrum in the supermarket, you want to be able to say, 'See that square on the floor over there? That's time-out. Sit there.' " If you're in the car, pull over at your first opportunity and wait it out. Make sure the child isn't hurting himself or others. You may need to hold him to keep him from injury even if you know restraining him will boost the tantrum to a new pitch for a short time. The point is to not give attention to the tantrum and to make it clear that the behavior is unacceptable.

■ Speak softly. Dr. Garbarino suggests speaking to the child in a quiet voice "so the only way the child can hear you is if he stops. Get close to him and make eye contact and tell him firmly that this behavior is not going to get him what he wants. You want to try to lead the child into verbal mediation of conflict as soon as possible. You do this by first modeling it yourself, then by helping him name what he is feeling: 'You are feeling really angry right now because you couldn't do this. I know that, but there's a good reason why you can't do this, and screaming and yelling isn't going to work. I want you to quiet down and then maybe we can do something about it.' "

■ Once the tantrum is over and the child is calm, don't punish or humiliate him. "Just pick up life where you left off," Dr. Garbarino advises.

■ If the child repeats the scene again later—and he surely will —remind him of how ineffectual his behavior was. "Say, 'Remember how angry you got and how angry I got and how nobody had a good time? Now, before that happens again, is there some other way you can show your anger?'" suggests Dr. Garbarino.

■ Breath holding, while a dramatic device, has never resulted in death, and there's no evidence it causes brain damage. "Before you can do any harm, you pass out," says Dr. Garbarino. "If you respond calmly, it should disappear rather quickly because it doesn't get the child anywhere. If, on the other hand, you show visible panic or you get enraged, it's likely to continue."

■ Tape him. Some researchers suggest recording your child's tantrums—on a tape or video recorder—and playing them back for him later, administering a verbal reprimand. They say this works, even with stubborn cases.

### WHAT PARENTS SAY

*When our toddler explodes, I remind myself that he is raging because he feels he must. Though I explain why I said no, of course he isn't satisfied with this logic. I let him rant and rage because I support his questioning authority while he learns to accept limits.*

*Kellen D.*
*Washington*

■

*When my son has a tantrum and starts screaming at home, I join in on the tantrum. The first time I did this he stopped what he was doing and got up and walked away. Now when he starts a tantrum, he looks at me and stops.*

*Cerene C.*
*New York*

■

*My solution when my daughter holds her breath is to take her in my arms and blow in her face so she tries to catch her breath.*

Susan S.
Pennsylvania

■

*When my three-year-old threw tantrums, I let her take a tape recorder with a story tape up to her room (or my room) and told her to listen to the story until she calmed down. She may have cried or listened through the story, but she did come downstairs refreshed.*

Ena C.
Minnesota

■

*I handle toddler tantrums by taking a deep breath, reminding myself that the very worst things I can do are, one, give in, or two, lose control myself. Then I just sit down and say as sweetly as possible, "Okay, honey, you have your tantrum if you need to. Let Mommy know when you're ready to be snuggled." Then I ignore her. Usually after two or three minutes (l-o-n-g minutes) she comes to me with her arms up and I scoop her up and we cuddle. Her tantrums only seem to occur when she's tired, hungry, or both, so once she's calmed down we solve the problem.*

Vicki W.
Oregon

■

*My alternative for giving candy at the checkout counter is to keep treats in my purse. I offer my child something special before the tantrum starts, to avoid being manipulated. A few suggestions include sugarless gum, raisins, crackers, miniature candy bars, or dried fruit. Providing the child with the novelty of opening a new package usually does the trick.*

Carol K.
Texas

■

*Instead of asking or telling our son what we wanted, we threw him a curve and phrased the request in such a way that he had to make a choice. For example, instead of saying "It's time for bed" or "Eat your vegetables," we would say, "Would you like to read the blue book or the green book for your bedtime story?" and "Do you want to eat your green beans with a fork or with a spoon?" Our son became so involved in choosing what he wanted to do that he usually ended up doing what we wanted him to do without a fight. Not only did we avoid tantrums, I think it boosted his ego a little to know that we valued his opinion enough to consult him on these matters.*

*Leslie S.*
*Pennsylvania*

### THE SITUATION ▪ Your Child Bangs Her Head

**What can I do about my daughter's head-banging? She's nine months old and she doesn't seem to do it out of anger or frustration, as my older daughter did when she was having a tantrum. Is this a sign of some neurological damage?**

### WHAT THE EXPERTS SAY

While head-banging can be a sign of a neurological problem, that's quite rare. More often it's the result of anger or frustration, as you've seen in your older child, or in infants, a need for rhythmic stimulation, says pediatrician George Sterne, M.D.

If the banging is severe, you may need to pad her bed or put a helmet on her. "I've heard of kids who bang their heads so severely it actually moves the bed across the room," says Dr. Sterne. If her head-banging is that extreme, she may have a neurological or psychological problem that will need a professional assessment. Certainly see your doctor if she seems to be injuring herself.

More than likely, though, she's just banging her head to help her gain some control over the stimuli in her environment, says Dr. Sterne. "Some children bang their heads at night to help them go to sleep. They have a need for this kind of rhythmic, self-stimulating behavior." Other children may adopt a more benign method, such as shaking their legs or rocking from side to side.

You can help eliminate the problem by bringing a little peace and quiet to your daughter's environment. Soft lighting and a moratorium on TV and stereo, particularly at night, can cut down on the overstimulation. "You can play rhythmic games with her, such as patty-cake or nursery rhymes. Having more of a quieting-down time before bed sometimes helps," says Dr. Sterne. Even an infant can benefit from a bedtime routine that will help her unwind.

As an expression of anger or frustration, head-banging can be frightening. But you need to react calmly. Hold the child to keep her from injuring herself (most of the time they don't). Use distraction or time-out to control it, but don't give the tantrum any more attention. Any behavior that gets a child what she wants is sure to be repeated.

## WHAT PARENTS SAY

*My son frequently bangs his head. About half the time I ignore him because it's one or two bangs and then he's up and running again. But if he seems particularly frustrated, I'll sometimes cradle his head in my hands, talk to him, kiss his head, or stroke his hair— just enough to let him know that I'm there and that I love him.*

*Jill J.*
*Pennsylvania*

◾

*Every time I said no to my two-year-old, almost regardless of my tone of voice, he bent over and with a great deal of finesse, banged or tapped his head on the floor. I thought it was extremely funny. My mother thought he would hurt himself. This child was no fool. He was not about to hurt himself because he was angry with me. I tried to limit the times I said no to only those things that were important and never mentioned what he was doing. His banging stopped after several months. As a postscript, he grew up to be a physician.*

*Cynthia S.*
*Pennsylvania*

## THE SITUATION ▪ Your Child Says a Dirty Word

My four-year-old son came home from preschool the other day with a note from his teacher. Apparently, he's been using a swear word very inappropriately there. I've heard him use it at home (which is where he first heard it, of course), and I've been ignoring it. Should I speak to him about it or continue to ignore it?

## WHAT THE EXPERTS SAY

Ignoring a child's use of "dirty words" usually works. However, says sex therapist Shirley Zussman, Ed.D., some parents find they can't. Since you use the word yourself (or live with someone who does), you're probably more comfortable with it. But you might want to tell your child that school is an inappropriate place to swear.

"Tell the child that 'those are words I don't like to hear. People use those words when they are angry and upset, and I don't want you to use them,' " suggests Dr. Zussman.

Then you need to erase them from your vocabulary, too. Unless you practice what you preach, your child will simply be reinforced in his use of "bad" language.

A small child quickly picks up that these words are emotionally charged, says Dr. Zussman, and may continue repeating them for their effect. Although the child may understand them in context —"People say these words when they're angry or frustrated"— it's unlikely he knows just what the words really mean.

You need to defuse the emotion attached to such words. The best way is to ignore the child's use of bad language and refrain from using it yourself. If you punish him or raise a fuss, you give those words power and magic, and your child may not want to give them up.

With older children—threes, fours, and fives—you can explain that you'd prefer they not use those words in public because they may offend some people. "They need to know that there are some words people don't like to hear and certain behaviors that aren't approved of outside," says Dr. Zussman.

But don't overdo your lecture. It should be handled as just another lesson in manners.

## WHAT PARENTS SAY

*Just tell them it's not nice to say and be done with it. The bigger deal you make out of it, the worse the situation gets.*

*Susan S.*
*Pennsylvania*

■

*My son and I started putting change in a jar when either of us said dirty words. We would mark on the calendar days when we didn't say dirty words. When a week was up with no dirty words, we'd treat ourselves to something nice.*

*Sharon K.*
*Ohio*

■

*In my house, everyone has words that belong to them, and there are words that do not belong to them. So when my children say a dirty word or insult someone by calling names, I ask them to please never repeat that word again because that word does not belong to them so they can't use it. Instead, I give them a word or expression they may have, such as "oh gosh" or "silly."*

*Mary R.*
*Puerto Rico*

---

## USING TIME-OUT FOR BEHAVIOR PROBLEMS
### Parents' Guidelines

### PREPARATION
1. Purchase a small portable kitchen timer.

2. Select a place for time-out. This could be a chair in the hallway, kitchen, or corner of a room. It needs to be a dull place (not your child's bedroom) where your child cannot view TV or play with toys. It should *not* be a dark, scary, or dangerous

place—the aim is to remove your child to a place where not much is happening, *not* make him feel afraid.

**3.** Discuss with your partner and your child's regular caregivers which behaviors will result in time-out. Consistency is important.

## PROCEDURES

**1.** Following an inappropriate behavior, describe what your child did in as few words as possible. For example, say, "Time-out for hitting." Say this calmly and only once. Do not lose your temper or begin nagging. If your child has problems getting to the chair quickly, guide him with as little effort as needed. If you have to carry him, hold him facing away from you.

**2.** Practice with two-second time-outs initially, until you are certain the child understands he must be quiet in order to get up. Gradually increase the length of time he must sit. After a week or so, when you should be using time-outs that are at least a minute long, begin to use the timer to signal the end of time-out.

**3.** The rule of thumb is a maximum of one minute of quiet time-out for each year of age. For children five years and above, five minutes remains the maximum amount of time. If your child makes noises, screams, or cries, reset the time. Do this *each* time the child makes any noises. If your child gets off the chair before the time is up, put him back on the chair and reset the timer.

**4.** After your child has been quiet and seated for the required amount of time, the timer will ring. Walk over to him, place your hand on his back, and simply say, "Okay." Apply gentle pressure to his back with your hand to let him know it's all right to get up.

**5.** After a time-out period, your child should start with a clean slate. Do not discuss, remind, or nag about what the child did wrong. Within five minutes after time-out, look for and praise good behavior. It's wise to take your child to a different part of the house and start him in a new activity.

## THINGS TO CHECK WHEN TIME-OUT DOESN'T WORK

1. Be sure you are not warning your child one (or more) times before sending her to the time-out chair. Warnings only teach your child that she can misbehave at least once (or more) before you'll use time-out.

2. To maximize the effectiveness of time-out, you must make the rest of the day ("time-in") pleasant for your child. Remember to let your child know when she is well behaved rather than taking good behavior for granted. Most children would prefer to have you put them in time-out than ignore them completely.

3. Your child may say, "Going to the chair doesn't bother me," or, "I like time-out." Don't fall for this trick. Many children try to convince their parents that time-out is fun and therefore not working. You should notice over time that the problem behaviors for which you use time-out occur less often.

4. When you first begin using time-out, your child may act as if it's a game. She may put herself in time-out or ask to go there. If this happens, give your child what she wants—that is, put her in time-out and make her sit quietly for the required amount of time. She will soon learn that time-out is not a game. Your child may also laugh or giggle when being placed in time-out or while in time-out. Although this may aggravate you, it is important for you to ignore her completely when she is in time-out.

5. You may feel the need to punish your child for doing something inappropriate in the chair (for example, cursing or spitting). However, you should ignore your child when she behaves badly in time-out. This will teach her that such "attention-getting" strategies will *not* work.

6. You must use time-out for major as well as minor behavior problems. Parents have a tendency to feel that time-out is not

enough of a punishment for big things. Consistency is most important for time-out to work for big and small problems.

**7.** Be certain that your child is aware of the rules that, if broken, result in time-out. Frequently, parents will establish a new rule ("Don't touch the new stereo") without telling their children. When children unwittingly break the new rule, they don't understand why they are being put in time-out.

**8.** Review the time-out guidelines yourself and with your child's regular caregivers to make certain all are following the recommendations.

Source: Adapted from *Little People: Guidelines for Commonsense Child Rearing* (3rd ed.) by Edward R. Christophersen. Published by Westport Publishers, Inc., Kansas City, MO, 1987.

## CHAPTER 12

# DISCIPLINE
■
# Friendly Persuasion

**THE SITUATION ■ Your Child Won't Use a Car Seat or Seat Belt**

My twenty-two-month-old son, the mechanical genius, has learned how to get himself out of his car seat and so far has escaped once during a short car trip. Is there any way I can keep him in his seat, short of tying him in?

### WHAT THE EXPERTS SAY

There's no intrinsic motivation for kids to want to stay belted in place during a car trip. Toddlers don't understand mandatory seat belt laws and don't see the danger in roaming freely around the backseat. You need to provide a reward for seat belt or car seat use. (And don't even consider tying the child in —that's as dangerous as his meandering.)

In fact, says child psychologist Lynn Embry, Ph.D., who received a federal grant to study which parenting techniques are most effective, you'll probably need to teach car safety by awarding prizes for compliance. Start by "playing car," she suggests. Put the car seat on the floor of the living room and strap the child in. Then sit in front of him on a chair and pretend to drive. If the child remains in the seat for a minute, give him a small prize or draw a happy face on his fingernail with a washable marker, a treat most toddlers find delightful. You can even use a chart, attached to the neck of your chair, on which you allow the child to place gold stars or stickers for every successful try at staying put. Work on this until you get compliance for a good five minutes (don't count on this the first day).

Now you're ready for a road test. "Choose a quiet neighborhood and plan on taking a twenty-minute drive," says Dr. Embry. "You need a quiet neighborhood because you need to be able to pull over and say, 'The car doesn't move until you buckle up.' You can't do that on a busy street."

Follow the same technique in the car as you did in your living room, rewarding compliance.

One very important caveat: Before you take your first test drive, make sure you buckle up your own seat belt with some ceremony, so the child sees the good behavior you want him to imitate. In fact, make sure you always buckle up. Not only will you be safer, but "you want the child to almost believe that the car cannot start unless everyone puts on his or her seat belt," says Dr. Embry. If you have a car that squawks until you buckle your belt, make a game of "shushing" the car.

If most of your trips are limited to a half hour and under, you probably won't have much trouble teaching your child car safety in no time. But if your trips are much longer, you're battling boredom. With nothing else to do, your child might very well occupy his time by planning his escape.

Denise commuted with her son for two hours daily from the time he was four months old. When he was an infant, he usually slept. But as he got older, he began to get antsy. She kept a box of toys (and later, books) within easy reach of his car seat and changed them every few weeks so there would be a new batch to hold his interest. Sometimes she played a children's tape. "When all else failed, we sang," she says.

With an older child—four or five—you might want to use a booster seat or a cushion that will allow you to buckle the seat belt across his hips and not his tummy, where he risks a soft-tissue injury if the car stops suddenly or there's an accident. It also allows the child to sit high enough to see out the windows both in front and on the sides. This not only cuts down on boredom but also on motion sickness, says Dr. Embry.

## WHAT PARENTS SAY

*The time that my kids started giving me grief about using the car seat coincided with that period of fascination about people in uniforms. So I told them that the law requires that they sit in the car seat, and that the police will stop cars where children aren't properly restrained. And I didn't hesitate to pull over and stop the car until they got back in their seats if they did climb out.*

Nicole W.
Connecticut

■

*I let my child decorate her car seat with her own selection of stickers. Now she enjoys riding in her personalized seat.*

Cheri M.
New Jersey

■

*From the time that my daughter was able to walk, she could get out of her car seat. I tried everything but nothing worked.*

*By the time she was three, I'd almost given up. Then I saw a child-safety videotape at my pediatrician's office. My doctor was allowing parents to take the film home for viewing. Once I watched it and saw that the scenes were tastefully performed, I had my daughter watch it with me. Among the situations they showed were crash dummies in various positions with and without safety restraints. Once she understood what would happen if she wasn't secured in the car, I never had any further trouble. She wears her seat belt faithfully and has for two years. She even reminds other passengers to buckle up.*

Kelly C.
New Hampshire

## THE SITUATION ■ Your Child Steals

When we got home from the store the other day, my three-year-old daughter had a can of modeling clay I'd never seen. When I asked her where she got it, she told me she took it from the store. I told her she shouldn't take things that don't belong to her, and I drove back to the store and made her give it back. Was that the right thing to do?

## WHAT THE EXPERTS SAY

"Absolutely," says Dr. Lynn Embry. "A child needs to understand that there are very serious consequences for this behavior."

The best punishment for stealing is forcing the child to 'fess up to her victim and make restitution. You want to get across to her that stealing is a serious transgression of social rules and punishment will follow whether the stolen booty is worth a penny or $100, says Dr. Embry.

"You want the child to get the message that this is serious," she says. "Don't pass it off, don't laugh, and don't base your punishment on the value of the item. Base it on the behavior. Kids don't understand the value of things. So a piece of gum or penny candy is as important as a diamond ring."

But don't overreact. A child of three doesn't really understand the moral implications of stealing, and unless it becomes chronic, it is not a symptom of a serious psychological problem, says Dr. Embry.

"Somewhere between three and four kids begin to understand that there are 'my' things and there are 'your' things," she says.

While an episode of stealing is a good time to pass on your moral values, probably the only thing your child will understand at this age is that you find this behavior unacceptable. It's another on a long list of no-noes she is accumulating.

"Don't get panicky. Don't overpunish. And don't think you can somehow teach these magic concepts of guilt and goodness to a three-year-old," Dr. Embry advises.

If your child takes something from another child, you might want to play upon her empathy. Ask her how she would feel if someone took something she treasured from her. When they're able to put themselves in another's place, children usually get the message quicker.

Though your child told you the truth about where she got her new toy, many children, even as young as three, will lie if they think the truth will get them into trouble. (See "Your Child Lies," later in this chapter.) Try not to get so upset about her lie that you forget the original crime. You want the child to learn that it's wrong to steal, not just that it's wrong to lie about it.

## WHAT PARENTS SAY

*One day we came home from shopping and I found a lollipop in my four-and-a-half-year-old daughter's closet. I asked her where she got it and she told me she had taken it from the store. I told her we would have to take it back to the store and she'd have to tell the manager that she took it. The kid was hysterical. But I knew I had to take her back to teach her a lesson. I called the store and explained to the manager what had happened. I asked him to explain to her what could happen to children who steal. When we got there, she gave it back to him and told him she took it and was sorry and said she'd never do it again. He told her that he could press charges and put her parents in jail (what a vacation that would have been!), and that she should never steal again. After all this, I don't think she ever will.*

*Susan S.*
*Pennsylvania*

## THE SITUATION ▪ Your Child Lies

Brandon, who is four, got into the Halloween candy that I had hidden in the back of a kitchen cabinet. Not only did he take the candy, he climbed onto the counter to get to it, which he knows isn't allowed. Then, when I confronted him, he lied about it. This is the second time he's lied to me about doing something wrong. I hate dishonesty. How should I handle this?

## WHAT THE EXPERTS SAY

Your son broke three house rules. Do you know why his lying seems the most important to you? "To most parents, a lie represents a failure in the interpersonal relationship between themselves and their child," says Michael Lewis, Ph.D., director of the Institute for Child Development at the Robert Wood Johnson Medical School in New Brunswick, New Jersey. "It's a violation of trust."

But Dr. Lewis, who has done research on why and how young children lie, says that's not the way parents should view their children's occasional dishonesty. Your child hasn't really betrayed your trust. He's simply protected himself from certain punishment, a display of precocious pragmatism that is part of the normal development of children. In fact, Dr. Lewis says, in his studies he and his colleagues found that the more intelligent, the more capable a child, the more likely that child will lie about doing something wrong.

Of course, that doesn't mean you should reward your child for his ingenuity. It does mean you shouldn't overreact, and most important, you shouldn't overlook the other offenses that prompted the lie.

To illustrate the point, Dr. Lewis tells the story of a little girl named Susie who, while visiting her friend Jane's house, steals Jane's favorite doll. When Susie's mother asks her where the doll came from, Susie tells her, "Oh, Jane gave it to me." Then Jane's mother calls and asks if Susie brought home Jane's doll. "Oh, yes," says Susie's mother. Jane's mother explains that Jane is heartbroken over the loss of the doll, which she certainly did not give to Susie.

"Susie's mother is horrified—'Susie lied to me!' If I were Susie's mother, what would I do?" asks Dr. Lewis. "I would have two choices. The first it to teach Susie that she has violated a moral rule in our family, which is not to take other people's things. I could explain to her the general rules of conduct in society, or ask her how she would feel if someone took one of her precious toys."

The second choice—and the one to which most parents are inclined—is to confront Susie with her lie, says Dr. Lewis. The deliberate lie then sends them into an emotional frenzy, and they completely ignore the moral transgression that prompted it.

"I don't think Susie, my daughter, has lied to me because there is a failure in the parent-child relationship," says Dr. Lewis. "She has lied to me because she is a clever little creature who knows survival rules. Though I do not want to teach her to lie, my ultimate goal is to teach her to be a moral, responsible citizen."

It might help you to sort our your priorities if you tally your own lies for a day. What do you say when you're confronted with these situations?

- Your friend arrives at your front door with her new Bride of Frankenstein hairdo and wants to know what you think.

- Your aunt Lucy knits you a crazy-quilt afghan with all the yarn she has left over from twenty years of knitting projects.

- You're watching your favorite movie on TV and your husband tells you that your long-winded neighbor is on the phone and wants to talk to you.

Those first two lies you'll tell ("It looks great!" "It's beautiful, Aunt Lucy!") are what Dr. Lewis calls "altruistic lies," kindly fabrications meant to spare another's feelings. The third is a self-protection lie ("Tell her I'm in the shower!"). "And we know parents teach children both kinds of lies," says Dr. Lewis. "We'll say, 'Listen, Grandma's going to get you a sweater for your birthday instead of the toy you wanted, but tell her you like it anyway.' We ask them to lie for us on the phone: 'Tell him I'm not here.' "

There are often ways around both kinds of lying. Instead of telling Aunt Lucy her quilt is beautiful, simply thank her for it and praise the effort she must have put into it. Your children can thank their grandmother for her thoughtfulness without gushing over the disappointing present. You can go to the phone and tell your neighbor the truth—you're watching *Casablanca* and you'll call her back after Bogey walks off into the fog. But you'll have to face the fact that in certain situations, the truth may hurt too much and you will, unfortunately, be encouraging your child to lie.

If your child is lying chronically, this could be a sign that something more profound is wrong and you might need some professional help. But most children will tell an innocuous fib or two or twenty, sometimes starting as young as two and a half, says Dr. Lewis. This is part of normal childhood development, and you need to deal with their lying calmly. First, ask yourself why your child might be lying. To avoid punishment? To make himself look better? To change reality to something more appealing? To protect the feelings of someone he cares about? If you can get at the reason he lies, deal with that issue as well as his dishonesty. Don't overlook the original sin because lying is an emotionally charged issue with you. Explain how you feel about lying and dishonesty in general. Tell him, for example, "I'm disappointed that you don't feel you can tell me the truth. When you lie to me, I lose my trust in you. How can I believe what you say if I'm never sure if it's true or not?"

Above all, don't lie to your child, even if it's to shield him from the ugly truth. You can preserve his trust in you if you explain to him what is happening in terms that he will understand, rather than avoiding a subject that may pain you more than it pains him. Children can sense when something is "off" about a situation, but are likely to misinterpret it as having something to do with them.

## WHAT PARENTS SAY

*During the last six months, my four-and-a-half-year-old daughter has told some tall tales. She claims to have accomplished an incredible feat. For example, she brought home a picture from school that an older student drew and said it was hers. If challenged, she indignantly proclaims that it is true. Sometimes, instead of confronting her, I gently interject some reality: It may not be her picture, but I bet she could draw one just as good. This lets her know I understand her tale and take it for what it's worth.*

*Other times, however, my daughter tells what I consider an outright lie. But I feel she generally fibs only to protect herself from punishment, and since the line between fantasy and reality is so easily blurred, I think she actually believes she has not lied. In dealing with this type of behavior, it is more constructive to forgo punishment. We talk, and I emphasize my appreciation for honesty. In this way, I hope to teach her that she has little to fear in taking responsibility for her actions.*

*Dore D.*
*California*

## THE SITUATION ▪ Your Child Runs Into the Street

I can't seem to get it across to my four-year-old daughter that it's dangerous to run into the street. I've scolded her, swatted her, made her sit in her room, but she still dashes into the street while she's playing. Is there a better way to handle this?

## WHAT THE EXPERTS SAY

That's what child psychologist Dennis Embry, Ph.D., wanted to know. "I had heard many professionals say, 'That's the time that you give them a good swat across the bottom.' In fact," says Dr. Embry, "I used to give that advice myself. Well, there's nothing like going out and watching the impact of your advice to find out whether or not it actually works."

Dr. Embry and his colleagues, after watching hundreds of youngsters at play, concluded it didn't. In fact, he says, "when parents reprimand, scold, or spank their kids for unsafe behavior, the probability of future unsafe behavior skyrockets!"

Not only did Dr. Embry discover what isn't effective in keeping kids out of the street, he found out what is. It's a simple matter of positive reinforcement. "We discovered that when parents made a fuss over a child's unsafe behavior, the children ran into the street. What we teach in parent training courses is to pay attention to and praise safe behavior. Don't just tell your child not to go into the street. Say something positive: 'Safe players stay in the safe places to play. Safe players stay on the grass or the sidewalk or in the yard.' And then you praise and reward the children for their safe actions."

What doesn't work is warning children that if they dash into the street, they could be killed. Kids who dash into the street two to ten times an hour (and this number of times is not unusual, according to research studies done in the United States, Australia, and New Zealand) and aren't killed aren't likely to take that seriously. "And what does that make mom or dad? A fool, a liar, not to be trusted. Though this is one of the leading causes of death for small kids, it is still an infrequent event," Dr. Embry points out.

The positive approach actually works, as evidenced in the research studies. And the best thing is that it also extends to almost every area of safety—from pools to playgrounds.

## WHAT PARENTS SAY

*A friend of mine instilled a healthy fear of running out into the road in her child in a very graphic fashion. One day one of the farm's chickens had gotten onto the road. Its gruesomely squashed body was there for all to see. The mother walked her child to the side of the road and plainly told the daughter that that was why she had to stay away from the road. That was what happened when a car hit something.*

*Heidi C.*
*Alabama*

## THE SITUATION ▪ Your Child Plays With Matches

**I recently caught my five-year-old son lighting matches. It really scared me because I've read so many stories about whole families being killed in fires caused by kids playing with matches. How can I teach him how dangerous this practice is?**

## WHAT THE EXPERTS SAY

First, call your local fire department and ask if they have a program for young fire-setters. Many do and will be happy to talk to your son about his match play.

What is probably prompting this frightening behavior is simply an innocent curiosity about fire, says John Thompson, M.S.W., a social worker at the burn center at Crozer Chester Medical Center in suburban Philadelphia. Although some fire-setting can signal a serious psychological disorder, many children your son's age and slightly older play with matches because they find it intriguing to see the flame leap from the matchstick and catch on to paper or cloth. You need to explain to your child why playing with matches is dangerous—but you also have to satisfy his curiosity. In fact, Thompson and child psychologist Dennis Embry, Ph.D., suggest you "oversatisfy" it.

Buy a large box of wooden matches and take your child outside with a large pail of water. Tell him to light the matches one by one, blow them out, and drop them into the pail while you supervise the procedure. "It becomes very boring to do this four hundred times," says Dr. Embry. "The scientific principle of this is called overcorrection and it works very, very well."

Also, look for positive behavior you can reward, suggests Dr. Embry. Tell your son that when he finds a match, he should bring it to you or another adult. Reward him with praise for his safety consciousness when he does. In fact, says Dr. Embry, you can set him up to succeed by placing matches in a conspicuous place where he's sure to find them. When he hands them to you, tell him how proud you are of him, and what a "safe player" he is.

"That way you don't have to scream and rant and rave in fear. Moreover, your child is learning that he has control over his environment and gains a positive sense of self. He is also becoming safety rather than danger conscious," says Dr. Embry.

## WHAT PARENTS SAY

*Telling a child that "playing with matches is dangerous, dear," won't convey much. Instead, take a child over to the sink. Crumble up some paper and put it in there. Set fire to it. Then say: "Playing with matches can make our house and everything in it go like that." Show him the crumbling, charred remains. "This could be our house if we play with matches."*

*Heidi C.*
*Alabama*

■

*We have always taught our children the importance of fire safety. We keep matches up and out of the way of little hands. When we go to other homes, I know they may not be childproof. I can't childproof the great outdoors either. I have found that by teaching them about fire safety right from the start, they will bring me any matches they do find. And I praise them for bringing them to me.*

*Kathy H.*
*Nebraska*

## THE SITUATION ▪ Your Child Hits or Bites

My two-year-old son has bitten me several times and has just started biting his playmates when he's angry. I've scolded him, and once I even bit him (lightly) to show him how it felt. Nothing works. How can I cure him of this horrible behavior?

## WHAT THE EXPERTS SAY

Children use physical aggression against others for a reason. They may bite or hit out of anger or frustration or to get attention. Some babies will bite for no apparent reason other than to try out their new teeth. Naturally, parents of a biter or hitter become concerned when their child resorts to such animalistic practices.

The truth is that a two-year-old doesn't have an arsenal of techniques at his fingertips that will help him appropriately get what he wants or express anger or frustration. Hitting and biting are two techniques that come naturally and frequently work.

Curing children of using aggression takes some time, effort, and consistency. Start, suggests Sirgay Sanger, M.D., founder of the Parent/Child Interaction Program at St. Luke's–Roosevelt Hospital in New York, by observing your child. When does he hit or bite? You've noticed your son bites when he's angry. What are the things that make him angry? The more you know about what causes his behavior, the better equipped you'll be to stop it.

In fact, says Dr. Sanger, you don't want to stop it before you know what's causing it. "A symptom like this should be looked at with great respect and care because you can stop a child from biting, but the symptom will simply go underground, resurfacing as something else such as scratching, stealing, or hitting," he says.

Knowing what precipitates your child's aggression will also help you head it off. If you see your child getting angry, remove him from the situation or distract him. For instance, some children get overstimulated when they've been playing for a long time with a group of other children. The hitting or biting could be your child's way of telling you it's time to go home for a nap or some quiet play alone. If your child is hitting and biting for your attention, give him more attention (at those times when he's not biting or hitting, of course) and give him alternate ways to get your attention. Even a two-year-old can learn that a touch on the arm, a spontaneous hug, or a big smile can elicit a parent's positive attention better than a right cross to a playmate's jaw.

One of the best ways to help your child find appropriate ways to handle frustration, says Dr. Sanger, is to frustrate him deliberately so he can learn patience. "If he wants food right away, give it to him. The next time, count to three before giving it to him. Then count to ten, then twenty. By doing this, you'll be teaching him how to wait for food. If it's a toy he wants, do the same thing."

You also have to approach hitting and biting in much the same way you do tantrums, which can often be a child's natural way of expressing anger and frustration. "It can't be allowed to succeed," says psychologist James Garbarino, Ph.D., president of the Erickson Institute. "A child needs to have some calmly applied negative consequences associated with hitting and biting."

Time-out, explained in "Using Time-out for Behavior Problems" in Chapter 11, is often an effective technique for curing hitting and biting because it removes the offender from society for a time. In effect you're telling the child, "People who hit and bite are not allowed to associate with other people."

"You've also got to tell the child that this is not the way people treat each other," says Dr. Garbarino. Try to help your child understand the reason for his actions (he's acting impulsively and may not know). Tell him: "I understand that you're feeling angry, but that's not what we do when we're angry. Next time you're angry, tell your friend how you feel and ask him to give you back your toy or offer him a trade."

Give your child praise when he handles conflict without resorting to violence. Absolutely do not hit or bite him! That does not teach the child that his behavior is wrong. In fact, if you use physical violence against him, you're just reinforcing his aggression.

It is often quite helpful to role-model appropriate behavior. This means allowing your child to see you handling conflict, anger, and frustration in positive ways. Another technique that some experts and parents swear by is to lavish attention on the victim of your child's violence, ignoring the offender.

## WHAT PARENTS SAY

*Take the child and firmly say, "No biting (or hitting)," and remove the child from the situation to a time-out place for a set amount of time. Never hit or bite the child. Just stay consistent in refusing to allow a biting child to continue to be with other children. Eventually they will get the message—especially when the others are having fun with toys or each other and your child is alone.*

*Linda U.*
*Pennsylvania*

■

*My two-and-a-half-year-old son has not deliberately hit someone to hurt them. He has hit back in self-defense, which I don't often like, but I recognize everyone's right to protect himself. We have talked about other "mean" children and how he doesn't want to hurt others like he has been hurt himself.*

*Angela W.*
*California*

# CHAPTER 13

# MANNERS AND DECORUM

■

## Beyond Please and Thank You

**THE SITUATION** ■ **Your Child Always Bothers You When You're on the Phone**

Every time the phone rings I can be sure of two things—that my phone is working, and that my toddler will be tugging at my sleeve and crying for my attention before the receiver reaches my ear. Right now, the only time I can carry on an uninterrupted conversation is when she is napping or in bed for the night. How can I get her to leave me alone for a few minutes so I can talk on the phone like a human being?

### WHAT THE EXPERTS SAY

As you probably know, the only people who haven't experienced this problem either don't have phones or don't have children, it's that common. And since you don't plan on getting rid of either, you'll have to find a workable solution, one where you and your daughter can coexist pleasantly even if a phone call comes along.

Believe it or not, this really is possible, says professor of pediatrics Edward Christophersen, Ph.D. What you need to do is teach your child independent play skills. That means your child must learn to entertain herself for a certain amount of time (from a few minutes at first to several continuous hours, eventually). It's a skill that will serve her well her whole life, insists Dr. Christophersen, because it's the same skill needed to do a good job with schoolwork now or out in the real world later. In fact, research has shown that the best predictor of adjustment as a teenager is how well a child in the three- to four-year-old range does with independent play.

This is not a particularly difficult skill for your child to learn even at her tender age, says Dr. Christophersen. Here's all you need to do. Every day make sure you have at least fifty to one hundred brief, nonverbal, physical contacts with your child. "Love pats" are what they are—a squeeze of her shoulder, a little ruffling of her hair, a hug, a kiss—but all without speaking a word. So while she is playing nicely with her dolls or crayons or books, you are reinforcing her good behavior. (Naturally, these contacts are over and above the usual verbal exchanges that occur numerous other times during the day.)

When you answer the phone or want to place a call, make sure your child is near you with one of her favorite toys. Move your chair close to her or walk over to her with the phone, and every minute or so fuss with her hair or pat her on the back. You will eventually be able to keep her playing contentedly for extended periods of time. She will not need to interrupt you because she knows that in this quiet way you are paying attention to her. Once you're off the phone, praise her by saying, "It's so nice when you play with your toys."

Suppose your child is four or five—old enough to know that it's wrong to interfere with your phone conversations. And suppose that although she is pretty good at independent play, she still seems to "need" you at that time. First, explain exactly what it is you want her to do by using simple directions, advises Sarah J. Fernsler, M.D., director of the pediatric outpatient clinic at Allentown Hospital in Allentown, Pennsylvania. And do it at some neutral time, not after a big blowup. You might say, "When Mommy is on the phone, I want you to play with your toys," or, "When Mommy is on the phone, you must wait until she is off to ask her a question." Remember, it is not reasonable to expect a young child to wait an hour for your attention while you chat on the phone. So keep your calls short when your child is with you.´

If she continues to disobey your instructions, remind her of the rules again. Give her several chances to get it right, since kids do have a way of forgetting some things. If she still disobeys, it's time for gentle discipline, says Dr. Fernsler, who also has a pediatric practice devoted to handling difficult children. Time-out for a few minutes often does the trick, even though you may have to repeat it several times before she finally internalizes the rules. (See Chapter 11 for a full explanation of time-out.) And she will eventually—probably sometime before she's old enough to talk on the phone to her own friends.

## WHAT PARENTS SAY

*I gave my twenty-two-month-old son and five-year-old daughter play phones. We have a game. Whenever the phone rings, I call to them, "Telephone, everybody pick up your phone." They don't hang up until I give the clue words: "Okay, bye-bye." And everyone hangs up. At first, I had to make my calls short, but now they just play along.*

*Cerene C.*
*New York*

*If I know I have a couple of calls to make, I set the kids up with a project (Play-Doh, water paint, or a videotape) to entertain them. When they were small, I kept a few little toys in a kitchen cupboard along with measuring spoons and cups to keep them busy. If I'm interrupted when on the phone, I send the kids to their rooms, and they can't come out until I'm done with the call.*

*Laurie S.*
*Ohio*

*I use a cordless phone so I can always go to where my child is, rather than having to get up and walk away from my call.*

*Judy K.*
*Pennsylvania*

## THE SITUATION ▪ Your Child Acts Up in a Restaurant

**When my son was a baby, we could take him to nice restaurants and he'd be content to look around and play with a few simple toys. Now that he's a toddler, he's become a terror when we try to eat out. He'll sit still for about a nanosecond, and then he'll squirm, fidget, and eventually throw things and cry. It's made eating out a nightmare for us and for any other patrons unlucky enough to be trapped near us. What can I do to make my child behave in a restaurant?**

## WHAT THE EXPERTS SAY

The simplest thing is to wait for your child to get older, about four or five, before attempting to take him out to eat again (except for fast-food-type restaurants, of course, which specialize in catering to kids of all temperaments).

Sitting through a long restaurant meal seems like cruel and unusual punishment to a child who's mobile. Of course, there are those mellow little kids who will sit there and play with toys or be happy to nibble on crackers. But reassure yourself that most people's kids are like yours or fall somewhere in between, says child and family psychologist Lynn Embry, Ph.D. If you're determined, however, to have your son master restaurant behavior before age four, or at least be able to get through a meal without an embarrassing scene, there are a few tactics you might try—none of which will get you arrested, by the way:

▪ Keep your expectations low. Your goal should simply be to get through the meal without incident. If you want to go out for a nice, leisurely meal, leave your child at home.

▪ Center the conversation around your child. Accept the fact that bringing a young child to a restaurant is for him, not for you, and so you'll need to pay attention to him most of all—not the latest office gossip, the new dress you just bought, or for that matter, the food.

▪ Have a few small toys on hand, preferably ones that don't make any noise. You could bring an old favorite, but sometimes one he's never seen before (bought just for times like these) can keep him happy for an extralong time.

- Bring food from home for your child and give it to him as soon as he appears to want it. Whatever attention span your child may have will no doubt be completely used up before the restaurant food arrives.

- Don't make a hassle about eating. If he is able to wait to be served, don't insist that he eat what's on his plate. If he refuses everything that's presented, ignore it and ask the waitress to wrap it up for later.

- Take your child to the bathroom if he should lose control. That's what restaurant bathrooms are for, aren't they? quips Dr. Embry. Or you could take him out to the car for a few minutes. But if you can't calm your child down in a reasonably short period of time, you may simply have to ask the waitress to wrap the food, then hustle yourselves out of there.

## WHAT PARENTS SAY

*Before we went into the restaurant, we outlined what behavior was okay, sometimes even role-playing situations. I also kept a small supply of interesting items in my purse: a tea strainer, a box inside a box, and other things that my toddlers only saw when we were out somewhere. It seemed unreasonable to expect them to sit with nothing to do.*

*Melissa M.*
*Oregon*

■

*We dine out quite often with our children. If one of them misbehaves, my husband or I give one warning, and if the situation isn't corrected, one of us simply takes the child outside. We tell him his behavior is not acceptable, and until he decides he wants to go back in and behave himself, we will stay outside. You would be surprised how quickly his attitude changes; a completely different child returns* to the table. Only once did this approach fail and we had to leave a restaurant.

Gail R.
Nebraska

■

As a single parent, it was important to me that my daughter be able to go to restaurants and other places and know how to behave. At the age of three, we invented "the restaurant rules." In order of importance they are: You must stay in your seat at all times (except to go to the bathroom). You must keep your voice low. You may not climb on chairs or sit under the table. If you don't like something on your plate, don't eat it, but never make a fuss about it. You may not eat sugar packets or salt from the shaker.

Before we go into a restaurant, I always ask my daughter to tell me the restaurant rules. And if she forgets during the dinner, I just give her a stern look and say, "Remember the restaurant rules!" That's all it takes. As a result we have had many splendid dinners in fancy restaurants with no problems.

Here's an added bonus that came as a result of my daughter's experience with restaurants. When I want her to help me at dinner-time, we play "waitress." She takes my order and then sets the table and carries the plates out—and she thinks it's a game!

Maria R.
Pennsylvania

■

When we do take our daughter to a restaurant—which she enjoys —we time it to be between the rush periods (breakfast at ten, lunch at two-thirty, or dinner at four), pick a place that caters to children (with crayons, their own menu, etc.), and remind her of the desired behavior.

Vicki W.
Oregon

**THE SITUATION ▪ Your Child Hates Long Car Trips**

We're planning a family vacation to a place that's seven hours away by car. No matter how much fun I'm sure we'll have once we get there, my kids (ages three and five) are sure to balk, bicker, and get cranky during the long drive. In fact, even a one-hour trip is no picnic with them in the backseat. How can I prepare for this vacation so that all of us reach our destination with more smiles than tears?

**WHAT THE EXPERTS SAY**

The best way we know is to make the car trip itself an active part of the vacation. This will require you to plan ahead, and we can't stress this enough. In fact, if you've never planned for anything in your whole life, including the kids you gave birth to, this is the time to learn how. Think of it this way. The four of you will be confined for many hours to a space that's probably no bigger than your bedroom closet.

If you plan it right, the hours spent in the car may actually border on delightful some of the time, and at least benign for the rest of it—which is more than most families can hope for. Here's what you need for a shot at a successful trip:

**Car Toys and Games**

▪ Give each child a bag (you determine what size) and have them select several of their favorite toys from home to bring along.

▪ Fill a bag of your own with "mystery" toys. These should be complete surprises to your kids and can range from stickers to comic books to sunglasses to, well, anything you think they'll like.

▪ Make use of your car's tape deck, and not just for music. You can get tapes of old-time radio comedy or mystery shows that the whole family will love.

▪ Use personal cassette tapes and earphones if all of you have different tastes in entertainment. You can get stories on tape for the littlest ones, for example, or you could record some of their favorite books from home before you go. Let older kids make their own choices.

■ Consider buying your kids a few travel-size versions of their favorite board games. For a real splurge, you could invest in Game Boy, the travel-size version of Nintendo. If your child is hooked on this at home, you won't hear a peep from him for the whole car ride.

■ Give each of your kids (if you think they're old enough) a map and a highlighter and show them how to plot your progress. This is a good way to teach kids the real meaning of travel time. In other words, how long does it take to go one inch on the map?

### Travel Food and Cleanup Supplies

■ Put a cooler in the car, a must when you're traveling with kids. It's not always possible to find food when they need it, and besides, you can control its quality and healthfulness if you bring it from home.

■ Bring food that's easy to handle such as cut-up fruit, cut-up raw vegetables, cubed cheeses, chunks of lean lunch meats, pretzels, crackers, cookies, and boxed juices or a thermos of cold water.

■ Make one of your breaks a special treat by stopping at a place that has ice cream.

■ Pack litter bags for garbage collection or you'll soon feel like you're traveling in a landfill on wheels.

■ Take moist towelettes along to clean up sticky hands and faces—not just the kids', but yours, too.

### Rest and Relaxation

■ Bring your child's pillow from home, her blankie, or a favorite stuffed animal. These are comforting to a child who might be missing the familiarity of home.

■ Take along a potty for newly trained toddlers. When they have to go, they have to go, usually without enough forewarning to make it to a rest stop.

## Miscellaneous Equipment

■ Put a flashlight in the car and make sure you have fresh batteries in it. A flat tire on a dark country road is no time to find out that the batteries are out of juice.

■ Pack a first aid kit. See "Your Child Gets Sick While Away From Home" in Chapter 5 for a complete guide on what to include.

■ Use removable tinted plastic shields on the windows to block the sun that shines directly on your little ones.

## WHAT PARENTS SAY

*I rinse out empty plastic syrup bottles, fill them almost full with water, and keep them in the freezer. Children then have a ready supply of cool water to drink as the ice melts. Even a toddler can open the pull top and drink with no mess.*

*When traveling with an infant, I always use the powdered baby formula. I can take my own water (kept warm in a thermos if necessary) and mix as much as needed. Another area's water may upset baby's digestive system, so using my own water eliminates this potential problem.*

*I also give each (older) child a roll of dimes when a long trip begins. Arguing, whining, and each "When will we be there?" costs a dime. The money remaining at the end of the trip is theirs to spend as they wish.*

*Jo Anne M.*
*Texas*

■

*Here are several games we play: ABC—The first person starts with A and must find a sign with a word that has an A in it. The next takes a B and we continue until Z. Colors—Everyone picks a color. When you spot a car with that color, you point and say its color. The first to get ten cars of their color wins. Map—Before we leave I write a list of cities, exits, and sites we will pass in order of their appear-*

*ance. When we get to the bottom of the list, our destination is soon to come.*

*Susan B.*
*Pennsylvania*

■

*Travel kits are available through our local library that include books, tapes, magazines, games, and songbooks. We always order one for every trip.*

*Laurie S.*
*Ohio*

■

*I collect small surprises to spring at anxious moments. These include a small flashlight, a magic slate, a washcloth mitt puppet, small memo pad, an old calculator, and a watch. Food is always important to bring along, but it should be made special. I call it "travel food" and explain how pilots, astronauts, and others eat these same nutritious snacks.*

*No matter how young your child, he must be made part of the "crew." That means talking together while en route about where we are going, how we will get there, and what will happen on the way (such as bridges, tunnels, or tollbooths).*

*Sheila E.*
*New Hampshire*

**THE SITUATION** ■ **Your Child Won't Put His Toys Away**

I have a four-year-old son who's a born slob. Every day there's a battle when it comes time for him to put his toys away and clean up any mess he's made. Even when we do it together, I wind up putting most of them away myself, while he seems to move in slow motion. How can I get my son to clean up after himself without being a nag?

## WHAT THE EXPERTS SAY

Kids certainly do take out their toys a lot faster than they put them away, don't they?

At four, your child is old enough to understand simple directions. In fact, even a child of two isn't too young. But ask yourself these questions first. Do you find yourself forever saying no to your child for one thing or another? Does it seem as though everything he does needs correcting, improving, or redoing? Are there more negative exchanges with your son than positive ones in any given day?

In that context, another order from you—this time to pick up his toys—can get lost in the shuffle. You need to set priorities and pick your battles carefully, advises Dr. Sarah J. Fernsler. Focusing on two or three problem behaviors will be much more effective than trying to fix ten all at once. Since neatness counts in your home, let a few other minor misdeeds go for now while you work just on that. Here's what you need to do:

- Explain the rules of your house regarding toy cleanup, but bring up the subject at some neutral time when all is peaceful. To get your son's full attention, says Dr. Fernsler, make sure he is looking at you even if it means taking his face in your hands and turning it toward you before you speak. Then ask him to repeat the rules back to you so you can be sure he's absorbed them.

- Make sure you've broken down the job into simple tasks. Just saying "Clean up your mess" doesn't do it. Instead you might say, "Put the blue toys in the blue box," or, "Put all the cars in the box next to your bed." The more specific you get, the easier it will be for him to know exactly what to do.

- Don't label your son as the slob of the family. A child will live up to his parents' expectations, or in this case, down to them. "If I'm a hopeless slob," he may think, "why should I try to improve?"

- Keep your standards reasonably low, especially at first. Just because every knickknack in your home sits squarely in the middle of a table doesn't mean your son should be expected to perform the same kind of precision housekeeping.

■ Don't sabotage your child's efforts by following after him to "fix" what he's done to meet *your* specifications. Fussy housekeepers are particularly guilty of this.

■ Talk about neatness as a team effort. You might say, "You are part of a family, and families all work together."

■ Reward good behavior. Tell him how proud you are of his splendid effort. Then spend some extra time together to reinforce it further. The message he gets is, when I put my toys away, mommy is happy and has more time to spend with me.

■ Set a timer and make a game out of putting toys away. But have your child try to beat his own time, not anyone else's, particularly not his sibling's.

■ Discipline your child when he fails to follow the rules. You need to have logical consequences for misbehavior, Dr. Fernsler stresses. "If you don't put your toys away, then I'll put them away, but you won't see them again for three days" is a logical consequence. Eliminating TV for a week is not. Your child is likely to test you on this, so make sure you follow through with your threat. In most cases you won't have to repeat it.

## WHAT PARENTS SAY

*I handled toy cleanup with the Tom Sawyer whitewashing-the-fence ploy. Putting toys away was never treated as a chore, but rather as the final game of the day, one in which Mom participated. First, everything had a place of its own on toy shelves, or on the floor under the lowest shelf. The exact spot was marked by a drawing or the picture cut from the box. I provided the format each day. One day it was, "Let's find all the red toys and put them away." Then each color in turn. Another day, it might start with the largest toys and work down to the smallest. Or the other way around. Or maybe by shape: round, square, etc. It was not only fun, but also a learning opportunity.*

*Ruth R.*
*New Jersey*

■

*When it's time to clean up, I put on a rowdy rock 'n' roll record and tell the kids, "Okay, it's time!" We all bop around and clean up, hardly noticing that we're doing a chore. And things are usually tidied up by the end of one good, loud song.*

Nicole W.
Connecticut

■

*Our house rule is always pick up one set of toys before getting out another. Our house is small, and it makes it much neater and easier at the end of the day to pick up a few instead of a whole roomful.*

Laurie S.
Ohio

■

*We decided to have our kids clean their rooms and paid them at the rate of $.25 per year of age. That worked out to $1 and $1.25 respectively, enough money to buy a toy or a coloring book as an instant reward for a job well done. And a job it is. We take this seriously. If you don't do your job, you don't get paid. And if you don't do your job and your sister does it for you, she gets your pay. Now that's incentive. My daughter may not want to clean her room, but she will certainly make sure her sister doesn't do* her *work and get* her *pay!*

Lori A.
California

■

*My children hate to clean up their toys, as most children do. I have a chart on my dishwasher with the children's names. Next to their names they receive a gold star for every cleanup job. When the chart is filled, they get a toy of their choice.*

Kelly C.
New Hampshire

## THE SITUATION ▪ Your Child Talks Too Much and Too Loud

My five-year-old son has an excellent command of the English language. Maybe too good. He hogs the conversation around the dinner table and other times. What's more, the longer he goes on talking, the louder he gets. I don't want to stifle his verbal abilities, but he's really starting to annoy us, and no doubt his friends, too. How can I make him understand that he must let others have their say, and that his loudness is offensive?

## WHAT THE EXPERTS SAY

Your son needs to learn to recognize when another person's body language says, "I don't want to listen to you anymore." And you are in a perfect position to help him do that, says Natalie Elman, M.A., an educational consultant, author, and director of The Summit Center for Learning, in Summit, New Jersey. When your child is interacting with you and you find him talking on and on, point it out to him right away—but only if no one else is around, she stresses. You don't want to embarrass him in public.

Teach your child to look for signals from others such as yawning, eyes wandering around the room, or body fidgeting. You can even show him what an impatient expression looks like. "Suggest to your child that when he picks up these signals, it's time to stop and ask the other person a question. This will get the other person talking and involved in the conversation," says Elman, who also conducts workshops in social skills.

Try role-playing conversations with your son, too, with each of you taking turns listening and asking questions. You might remind your son that there needs to be a give-and-take in any conversation, or the one doing all the listening will get bored. During role-playing you can stop anytime and make gentle corrections when you see him going wrong.

The fact that your son gets louder and louder as he talks suggests that he knows deep down that he's losing his audience, and this is his way to keep them listening. It's possible that as he becomes more aware of other people's body language, and as he learns to stop and ask questions to involve others in the conversation, the loudness will resolve itself naturally.

If your son continues to keep the volume up, however, you might try a little exercise with him. Ask your son when you two are alone to repeat his loud comment in a soft voice. Demonstrate for him first, says Jay Belsky, Ph.D., professor of human development at Pennsylvania State University. Whenever he talks too loud, ask him in a whispery tone to repeat what he said, only this time with a softer voice. Eventually, he should get the decibels down, says Dr. Belsky.

As with any unacceptable behavior, don't expect your child to change overnight, says Elman. There'll be many times when you'll need to step in with help, but remember to use patience and understanding when you do.

## WHAT PARENTS SAY

*One of my children talked constantly. I gently had to explain to her that there will be times when I'll be "all ears" and eager to hear her stories. Other times I'll want quiet or I'll find it hard to pay attention to her, such as when I have a sizzling frying pan on the stove. While she now understands that I can't always listen to her, I make sure that I set aside a certain time just to sit down and hear what she has to say.*

*When my child is talking too loud, I close my eyes and cover my ears and turn my head. He then realizes that I'm not listening. I gently remind him that I'll hear him just fine if he just lowers his voice a drop. When he does this, I praise him and show him that I am now enjoying the conversation.*

*Connie H.*
*New York*

■

*I tell my child that Mom and Dad need quiet time. Each day I set aside a fifteen-minute period when my child must be silent (while I read the paper, etc.). I use a timer, and if he makes it, I put a mark on the calendar. At the end of a week I reward him for good marks*

*with a trip to the library or some small, desirable activity, such as*
*my undivided attention.*

*Linda U.*
*Pennsylvania*


**THE SITUATION ▪ Your Child Makes Comments About**
**People Who Are "Different"**

The first time my child noticed someone's black skin color,
she pointed and asked well within earshot of the person, "Why is
that man's skin so dirty?" Of course, I was embarrassed and explained immediately that it wasn't dirty, just a different color
from her own. She's also pointed at and asked questions about
a lady in a wheelchair and a man who was bald. How should I
respond to her outspokenness? And should it be done immediately in front of the "different" person, or later in the privacy of
our home?


**WHAT THE EXPERTS SAY**

Every parent of a two-, three-, or four-year-old has a story to
tell like yours. Children not only *"say* the darndest things," they
say them loud enough for everyone to hear, as you've recently
discovered. When your daughter notices the "differences" among
people, she's not doing it to be cruel. Rather, she's demonstrating
her powers of observation. To ignore that these differences exist
gives your child the impression that there is something innately
wrong with black skin or a bald head or needing a wheelchair,
and something wrong in talking about it, too, says human development teacher Louise Derman-Sparks.

That's why it's important for you to answer your child's remark
at the time it happens. It's unlikely that you will offend the person
about whom the remark is made, because most people realize that
there is no malicious intent in a child's comments. In fact, most
welcome the chance to teach a child about their particular "dif-

ference." The worst thing that can happen (and probably won't) is the offended person may go off in a huff, which brings up another learning experience for you and your child.

How you respond to your child's comments depends on her age. Your response about skin color was on the right track, but could have gone even further. You could also explain to your child that a person has dark skin because his mother and father had dark skin, too. An older child can understand how the amount of melanin each person has determines how light or dark our skin color will be.

Children often ask if the brown color will wash off in the tub, says Derman-Sparks. "This is a fairly common question," she says, "because children are influenced by the racist equation of dirtiness and dark skin in our society." An appropriate response would be: "No, it won't wash off. When a black person takes a bath, the dirt on his skin washes off just like when you take a bath. Everybody gets dirty, and everyone's skin stays the same color after it is washed. And everybody's skin is clean after they wash it."

If it's a person in a wheelchair your child has noticed or commented about, your response might be: "That person is using a wheelchair because her legs are not strong enough to walk. The wheelchair helps her move around." For an older child you may want to talk about specific conditions that might require a person to use a wheelchair, such as a spinal cord injury, arthritis, or cerebral palsy, says Derman-Sparks. Resist the impulse to say it's not nice to ask about someone in a wheelchair. That won't quench your child's curiosity; rather, it will leave her without the ability to interact comfortably with a disabled person, she says.

The idea is to be truthful when discussing a person's "differences," and to explain them in a very matter-of-fact way. You also want to get across the fact that some words can hurt. You might want to remind your daughter how bad she felt when other kids made fun of her buck teeth, for example.

You can begin to teach your child the essence of tactfulness when she first begins to point and comment about a person's unusual appearance, whatever it is. About an overweight person, you might say to your child, "People come in all different sizes and weights." A similar response would work for many other situations, from baldness to a big nose. And make it clear, adds Derman-Sparks, that a person's physical characteristics, however unusual, are no reason to tease or reject someone.

## WHAT PARENTS SAY

*My son noticed a boy who had no arms. We talked about what could have happened to him. And we discussed what life is probably like for him because he has no arms. I told my son about someone I once saw who had no arms and used her feet to eat and pick up objects.*

*My son was born with a cleft lip and palate and we have experienced people's stares. Children would often ask questions only to have a parent whisk them away. I wish more parents would let the person asked answer the questions.*

*Kathy H.*
*Nebraska*

■

*I am legally blind and walk with a guide dog, and I use hearing aids because I am hard of hearing. My wife and I have kept no secrets from our daughter, nor do we act any different around her. Therefore, her views of handicapped people are just the same as for other people. We always taught her that we all love her very much, and that there are different kinds of people in the world who also love her. Our view is to treat handicapped people without any pity, just with love and respect. Consequently, our daughter does not point, stare, or act any differently to someone who's different from her, including my guide dog.*

*Lewis C.*
*Texas*

■

*Try to find something positive about the "different" person that your child can focus on. Aunt Nell laughs too loudly, but she can do some terrific tricks with a quarter. Cousin Todd never smiles, but he makes great chocolate sundaes. In all fairness, grown-ups aren't ex-*

*pected to like everything about everybody, so why should you expect
a child to be any different?*

*Susan B.*
*Washington*

## THE SITUATION ▪ Your Child Says She Doesn't Want to Be Black

Recently my five-year-old daughter said something to me that I didn't know how to respond to. She said she didn't like being black. I think she has started to experience society's intolerance of blacks and feels she will be limited by her color. It made me so sad that one so young should have to be burdened with racism. How can I help her accept and be proud of who she is?

## WHAT THE EXPERTS SAY

For starters, reassure your child that *you* think her color is wonderful, says human development teacher Louise Derman-Sparks, who is also the mother of a biracial son. Explain to her that we can't change our skin color, that it comes from our mom and dad.

This problem may come up even more often with middle-class kids of color because they are more likely to be in an integrated situation or in a white-majority situation. A child of color needs to see herself reflected in others around her to help build a positive identity. Actually, we all do, but for whites it's never been a problem, says Derman-Sparks. Society has always catered to whites. For blacks it's a little easier than it was a decade or so ago, at least as far as television goes. But there's more to building a positive self-image than that. Your child needs to see herself reflected in the real world around her, too.

To do that, encourage the "black is beautiful" theme started in the sixties. Buy magazines and books with pictures and stories about blacks and page through them together. Look and find service people (doctors, fire fighters, teachers) to whom your child can relate.

Try to find out if a particular incident precipitated her displeasure with her color. Derman-Sparks says her son decided he didn't want to be black, either. Upon questioning, she discovered that he wanted to be a paramedic like the ones he saw on the television show "Emergency." There were no blacks on that show, she explains, and so he thought that he'd have to be white, too.

"I told him that that wasn't fair, and that there was something wrong with the people who do 'Emergency,' not with *him*." Derman-Sparks and her son also wrote a letter to the producers of the show to tell them that they should show all kinds of people of all color on TV. Although nothing ever changed for that show, it did for many others that came later. What's more, writing that letter gave her son a message that he could take action, and that there would be other times when changes would occur. You could, for example, ask your local stationery store to sell greeting cards that show children of color, she suggests. And you could talk to your local toy store managers about stocking more toys that reflect ethnic and racial diversity.

There are different interpretations as to why a child might say she doesn't want to be black, says Derman-Sparks. "I think the major reason is that kids begin to sense or know or fear that they are going to be constrained or restricted by society because of who they are. So giving your child the support and the knowledge that you will help her do whatever she wants to do in her life is what's really critical."

## WHAT PARENTS SAY

*During a trip to visit my children's paternal grandparents, my son told his grandmother that he wished he were white. This very honest remark brought tears to my mother-in-law's eyes.*

*I realize that a lot of what he thinks and feels is a byproduct of what he gleans from my husband and me. He does attend primarily white private schools. We do do most of our shopping in the suburbs. I have made comments on occasion how certain parts of our city were once beautiful, thriving areas, but now are scary eyesores since the whites moved out and the blacks moved in. And yet when I hear* my children's wishes to be something other than who or what they are, like my mother-in-law, it hurts me.

I am proud of my black heritage, and I want my children to have this sense of pride. I want my black children to aspire toward the high ideals and goals as did their forefathers and not become complacent and contrite as young men and women have become in recent generations.

Children are not born prejudiced, but sadly, I feel, we parents consciously and unconsciously instill this syndrome in our children.

Vanessa S.
Michigan

# CHAPTER 14

# SIBLINGS
▪
# A Love/Hate Relationship

**THE SITUATION ▪ Your Child Hits His Sibling**

Every time my four- and six-year-old sons argue, it quickly escalates into a slugfest. I can understand that they will disagree at times, but does it always have to turn physical? How can I get them to stop before someone gets seriously hurt?

**WHAT THE EXPERTS SAY**

Screaming, spanking, and reasoning won't work. Neither will asking them what's going on or who started it. These are the tactics many parents try, however, and who can blame them for wanting to get to the bottom of the matter any way they can? The point is, says professor of pediatrics Edward Christophersen, Ph.D., it really doesn't matter why your kids are hitting each other, just that hitting is unacceptable behavior and it must stop.

Dr. Christophersen says the best way to accomplish that is to use the time-out technique. (See "Using Time-out for Behavior Problems," in Chapter 11.) Time-out consists of nothing more than a temporary interruption of time-in or, the good life. Think of time-in as the pleasant interaction of your kids with a toy, a game, a sibling, a parent, says Dr. Christophersen. It's also talking with your kids, hugging and kissing them, playing games with them, listening to them, and taking them places. Who wants to be removed from that? Not your kids, at least, not for long. And that's why time-out works.

Remember, it doesn't matter who's at fault in this or any fight. Both kids go to time-out immediately. "If you punish both," says Dr. Christophersen, "you're certain to get the one who started it. You're also certain to get the one who reciprocated."

When you see your kids start hitting each other, here's what you need to do:

- Call time-out. (Your kids will know what that means because you will have explained it to them previously.)

- Set a timer for a maximum of five minutes.

- Separate your children where they can't see each other, but where they can see you, if possible.

- Show them that you are not angry by just going about your business.

- Do not mention their fight during time-out or once it's over.

- Repeat time-out as often as necessary until you get the desired effects.

Don't be surprised if you need to send your kids to time-out twenty or thirty times at first, Dr. Christophersen says. Whether you're trying to teach children French, piano, or how to get along with each other, it takes practice to get it right. That means rather than keeping your kids separated, you *want* them to play together again as soon as possible after time-out. And if they start hitting each other, put them right back into time-out. When they are calm, they can come out of time-out and should be encouraged to play together again. Eventually, they will learn to handle their disagreements without hitting each other, and consequently, without incurring a time-out.

One final note: It's possible that one child will quiet down quickly while the other won't. In that case, Dr. Christophersen says, the calm one can come out of time-out and join mom in some play where the other sibling can see them. This reinforces the purpose of the technique—that time-*in* is much more fun than time-*out*.

## WHAT PARENTS SAY

*Under age two: Look the offender in the eye, hold tight, and say firmly, "No hitting." Then comfort sibling.*

*Over age two: Put child in time-out seat. Say, "No hitting allowed." Afterward discuss child's feeling and ways he might handle anger as covered in the book* Siblings Without Rivalry.

*Muriel B.*
*Pennsylvania*

## THE SITUATION ▪ Your Child Quarrels Over Everything With Her Sibling

My two daughters, ages three and five, sometimes play together nicely, but most of the time one or the other winds up screaming or crying. They tease and torment each other or argue over such things as who got the bigger piece of cake or whose turn it is to sit next to Mommy. Frankly, it's easier for me if I just separate them and make them play alone. Yet, no sooner are they apart, they're begging to play together again. What should I do about these sisterly squabbles?

## WHAT THE EXPERTS SAY

For the most part, nothing. As you've already witnessed, your kids may appear to be mortal enemies one minute and truly devoted to each other the next. If it's any consolation, the older your kids get, the closer they're likely to become, according to the American Academy of Pediatrics, the group who knows best about such things. The peak period for sibling rivalry usually occurs between the ages of one and three, they say. And it's more intense if the siblings are close in age and the same sex.

On the positive side, there are valuable lessons to be learned from sibling rivalries—how to compromise, cooperate, share, persuade, and negotiate—although you may find this hard to believe right now.

Don't interfere unless there is blood or the fighting is so cruel that one is falling apart, says Nancy Samalin, M.S., founder and director of the Parent-Guidance Workshops in New York City. Don't ask who started it unless you want to be put in the middle —a no-win situation for you. Don't assume that the younger one is the innocent victim or that the quiet one is the guilty party. Give your kids a chance to work out their differences without your input. And don't be surprised if they are eager to play together again as soon as the current crisis passes.

If your kids continue to have frequent sibling squabbles, you could also give time-out a try, a technique that works for any number of kid problems (see "Using Time-out for Behavior Problems," in Chapter 11).

Nancy Samalin also recommends using a tape recorder for screaming battles. "Tell your kids they can continue their fight, but you think they should have a recording of it. Most likely that will stop the argument," she says, "but even if it doesn't, they'll have a good giggle when you play it back."

Separating your kids when they fight will certainly end the situation for the moment. If nothing else, it gives mom and dad a moment of peace and quiet, which is a great recommendation in itself.

One final note: Expect your kids to react with increased sibling rivalry if you and your spouse (or ex-spouse) are arguing and yelling all the time. Your kids will take their cues from you, and so a bad marriage may teach children that fighting is how you behave with another person. Consider trying to work out your differences in private, and try to keep your feelings about your spouse to yourself.

## WHAT PARENTS SAY

*If the fighting is based on something general (which means no one really knows how it started), I suggest they both put on paper how they're feeling as well as a suggested solution to the argument. The only rule is that they can't talk to each other until both have completed their drawings. My son drew a series of heavy red and black circles surrounded by blue lines. He said the circles described how*

*mad he was and the blue lines represented talking things over. This
activity seems to give them time to "defuse" their anger and an opportunity to really listen to one another.*

*Melissa M.
Oregon*

■

*My kids always argued about who would sit in the front seat of the
car with me. To settle the discussion, we checked the calendar before
leaving home. If it was an odd-numbered date, one sat in the front;
if an even-numbered date, the other. Before long, one began to forfeit
her turn, and eventually, they both took the backseat.*

*Deborah M.
Ohio*

■

*To stop arguments in our home we have what's called a V.I.P.
chart. The Very Important Person for the day gets to sit in the front
seat of the car, choose TV programs, say mealtime blessings, gets
extra candy, the last piece of cake, etc. The chart has the days of the
week listed. Above each day is a card with the person's name and
picture, so even those who can't read can tell whose turn it is to be
V.I.P. There are seven in our family, so we each take one day of the
week to be the V.I.P. You can alternate which day of the week each
child is the V.I.P. so no one always gets the same day. This system
really works.*

*Kimberly H.
Oregon*

■

*My two sons went through a period in which they could not spend
five minutes alone together without ending up in an argument. I let
them know from the start that as soon as one or the other came to
me with a complaint,* both *of them would be punished*—no questions asked or explanations allowed! *This usually meant the end of
the game and a boring time-out in the bedroom they share together.
It took a little time, but it worked. My young son learned to hold his*

*own in an argument, and my older son got less enjoyment out of teasing once his brother refused to squirm.*

*Pattie S.*
*Florida*

■

*Our children, ages seven and six, were always bickering and fighting. I sat them down together and gave each one ten dimes. I told them that this money would be given each week, but that every time I caught them arguing or fighting, they would lose a dime for each offense. At the end of the week, if there were any dimes left, the one with the most money could choose either to buy something or to put his money in his bank. If he chose to spend it, the other child had to go along on our shopping trip. The one with less money had to save it in his bank. Not once in the time I used this technique did they ever have the same amount of money left at the end of the week. Today they are both richer in more ways than one.*

*Julie W.*
*Kansas*

## THE SITUATION ■ Your Child Thinks You Love His Sibling More

No matter how evenhanded I think I am when dealing with my two sons, Michael (the older one) feels that I favor his younger brother, Sammy. Michael says I pick on him all the time, and he's sure I love Sammy more. It's true that the boys are very different, and Michael is more difficult than Sammy, but I love them both very much. How can I convince my older son that I am not putting his brother first?

## WHAT THE EXPERTS SAY

Actually, you probably are putting your younger son first, at least some of the time. But then again, there are probably times when Michael has been favored, too, although he may not be focusing on that right now. The point is, neither praise nor punishment can be doled out evenly like so many Milky Way bars.

As you've noticed, it's easier for one of your sons to behave well than it is for the other, and consequently, easier for you to praise him. "Some are just born with a more pleasant, easygoing temperament, but that doesn't mean those kids are intrinsically better," stresses professor of pediatrics Patricia Keener, M.D. Nevertheless, perhaps your "difficult" child has it in his head that that's what you believe. In which case it's especially important to find reasons to tell him that he's doing a wonderful job, or that you see him for the unique individual that he is.

Aside from that, Dr. Keener recommends a few other dos and one don't that may help your sons know that they are loved for whom they are:

- Don't compare your kids to each other or assign labels to them. In other words, says Dr. Keener, don't refer to Michael as the "neat one" or to Sammy as the "smart one." No matter who is getting the points for one particular role, there's somebody else who can't measure up. Instead, simply comment on an accomplishment as an individual achievement. "Michael, nice job on your homework," or, "Sammy, what a pretty picture you drew."

- Do have fun with each of your children separately. What free-time activities do each of your children naturally gravitate to? Take advantage of their attraction to them, cultivate them, says Dr. Keener, and then share in the joy together, just the two of you.

- Do give to your children according to their needs, recognizing that that will vary. You want your children to have confidence that you will be fair, says Dr. Keener. That is, although your attention may not appear equal from day to day, your kids should know that over the long haul, each will get his due.

## WHAT PARENTS SAY

When a friend's three children complained that "it's the worst being the oldest/the middle/the youngest," she sat them down at the kitchen table with these instructions: "Before you leave this table, each one of you has to write down three things that are good about where you fall in this family." The best thing in this mother's eyes was that each child had so many good things to write, they needed more paper.

Lisa B.
Pennsylvania

■

When our four children were younger and believed that a rule or request was "unfair" to one of them, I immediately agreed to make everything equal for all four! For example: When baby/toddler naps, everyone naps; no one can sleep over at a friend's house because baby/toddler is too young; everyone gets extra chores so jobs are distributed equally, and so on. Invariably, the children decided to forfeit total equality and trust parental judgment.

Judy G.
Maryland

■

I try to include all the children in games and activities, but sometimes that just isn't feasible and one child would get jealous. That's when a sitter takes the other kids and a one-to-one outing is in order. It's easy to incorporate this into one's schedule by running errands with the child and building her self-esteem by telling her of her importance in helping. Ask her for her input and opinion and allow her to be a decision maker in small projects to demonstrate her significance in the family.

Deborah M.
Ohio

## THE SITUATION ▪ Your Child Tattles on His Sibling

My five-year-old son is forever coming to tell me what his four-year-old sister is doing, and believe me, it's never anything good. I'm not sure if his tattling is for personal gain or if he is truly trying to be helpful. Either way, though, it's getting on my nerves. How can I get him to stop without hurting his feelings?

## WHAT THE EXPERTS SAY

There's no need to be accusatory when trying to change a behavior in your child that displeases you, especially when you don't know for sure what his motives are. It's true your child may be tattling on his sister because he wants her to "get in trouble." But perhaps you once praised him for telling you of something dangerous his sister was doing. That might explain his eagerness to "tell on his sister" again and again. Either way, this is a good opportunity for you to explain to both your children the difference between "good" tattling and "bad" tattling.

You might say, "Good tattling is when you come and tell me if you see your brother/sister doing something that you think might harm him/her. That would be a loving thing to do. Bad tattling is when you come and tell me things he/she is doing that are not harmful." Then give them clear examples of each that they can understand, such as incidents that happened in your family.

Once you've established the ground rules, follow through by praising good tattling while giving bad tattling as little notice as possible, advises behavioral specialist Patrick Burke, M.D., Ph.D. Most likely there will be far more bad tattling than good, and you will find yourself cutting off the tattler more than praising him. When your child sees that you are not going to punish the one he's tattled on, that you are, in fact, going to ignore the whole thing, the bad tattling will come to a stop.

## WHAT PARENTS SAY

*Provide two boxes: the Good News Box and the Bad News Box. If your children are too young to write, direct that they make a drawing of the offender and the offense and submit it to the Bad News Box. The Bad News Box will need frequent emptying. The Good News Box will need only occasional dusting.*

*Jerry S.*
*Pennsylvania*

■

*We ignore tattling unless someone is getting hurt or getting into something she shouldn't. If the tattling concerns not getting along or trouble sharing toys, we let them work it out among themselves.*

*Mr. and Mrs. Stephen W.*
*Oregon*

## THE SITUATION ■ Your Child Takes Out "Sibling Rivalry" Feelings on Others

I've been very proud of my three-year-old son's reaction to his new baby brother. He's been so gentle with him and hasn't shown any of the signs of sibling rivalry I was told to expect. Lately however, I've noticed that he's become quite aggressive when playing with his friends, pushing and hitting them at times, and rather destructive with some of his toys. Could this be a form of sibling rivalry, too? If so, how should I handle it?

### WHAT THE EXPERTS SAY

According to Dr. Patricia Keener, children can indeed transpose their hostile feelings to a friend, a toy, or the family pet when a new sibling arrives. Tearing his favorite stuffed animal to shreds or hitting his friends may be your son's way of showing that he's feeling some displacement and is threatened by or anxious about the new addition to the family.

You need to get the message across to your son—and this can't be stressed enough—that he is special and loved. Children need constant reassurance that no one can replace them in their parents' hearts. To help your child know where he stands, you could try the play-therapy approach, says Dr. Keener. Stuffed bears, for example, could represent mama, papa, and baby. See how your child plays with this "family." Then introduce the new baby brother bear and watch your child's reaction. You might say to your son, "See how the mama bear loves both babies and the daddy bear loves both babies?" Just that simple message can do wonders, she says.

It's not a good idea to confront your child with the cause of his aggression, advises Dr. Keener. He'll deny it. Rather, look for natural opportunities to open conversations that allow your firstborn to tell you how he feels. When the baby cries, for example, you might say, "Oh, Johnny's crying. Does it bother you to hear Johnny cry?" Your son may respond with, "Yeah, he's crying again." Or, "I hate it when he cries." That's your cue to pursue the conversation further.

Don't be surprised if your son says, "I hate him. Send him back." Your response here is especially important. Resist the impulse to say, "You don't hate him." Instead, be very supportive, says Dr. Keener, and deal with the situation so that your child actually *wins* by sharing his negative feelings with you. You might respond, "Why do you hate him?" And your son might counter with, "Well, because he takes all your time." Now rather than talking about hate, you can talk to him about the cause of the "hate," which really is his belief that mommy doesn't have time for him anymore, or that he is not important anymore.

Explain to your son that the baby takes a lot of time now because he can't do things for himself like his big brother can. And that while you have to spend time doing those things for his baby brother, there are lots of other things that only a big boy can do. When you both do those things together, then you will be giving all your attention only to him.

By working with the cause of your son's negative feelings, he will be more inclined to speak openly about them and not feel guilty or ashamed for having them.

Once you've reassured your son of your love, you might want to follow up with some or all of the following tips, if you haven't already done so.

- Encourage your friends and relatives to make a fuss over your older son *first* when paying a visit to the new baby. He's the one who will appreciate it, after all.

- Keep a supply of small gifts wrapped and ready to give your older child when the new baby is receiving gifts.

- Get books especially geared to young children that deal with sibling rivalry, then make it a point to read the story as frequently as your child wants.

- Enlist your firstborn's help in caring for the new baby. (Even a two-year-old can fetch a diaper.) Make sure you lavish praise on your son and tell him how lucky his baby brother is to have such a helpful brother.

- Set aside a time each day that is devoted entirely to your older child. You could take a walk together, read a book, play a game, or just talk.

## WHAT PARENTS SAY

*Apart from the inevitable run-ins from time to time, we are not much troubled with sibling rivalry. One of the reasons may be that from the time of my second pregnancy and the birth of my daughter, my son has been a part of everything we do with her. He felt the kicks, he learned about how she grew inside me. He knew about nursing, crying, and the helplessness of babies before it happened.*

*When my daughter was born, my son received a small gift from us to congratulate him for his new baby. He sat with big eyes on my chair as we breast-fed, and he promptly decided to breast-feed his doll. He got to hold his baby sister, kiss her, lift her arms. He was eagerly watching, and actually taking a picture, when she lifted her head for the first time. It takes time and conscious effort to make sure the older sibling feels as much a part of the family after the new arrival as before.*

*Heidi C.*
*Alabama*

*In our house, sibling rivalry varies directly with adult bickering. When my husband and I feel good about our relationship, the kids get along very well. Unfortunately, we contributed to sibling rivalry by not being close through all the adjustments after the new baby came home. Over the year, as we worked things out, our preschooler accepted his new brother more and more.*

*Kellen D.*
*Washington*

# CHAPTER 15

# FRIENDS AND ENEMIES
•
# Handling Both

**THE SITUATION ▪ Your Child Is Rejected by a Friend**

Until recently, my five-year-old daughter, Molly, played with a little girl in our neighborhood named Jane. Lately though, this girl wants nothing at all to do with my daughter. The two of them still ride the same school bus, however, and are even in the same kindergarten classroom, so Jane's rejection of Molly is a daily torment. It breaks my heart to see Molly so hurt. How can I make my daughter understand that Jane's friendship just isn't worth the pain she's experiencing?

## WHAT THE EXPERTS SAY

It's always agonizing for a parent to witness her child's pain, whether emotional or physical. So comfort your daughter, first of all. Tell her you know how much it hurts when someone you like doesn't like you back. Ask her to tell you how badly she feels about it, so she can get it out of her system. You might even empathize with her and tell her of a similar incident from your own childhood, advises Lonnie Carton, Ph.D., psychologist and broadcast journalist for CBS radio in Boston.

When she has calmed down, ask your daughter if she might have done something to displease her friend. Could she have made fun of Jane's hair? Or broken one of her toys? "You'll want to choose your words carefully," says Dr. Carton.

On the other hand, points out Dr. Carton, a lot of times people have no reason at all for dropping a friend, and if that's the case, you'll want to stress that fact to your daughter. Then Jane has made the mistake and has lost *Molly's* friendship, even though it's Molly who feels the pain.

You can help your daughter move toward new friendships now, instead of concentrating on one that doesn't work. Is there a girl Molly would like to get to know better? Ask your daughter if she'd like to invite her over to play.

"The point is," says Dr. Carton, "there will be many times in your child's life when the one she wants to play with, for one reason or another, doesn't want to play with her. It's your job as a parent to help your child master the ability to make new friendships."

## WHAT PARENTS SAY

*I tell my daughter that a real friend will always be your friend even if you sometimes don't share your chips or play with her. When a friend says, "I won't be your friend unless . . . ," tell her that's okay because you have other friends. Nine times out of ten, the friend will come right back.*

*Cerene C.*
*New York*

■

*A child's need for acceptance begins early, and rejection at any age isn't easy. When it occurred in a nursery school situation, my child was hurt and confused. I explained we cannot be accountable for anyone else's behavior. I told her this was an opportunity to meet new friends, and that she should try to accept people as they are, not try to change them to be like anybody else.*

*Deborah M.*
*Ohio*

■

*Use this as a learning experience for your child. Remind your child that its doesn't feel nice to be treated like this. That's why we never treat anyone else the way you've been treated.*

*Debbie V.*
*Pennsylvania*

## THE SITUATION ▪ Your Child Is a Sore Loser

**Although my five-year-old son has several playmates, I'm afraid he's going to lose them all because of his "must win" attitude. Whenever he loses a game with his friends, he becomes either sullen or he stomps off in a rage, leaving his friends bewildered and uncomfortable. How can I teach my son that being a poor loser is going to cost him more than the game?**

## WHAT THE EXPERTS SAY

First, take a look beneath the surface of these outbursts to see why they might be happening. There are two possibilities, says William Carey, M.D., a clinical associate professor of pediatrics at the University of Pennsylvania School of Medicine and a senior physician at the Children's Hospital of Philadelphia. One, you could have a fiery-tempered child who blows up at the slightest frustration. Or two, it could be that you've taught your child always to strive for the top and never to settle for second best.

If you've been guilty of number two, you should consider modifying the importance of winning in your child's eyes. Kids take their cues from their parents first, particularly at such a young age. So if winning loses its top priority with you, it will with your son, too, in time. Stress instead the value of having fun with friends. In the long run, friends give far more pleasure than a momentary victory. And reassure your child that he is loved and admired whether he wins one game a year or one game a day.

That's good advice for those who have a child with a fiery temperament, too. A child who is highly driven and unwilling to adjust to defeat needs to learn that losing is not the end of the world

—that life has its bumps. Changing a child's basic temperament is not easily done, admits Dr. Carey. Rather, your strategy should be to help your child live with his behavioral characteristics, to curb them and modify them so they are not self-defeating, as they are during a sore-loser episode.

The following tactics can help your son learn how to lose, if not gracefully, at least without alienating his playmates or siblings:

■ Don't deny your child's feelings when he is frustrated by losing a game, says professor of human development Jay Belsky, Ph.D. Acknowledge them instead. You could say, "I understand you like to win, and it doesn't feel good when you lose." That will encourage him to share more of his feelings with you.

■ Explain to your son that acting nasty when he loses turns his friends off. Let him know that they may not want to play with him again if he makes them feel bad.

■ Remind your child of how much fun he had during most of the play, that it was just at the end when he realized he was losing that he became so unhappy. Dr. Belsky likes to use a comparison for emphasis. Say to your child, "It's sort of like eating a whole ice cream cone and dropping the last mouthful, then crying profusely and ruining *all* the pleasure."

■ Try some advance planning, advises Dr. Carey. Before your son sits down to play a game with his friend, you could say, "I hope you do well, but if you don't succeed, what do you think will happen? Is it going to be the end of the world?" Ask him if he thinks he can control his anger. Could he just think to himself that maybe he'll do better next time? (It's probably asking too much of a five-year-old to expect him to congratulate the winner, by the way, but you could explain that that's what good sports do.)

■ Practice game-playing with your child. Some of the time let him win and other times let him lose. Talk about his feelings after his victories and his defeats. Remind him that he'll get better at whatever game he's playing the more he plays it.

■ Use time-out at the first sign of sour grapes. (See "Using Time-out for Behavior Problems," in Chapter 11.) You're saying to him that you're not interested in that kind of behavior, explains Dr. Belsky.

▪ Try leverage as a last resort. In other words, be prepared to withhold something your child really enjoys—a favorite television show or a trip to the comic book store, for example—to elicit the kind of behavior you want. Dr. Belsky says that's better in the long run than letting your child lose control of himself and learn a negative style of behavior.

One last note: Don't get angry at your child. He won't change because you get mad at him. Ultimately he'll change because he comes to realize that his behavior is counterproductive.

### WHAT PARENTS SAY

*There seems to be a strong, ingrown sense of competition in children, and unless you make a conscious effort to modify their emphasis on winning, children will be in for much pain and disappointment. Not to mention stress.*

*Whether they win or not, say things like, "Boy, you ran so well. You are really getting better. I'm so proud of you." Or, "Wasn't that game fun? I really enjoy sitting here playing with you and your sister."*

*Try to teach them to have fun and feel special whether they win or lose, but do not expect them to forget about winning. They won't.*

*Heidi C.*
*Alabama*

### THE SITUATION ▪ Your Child Is Picking Up Bad Habits From a Friend

Every time my five-year-old daughter comes home from playing, I can tell which friend she's been with. If she suddenly starts to whine, then I know she's been playing with "whiny Whinnie." If she displays sassiness, I know she's just visited with "sassy Suzie." Her latest gimmick is jumping on the sofa because "Judy's allowed to." **Doesn't my child have a mind of her own? How can I get her to stop picking up bad habits from her friends?**

## WHAT THE EXPERTS SAY

If you look closely, you'll probably see that your daughter is picking up some good habits from her friends, too, although it's the bad ones that are always the most obvious. Little kids are like sponges, soaking up everything that passes by, including the many good and bad behaviors they see around them. Think back a moment. How many times have you noticed your child imitating your gestures or, much to your embarrassment, parroting your occasional bursts of four-letter words?

At this young age, kids are not busy weighing the good and bad of their actions. They're copycats more than anything. Lucky for you, however, it's parents whom kids copy most at this time, says child psychiatrist Kenneth Gordon, M.D. Which means you have the upper hand in this situation and without too much difficulty, can change unacceptable behaviors simply by setting a good example yourself, along with letting her know the rules you want her to follow.

Remember, it will be easier to get your daughter to stop jumping on the sofa or being sassy at age five than it will be to stop her from drinking alcohol at age sixteen. By that time outside influences will play a much bigger role in your child's life.

Don't be afraid, first of all, to tell your daughter that she is doing something you disapprove of, advises Dr. Gordon. "Every child would like to use the couch as a trampoline," he says, "but that doesn't mean you should let her do it." You might say to her, "The rule in this house is no jumping on the sofa." Period. There is no need to try to reason with her over this.

As you've discovered, your child is likely to counter with, "But Judy is allowed to jump on the sofa." Then your response can be, "Well, you're not Judy, I'm not Judy's mother, and this isn't Judy's house." Then repeat the rule for *your* house. Simple and straightforward.

When your child's copying takes on more subtle forms—such as whining or sassiness, as in your child's case—you might want to bring it to her attention without mentioning the friend you think it came from, adds Anne Bernstein, Ph.D., a practicing psychologist and professor of psychology. She may not be aware that she is emulating a friend, and even if she is, she may not want to admit it because of loyalty to her buddy.

It's our job as parents to say no to our children, points out Dr. Gordon, whether they like it or not. We don't hesitate to tell them to come in out of the dark, for example. We know that if we didn't, they might be in grave danger. At times, it's just as important to say no when the behavior is not life threatening. It is, after all, how we teach our kids to get along in our complex society.

## WHAT PARENTS SAY

*I say to my child, "That sounds like something so-and-so would do, but you aren't so-and-so. You are Molly, and you don't do that."*

*Helene M.*
*Maine*

## THE SITUATION ▪ Your Child Is Being Bullied

**My five-year-old son is constantly being teased, pushed around, or punched by another little boy in the neighborhood. I've tried to get my son to hit this boy back and give him a taste of his own medicine, but he's not a fighter and refuses to do it. This has been going on for about two months, and now my son is reluctant to leave the house for fear of an encounter with this little terror. Short of moving to a different town, how can I help resolve this situation?**

## WHAT THE EXPERTS SAY

This is a tough one, and a problem that is likely to crop up again in the future. Research shows that about one in ten children is victimized by a bully sometime during his school years. At age five, your child is getting an early taste of what could lie ahead.

Bullies have problems all their own, and perhaps if you understand some of those it will help you with your son's situation. Consider these facts:

- A child who bullies is sometimes being bullied by other kids, an older sibling, or even his parents, says William Koch, M.D., child development specialist and director of the Skhool [*sic*] for Parents at the Lenox Hill Hospital in New York City.

- A bully may have learned from his parents' aggressive behavior that fighting is the only way to solve problems or get what he wants.

- Bullies generally have a more positive attitude toward violence, are often impulsive, and have a strong need to dominate others, say researchers in Norway who have studied bullies for years.

- Bullies are five times more likely than their classmates to grow up with criminal records and have job and family problems if their behavior goes unchecked, according to the National School Safety Center in Encino, California.

Of course, your first priority is to protect your child from potential harm, and rightly so. Bullies generally pick on someone they perceive to be weak, says Dr. Jay Belsky. Someone who is sensitive, shy, or quiet is particularly vulnerable to be bullied. Although your son is only five years old, it is never too soon to teach him how to handle himself when confronted with a tormentor. Here are the expert's suggestions:

- Instruct your child to say to the bully, "I don't like it when you push me around. Stop it." Some victims have never told the aggressor that they don't like being bullied, says Lynn Embry, Ph.D. If your child's tormentor is not a major bully, this simple tactic often works and the bully backs off.

- Tell your child to walk away from a bad situation. If the bully refuses to stop his harassment, your child needs to know that he doesn't have to put up with it.

- Have your child try the friendly approach, but be careful he doesn't overdo it or it will be taken as a sign of weakness. Believe it or not, sometimes bullies just want to be friends but they don't know how to go about it.

■ Tell your son of a similar incident from your own childhood, says Dr. Belsky. Children need to know that they are not the only ones who've had this problem, and that successful solutions can be found.

■ Teach your child the power of a verbal attack. "You've got to think of the perfect thing to say to the bully that will totally disarm him," Dr. Belsky says. And for maximum effect, deliver the comeback when others are around. A word of caution: A bully who is nonverbal may become frustrated when he's on the receiving end of a verbal taunt and may respond with more violence.

■ Tell your child it's okay to hit back. Although child development experts don't often advocate violence, this is one exception that most can live with. Explain to your child that you don't like the idea of fighting, but there comes a time when it may be necessary to defend yourself, says Dr. Belsky. "Slug the little stinker right back the next time he bothers you," you might instruct. And he might even do it if he gets mad enough. But don't be surprised (and don't berate him) if he doesn't. A child who is a born pacifist will do anything he has to to avoid a physical fight.

■ Talk to the parents of the bully. When all else fails, it's time to confront the parents. You may find that this child is bullying them, too, and they are looking for help, says Dr. Embry. It's also possible that the parents will be completely unreceptive to your complaints. Nevertheless, doing nothing and letting the situation continue doesn't help anyone. Besides, if you're not the first parents to complain, it will be easier for them to accept that their son has a problem that needs attention.

■ Enlist the help of your child's teacher if your child is being bullied at school. She may be able to help you most of all. She will know who is bullying and who is being bullied. Ask her to talk to the class about this problem. She should make it clear to everyone that bullying will not be tolerated and will be punished. If necessary, your child's teacher can even arrange to have a meeting between you and your child and the bully and his parents. Make sure the teacher follows up on any intervention, however, or the situation could become worse for the victim. Don't assume that once bullying is talked about it will magically go away.

## WHAT PARENTS SAY

*When our son was nine years old, he encountered his first experience with a bully while riding the school bus. After trying several suggestions, he was still coming home in tears.*

*Finally, not wanting to solve all his battles for him by going to the teacher or the bus driver, we decided to try to make this enemy his friend. Even against his disbelief he was to share with this child and others on the bus some sugar-free gum one night and nuts the next evening. To his surprise the older boy, although refusing the treats, actually became his friend.*

*Martha F.*
*Indiana*

■

*With the first few encounters, I helped my son and the other child work it out so that my son could see some coping skills demonstrated. Now I let him work it out by himself, unless I feel that the situation is accelerating or getting out of hand. He has also been taught that it's okay to defend himself, but only as a last resort.*

*Angela W.*
*California*

## CHAPTER 16

# DAYCARE AND SCHOOL
■
# The First Good-bye

**THE SITUATION ■ Your Child Cries When Left With a Sitter**

My two-year-old daughter cries and carries on when I leave her with her regular sitter in the morning, although when I pick her up at the end of the day, she looks as if she's been having a wonderful time. She's even worse when we have our teenage neighbor baby-sit for us during our rare excursions into the outside world. How can I ease her obvious discomfort with being left with a sitter?

## WHAT THE EXPERTS SAY

Most children go through several bouts of separation anxiety in the preschool years. A baby who previously smiled and cooed at strangers may begin reacting fearfully to a gootchy-goo from someone she doesn't know when she's about six months old. That's called stranger anxiety. A few months later, stranger anxiety blends into a bout of separation anxiety, her fear of being apart from her parents on whom she depends for everything. She may get over that, only to have it recur at about eighteen or twenty months, when she's beginning to explore her independence from you (see Chapter 6, "Your Child Clings"). And you

may see it again when she's about to enter preschool or kindergarten, although you're more likely to think of it as "first-day
jitters" by that time. Some children may even find transitions
rocky their whole lives, which is a temperamental trait. They're
the children who need to be dragged kicking and screaming to a
good time.

If your daughter's resistance to being parted from you is
the result of her temperament, it may help you to prepare her
in advance for separations, even the daily ones. A predictable
daily routine—both at home and at the sitter's—can be helpful
even with transitory separation distress. "It's very important
to tell children what's coming next," says Susan Weissman,
M.S.W., founder and director of the Park Center Preschools
in New York. "Giving them that kind of control over their environment enables them to handle it better. Try to get into the mind
of a baby. It must be terrifying not knowing what is going to
happen."

If you're certain she enjoys the time she spends with her sitter
(save for those few moments in the beginning), ask the sitter how
long she cries after you leave. "In most cases, two minutes after
the parent leaves they're perfectly okay," says pediatrician
George Sterne. "If the sitter says the child just doesn't stop for
hours and hours or if the child seems to be unduly upset with a
particular sitter, then there may be more concerns. But most of
the time this is simply a test and the parent has to steel her nerves
and keep walking. If you're not going to leave your child ever, it's
going to start to interfere with your life and with the child's development, because sooner or later the child is going to have to
learn to separate."

Separation anxiety is one of those painfully taught lessons of
human life, one from which parents should never attempt to protect their children. It signals the budding of a child's independence, something you should welcome and encourage. It also
offers fairly reasonable assurance that the child has become attached to her parents.

But there are also things you can do to ease your departure.
One we especially like comes from Sirgay Sanger, M.D., coauthor
of *The Woman Who Works, the Parent Who Cares.* "I advise parents
to have an enthusiastic departure," says Dr. Sanger. "The mother
should not change her personality. Before she drops the child off,
she should be warm and charming and pleasant so, in effect, she's

leaving the child on a 'high,' just as you would leave a party on a high. It's also important for her to have projects that she does with the child that will bridge her absence."

For example, says Dr. Sanger, begin a project—cooking, model-building, a drawing—that you leave incomplete, so the child knows that when you return, you'll pick up where you left off. It gives the child something to look forward to when you come back —and assures her you're coming back. It takes a long time for some children to grasp the idea that out of sight doesn't mean gone forever.

Dr. Sterne recommends that parents prepare their children as infants for separation by playing peekaboo or stepping out of the room even when the child wails. "They need to get used to the idea that people that they don't see still exist," he says.

Susan Weissman recommends that parents never try to escape the good-bye scene, however lugubrious it becomes. "Always say good-bye. Tell the child where you are going and when you will be coming back. Tell them you know they are going to have a good time and make it brief. The more you hang on, the more miserable the child becomes."

One reason for that is that parents who prolong their good-byes tend to be suffering from a little separation anxiety themselves, and just as often from guilt. "What we have seen is that for children to really separate well, parents have to really believe that their kids are going to be well taken care of," says Weissman. "If the parent shows ambivalence vis à vis whom they are leaving the child with, the kids will figure it out in a minute."

You need to be confident in your sitter and confident in your decision to work (or to enjoy a well-deserved evening out). Otherwise you'll be transmitting your doubts to your child. You should greet the caregiver warmly, spend a few minutes talking to her, and show your child that you like this woman with whom she'll be spending the day or night. If you're upset leaving her, how can she be anything but weepy and clingy?

"If possible, have the caregiver hold the child and comfort her or have a favorite activity ready for the child in the morning," says Weissman. If your child can plunge into something fun first thing, she might feel a little better about your leaving.

Some parents find that leaving the child with a picture or photo album of parents, family members, pets, and friends can help the child deal with occasional homesickness during the day. A blanket or favorite teddy can also ease the transition, since they're part of the child's home security system.

As for your occasional baby-sitter, perhaps she ought to be more than occasional. Your daughter may need to spend more time with her, to get to know her and feel more comfortable with her. Many working parents tend to avoid leaving their children with sitters on the weekends because they feel guilty. After all, their children are with sitters or in daycare forty hours a week. But you need a life, too, and your child will probably do better with a sitter who is less of a stranger.

The bottom line is that your child is probably always going to prefer you—that is, until a few years down the line when friends seem to become more important than parents. That's not a bad thing. It may mean you have to put up with some melodramatic partings, but if you're confident in your sitters, you can be confident that your child will grow from the experience of being separated from you and relating to other people.

## WHAT PARENTS SAY

*I've found that separation anxiety can be eased a little if the baby-sitter is invited over thirty or forty-five minutes before my husband and I leave. I socialize with the baby-sitter and allow my son to interact with her. I'll even leave my son and the baby-sitter in the room while I finish getting ready. This way my son gets the idea that when I'm away, I will return. Then I instruct the baby-sitter that once we leave, to do my son's most favorite thing: give him a bath. As soon as the water is turned on, my son's troubles are over, no matter what. After the bath comes his second favorite thing: a night-time bottle. And then to bed. I've used this routine with several baby-sitters, and they all were delighted to baby-sit again.*

*Two other suggestions:*

*1. Use the same baby-sitter as often as you can.*

*2. If another mother doesn't mind, use her as a baby-sitter. My son loves other buddies.*

*Vicki F.*
*Michigan*

■

*When I leave the twins with a baby-sitter, I give them a kiss in the palm of their hands. They put the kisses in their pockets. When they need a kiss at a later time, they take it out and put it on. For my older boys, I write a special note on their lunch napkins. At lunchtime, they read the note, which puts large smiles on their faces. I even find my older boys still asking for a pocket kiss!*

*Rosemarie L.*
*Pennsylvania*

■

*Over time, I discovered a combination of things that helped my two-year-old to accept our separation better. Since comforting her only prolonged the crying, I learned to be cheerful but firm. Mommy had to go to work. Each morning as I dressed her, I would talk about something fun we would do together when I returned. The older she became, the better she was able to accept going to the baby-sitter.*

*Kathleen T.*
*Wisconsin*

■

*I read once that when you leave a small child, she thinks you have died—wow! Some children respond better when you prepare them, telling them where they are going, what you'll be doing, and reassuring them about when you'll be returning. Other children seem to do better if they just get there and you leave as quickly as possible. Preparing them with all the details just seems to drag out the process and accelerates the anxiety until the children are hysterical by the time you get to the baby-sitter's. You have to decide which is best for your individual situation, and always remember that just because it worked with one child certainly doesn't mean it'll work with another.*

*One helpful hint: Leave a pocketbook (or anything else very personal that your child will know is yours) on a shelf in the room where your child will be. This will reassure the child in a concrete way that you are indeed coming back.*

*Maree D.*
*Florida*

## THE SITUATION ▪ Your Child Complains About a Sitter

My two-and-a-half-year old son has been with a new sitter for a couple of weeks and he's miserable. He cries when I leave and she tells me he cries for several hours a day. He tells me he doesn't like it there. I don't know whether he's got separation anxiety, misses his old sitter, or if there's a real problem going on. How can I tell?

## WHAT THE EXPERTS SAY

Listen to your child. If he's verbal, isn't a chronic complainer, and has never complained about a sitter before, there may be a real problem, says pediatrician George Sterne.

Your son and his sitter may have a poor fit, a personality clash. For example, if she's authoritative and he's the rare child who listens to reason, they may simply not get along. There may not be enough children his age to play with or not enough age-appropriate toys. Perhaps she's more inclined to keep the kids indoors, working on quiet projects, while he's the kind of child who needs to run and romp. Or perhaps there's neglect or abuse going on. Hundreds of things could be going wrong, from minor to major. Investigate.

Drop in on the sitter unexpectedly (all good sitters and daycare centers make it clear that parents are welcome at all times). That way you won't see the situation spit-polished for your inspection.

At home, engage your child in doll or puppet play, suggests Dr. Sterne. "You can tell a lot about what's going on by listening to them when they play. If they are suddenly saying things you know they didn't hear at home, and you don't like what you hear, or if they're doing things with their dolls or toys that show a kind of relationship that you don't approve of, they may be learning this from daycare."

If you listen carefully, your children, even if their vocabularies are limited, will give you clues to what is wrong. For example, Denise's son, who has always had a problem with separation anxiety, was having trouble adjusting to a new baby-sitter. He cried inconsolably when Denise left him in the morning, and his eyes were still puffy and red when she picked him up in the afternoon. But she wasn't sure whether there was a real problem until one day, out of the blue, Patrick asked, "Mommy, are you in charge?"

"Neither my husband nor I use that phrase so I was suspicious," she explains. "I asked him, 'Who says that?' He told me it was his new baby-sitter. I could only assume that was the authoritarian way she controlled the kids in her charge, and knowing Patrick was a strong-willed, independent thinker, I knew this was the wrong combination. When my neighbor, a gentle, reasonable woman who believes in explaining things to children, started watching Patrick for me, his whole demeanor changed. He still cried a few mornings, but most of the time he seemed happy to go to her house."

Daycare expert Sirgay Sanger also suggests that parents, in an attempt to get at the bottom of their children's upset, agree to do whatever it will take to calm them down. Says Sanger, "If they calm right down and it seems as if they were just trying to manipulate you, then you could say, 'Oh, my goodness, you really wanted some attention, so here's some attention,' and put some pretend attention in their hands." You can both have a good giggle.

But a child who is really upset may not calm down even when you offer to do whatever he wants. "Often they will still whimper and weep and cry, and then you know something really is upsetting them," says Dr. Sanger.

Encourage the child to tell you what is troubling him, using dolls or puppets to help him recreate the daycare situation.

It's usually harder to judge a daycare situation with an infant, but there are some signs you can look for:

- excessive crying and clinging

- signs of neglect, such as diaper rash or a bald spot on the back of the head, which usually means the child is left in one place for hours

- developmental regression

It's important that, when selecting daycare for your child, you visit the sitter's house or daycare center several times, at least once unannounced. Watch the other children. Do they seem happy? Are they relating well to the daycare personnel? Don't let the physical atmosphere sway you; look at the human relationships.

Needless to say, always check references, although no daycare provider with half a brain is going to give you the names of clients who will give her a poor reference.

## WHAT PARENTS SAY

*Over the years, my children have been in four different daycare homes, and they complained about two of them for different reasons. I started to watch more when dropping them off and picking them up. I started to notice things I did not find acceptable. They weren't being harmed physically, but emotionally they were. We are very happy with our provider now and it shows in the children.*

*Gail R.*
*Nebraska*

■

*When my son began complaining about the new sitter, I brushed it off as a phase he was going through. I figured he just didn't want me going to work and that was his way of showing me his feelings. Then when his brother (who couldn't talk yet) began showing signs of something bothering him, I started to listen to my older son's complaints. I asked questions and was shocked at his answers. Then, one day, I hid a tape recorder under the bed and taped thirty minutes of his sitter's stay. That night I was in tears, listening to what happened after I kissed them all good-bye in the morning. And I had faithfully checked the sitter's references and looked into her background. I learned a very important lesson: Always listen to your children's complaints and take them seriously.*

*Kathy H.*
*Nebraska*

## THE SITUATION ▪ Your Child Seems to Prefer the Sitter to You

My two-year-old daughter loves our live-out nanny. She stands at the door every morning waiting for Wendy to come, even on Saturdays and Sundays, when Wendy doesn't work. I can't tell you how depressing that is. I feel like a failure as a mother. I've even been tempted to hire a new nanny, but I think my daughter would be heartbroken if Wendy left.

### WHAT THE EXPERTS SAY

If you and your daughter have a close, loving relationship otherwise, her love for her nanny shouldn't trouble you.

"The first thing every mother needs to know is that regardless of everything, mommy is still mommy," says Susan Weissman, coauthor of *The Parents' Guide to Daycare.* "The caregivers, while they are performing a wonderful service in taking care of your child, will *never* take your place."

When your daughter is sick or wakes up frightened in the night, does she call for you or for her nanny? When you're alone together, is she affectionate and does she seem to enjoy your company? If so, you need to look at this other relationship she has from the positive side.

It's natural for your daughter to love her nanny. She's the object of her nanny's undivided attention. After all, all emotions aside, your child is her nanny's *job.* You may not be able to give your daughter that same focused attention when you're together because you have other things to do as well. But that doesn't mean your daughter's feelings for her nanny will ever displace her feelings for you.

In fact, says Weissman, seeing that your child can form a close attachment to another person ought to give you assurance that she's developing well. It means the original attachment—to you —is solid. She now feels confident enough that you're "hers" that she can establish other loving relationships. You've done something right! "It's more to worry about if a child can't form a positive relationship with her caregiver," says Weissman. "That signifies that the initial parent-child relationship never really got off the ground."

Think of your alternative: How would you feel about leaving your child for eight hours with someone she doesn't like and who doesn't like her? Or someone with whom she has a lukewarm relationship?

Your relationship with your caregiver should not be "adversarial," says Weissman. "You are not in competition for your child's love."

In fact, you are comothering your child. Don't let that relationship erode because of jealousy, which may be brought on by your low self-esteem, feelings of inadequacy as a mother, or guilt because you aren't with your child all the time as your mother probably was. You're still a good mother. Your child's love for her nanny proves that.


## WHAT PARENTS SAY

*All three of my children preferred the sitter to me because the sitter was their grandmother. My mother lived close by and helped out quite a bit. Whenever my husband and I returned from a day or evening out, and Grandmom had to leave, they all stood at the door crying. Fortunately for me they never expected to get the same treatment from me as they did from their grandmother. The crying lasted only a few minutes and things would get back to normal.*

*Cynthia S.*
*Pennsylvania*

■

*If your child prefers the sitter to you, the sitter may be spoiling the child and letting him do things that you don't allow. Don't take it personally and find out why your child likes the sitter so much. You may have to tell her what your child is and is not allowed to do or eat.*

*Kelly T.*
*Florida*

**THE SITUATION ▪ Your Child is Exposed to Different Religious Customs at a Sitter's**

My husband and I aren't religious people, but my son's babysitter is. While he is at her house, he says prayers before meals and now occasionally wants to say them at our house. He has asked us about God and Jesus, and we've tried to explain them as simply as possible, without telling him that we don't believe in the same things as his sitter. His sitter is a wonderful person, and I certainly can't tell her not to pray in her own house, but the whole thing bothers me.

## WHAT THE EXPERTS SAY

Of all the sticky situations we encounter as parents of the nineties, religion certainly ranks up there as one of the stickiest. Do we raise our children in the religion of our parents? Do we raise them in any religion at all? Parents who haven't seen the inside of a church or synagogue for twenty years, except for the occasional wedding, often find themselves carting their youngsters off to Sunday school or Friday-night services. Others, who think they would become the role model of hypocrisy if they stepped onto holy ground, grapple with what they're going to tell their children they believe in. We would not presume to tell you how to handle this. Religion is a personal matter. But you might want to get your beliefs in order. Your child is going to want to know how you feel.

In fact, you can use his exposure to another person's religion—which would have happened sooner or later—as a teaching experience. Parenting counselor Joanna Lerman, M.S.W., suggests you take advantage of it as an opportunity to impart your own views and values, and to teach your child the rudiments of tolerance. After all, this is not a homogeneous world. He's going to encounter people who hold beliefs different—even alien—from his own. He's going to need to learn to tolerate and respect them—even when, sometimes, they won't tolerate or respect him.

Certainly, if your sitter is proselytizing or if your little Jewish son is coming home singing "Jesus Loves Me," you have a right to ask your caregiver to stop. If she won't or can't, then you probably need to remove your child from her care.

But if your son is simply being exposed in a natural way to another's beliefs and practices—which can also happen in a religious-oriented preschool—you can probably take a more relaxed attitude. It doesn't mean he's going to join up.

"Keep in mind," says developmental psychologist Carolee Howes, Ph.D., professor of education at UCLA, "that kids learn very quickly that there are different rules in different cultures. You can say even to a three-year-old, 'In our family we do things this way, and in childcare you do things another way.' "

## WHAT PARENTS SAY

*My husband was raised Protestant, I, Catholic, and our son attended a Jewish preschool. We explained to him that different people believe different things, have different customs, and celebrate different holidays. Now that he attends a public-school kindergarten, he is very accepting of people who are different from him. He sometimes questions us on what other children say to him ("John said God can run faster than a car"), and we provide him with answers we feel are right.*

*Christine M.*
*Pennsylvania*

## THE SITUATION ■ My Child Doesn't Seem Ready for Kindergarten or First Grade

I had always assumed my son would go to kindergarten when he turned five (he was born in September), but I'm beginning to wonder if he's ready. He can count to twenty, knows all his colors, and can even write his name, but I don't think he's emotionally ready, even for half-day sessions. I can't exactly put my finger on what makes me feel this way. Call it parent's intuition. Should he be tested first?

## WHAT THE EXPERTS SAY

You're right to be concerned. A spate of new research lately seems to indicate that the youngest children in kindergarten are at higher risk of repeating a grade or being labeled learning disabled than their older classmates. Some experts believe that these so-called "summer and fall children"—a label that refers to their birthdays—are being set up for a lifetime of failure and damaged self-esteem because "they are expected to do too much too soon," says Louise Bates Ames, Ph.D., associate director of the Gesell Institute in New Haven, Connecticut, where the Gesell school-readiness test was developed.

Today, a disproportionate number of children are judged "too young" for kindergarten. Many experts, including the National Association for the Education of Young Children (NAEYC), believe the fault lies not in the children but in the kindergarten curriculum, which is developmentally inappropriate for some four- and five-year-olds.

If you're a Baby Boom parent, a trip to a kindergarten classroom may surprise you. In some places, where the water table once stood you're likely to find a computer. "In the typical American kindergarten, what the kids are expected to do is what you were learning in the late first grade and early second grade," says James K. Uphoff, Ed.D., professor of education at Wright State University in Dayton, Ohio, and coauthor of *Summer Children— Ready or Not for School* (J&J Publishing).

Part of the reason kindergarten has gone academic is the public perception that kids can learn more from workbooks than from a sandbox, something most early-childhood experts dispute. Children, they agree, learn by doing. "Kids learn from hands-on experience, figuring out and manipulating things, rather than sitting and listening, which many of them can't do anyway," says Barbara Willer, Ph.D., an early-childhood specialist and spokeswoman for the NAEYC. Nevertheless, the administrations of many public and private schools—people who ought to know better—have bowed to public pressure to make kindergarten more "competitive."

Another reason kindergarten has been overhauled is that in these days of infant flash cards, the average kindergartner is more sophisticated, if not more mature. Given a head start by "Sesame

Street," nursery school, and in some cases, competitive and highly academic "Ivy League–prep" preschools, many come to school already knowing their numbers, letters, and their way around an Apple Macintosh.

But not even the best prepared are guaranteed smooth sailing through school. As Dr. Uphoff says, "Being bright and being ready for school are not the same things. An inappropriate start in school too often tarnishes that brightness."

It's not unusual for children to flunk kindergarten, or to be placed in pre-K or pre-first-grade to get them ready for the real thing. Even very bright children may be held back. In Grosse Pointe, Michigan, for instance, school administrators abandoned an early-entrance program for bright children after a fourteen-year study found that nearly a third of the early entrants were poorly adjusted and about one in four was either below average in school or had to repeat a grade.

Call it flunking or being held back or retained, most parents—and their children—can't help thinking of it as failure. And an early experience of failure, like a first impression, tends to be lasting.

Most local school districts—and in some cases, state legislators—have recognized the problems of the so-called "age effect" in kindergarten. But rather than changing curriculums to counter it, they have moved up cutoff dates for admission. Once, children had to be five by December to enter kindergarten. Today in some places they must be five by June 1. Check your district's policy.

Districts may also test for readiness, using one or more of a number of tests designed to assess a child's emotional, physical, and intellectual maturity as well as academic skills. The Gesell test, used in about 20 percent of schools nationwide, compares a child's performance with the performance of a large group of children the same age. One of the most common achievement tests is the Metropolitan Achievement Test, which assesses a child's proficiency in reading and math.

Should you allow your child to be tested? The NAEYC takes the stand that testing is only appropriate when the results are used to screen for learning problems or design an appropriate learning plan for a student. If they are being used for entry or placement, that should be a warning that the district has a kindergarten curriculum that may be inappropriate for some four- and five-year-olds, says Dr. Willer.

The pitfalls of standardized testing are many. First, there is documented test bias. Testing also leads to what most experts consider a dangerous practice in education: teaching for tests. Rather than being encouraged to take delight in problem solving and learning, children are fed facts and figures to memorize so they get the high test scores by which legislators and school districts measure educational excellence. There's also the risk that a child will be labeled on the basis of a test score that may or may not be an accurate gauge of his ability to learn or his special strengths. Unfortunately, a label tends to stay with a child and in many ways dictates what parents and teachers expect of him. It may also dictate what the child expects of himself. Also, a test is often only as good as the examiner who gives it, and with young children the examiner has to be top-notch because young children are notoriously poor test takers.

Tests are fine diagnostic tools—in the right hands and given with the right motives. But, says Dr. Uphoff, you should insist on a multifactor assessment, one that gives equal weight to the opinions of your child's preschool teacher and *you* as to a standardized test. Parent's intuition counts! You know your child better than anyone, finely calibrated tests included.

What do you do when your child's September birthday is approaching and you've got to make a decision? If your child is facing what Dr. Uphoff calls "the standard American sit-still, pencil-and-paper-workbook-curriculum school," you might want to consider keeping your child home an extra year. Your child may need that "gift of time" to mature so that instead of being the youngest (and perhaps, slowest) child in kindergarten, he can be one of the oldest and have a better chance of experiencing success. After all, before reading, 'riting, and 'rithmetic skills, the most important factor for a child's school success is a desire and enthusiasm for learning, something that occurs naturally in kids but can be killed by early failure.

If you can't keep your child at home, look for a nursery school that offers a program for five-year-olds (most Montessori schools do), or pre-K or transitional classes that some private and public schools have introduced.

Dr. Uphoff believes that most parents can judge whether their child is ready to start school "with guidance." He has come up with a list of "red flags," factors that *may* signal your child needs to delay entry into a fast-track kindergarten. These include:

- His chronological age. "Children who are less than five and a half at the start of the year in this kind of school are more likely to experience problems," Dr. Uphoff says. Dr. Uphoff's research and that of many others has found that younger children are at greater risk of being misdiagnosed as "learning disabled" when they are actually only immature. Young children have short attention spans, are unable to sit still for long periods of time, and may have difficulty manipulating pencils because they lack fine motor control. Their social skills may be lacking. Children who are too young for school may become clingy and tearful, have toileting accidents, and "act out" by becoming hostile and aggressive.

- His early health. Children who have had chronic ear infections, allergies, or asthma may have suffered damage to their hearing that can affect their ability to learn to read. "One of the key ingredients to reading is the ability to pick out sounds, and many of these kids don't hear some consonants clearly," Dr. Uphoff says. Any illness that caused the child to be "passive" for any length of time may have slowed down his physical development. Of particular importance to his academic success is his hand-eye coordination.

- His speech. A child who was a late talker or who has significant speech problems "is going to take longer to learn to read," says Dr. Uphoff. "Talking is to reading what crawling is to walking." Also, there is a correlation between "monosyllabic homes"—where there's not a lot of conversation—and school difficulty, says Dr. Uphoff. "If you're not used to hearing full sentences, how can you be expected to sit still and decode them?"

- Birth problems. Long and short labors, difficult labors, and C-sections have been associated with learning problems and reduced social-skill development, says Dr. Uphoff.

- Low birthweight. A premature child may actually be younger than his chronological age and experience significant developmental delays, Dr. Uphoff notes.

- Sex. At birth, boys are about a month behind girls developmentally, and the gap only widens until young adulthood.

"Boys need extra time," says Dr. Uphoff. "But if you give a girl the extra time, the benefit is increased because she's already ahead."

■ Birth order. A second child who is less than three years younger than an older sibling is more likely to have problems in school.

■ Family status. Any problem that causes insecurity in the family may affect school success. These include a death in the family, a recent move, separation or divorce, birth of a sibling, or addition of a sibling through a second marriage. The closer these occur to the start of school, the more likely they will have a negative effect on the child in school, says Dr. Uphoff.

Other warning signs include:

■ Lack of interest in books, being read to, or in watching a TV program through to the end.

■ Memory difficulties, such as an inability to recall his home address or the words to prayers or songs he often hears.

■ Easy distractibility, which can lead not only to learning problems but discipline problems in a school where children are required to sit quietly and follow rules.

■ Vision problems. Young children may not be able to focus clearly because their eye muscles only strengthen over time.

While all of these factors may mean your child isn't ready for a *standard* kindergarten class, they are not proof. A child with one or more of these problems can do fine in kindergarten, but would probably do better if the class was less academically oriented, says Dr. Uphoff.

What do you look for in a good kindergarten classroom? Most experts agree that a classroom should have age-appropriate learning toys—things such as blocks, scaled-down tools and household items, games, and puzzles. There should be books, perhaps a dress-up area where pretend play can go on, musical instruments and/or record players, arts and crafts materials, and a well-equipped and safe playground. The children inside should look as if they are having a good time. What you shouldn't see are workbooks and homework and small children struggling to sit still to listen to a teacher.

It's important that you not dismiss those feelings you have about your child's school readiness. You may instinctively know what a dozen tests may or may not tell you. Besides, there's no evidence that delaying a child's start in school is damaging in any way, while there is clear evidence of the negative effects of early failure. It might be better in the long run for your child to start school at six than to be held back when he's eight or nine.

## WHAT PARENTS SAY

*"Who will tell me what I am failing?" my best friend asked me in our freshman year in high school. I asked her what she was talking about. "My counselor told me that my IQ is only ninety-six. She said I would need a scholarship to get into college because with an IQ that low my grades will be no help at all!" My best friend had always done well in junior high. She had a B average since sixth grade. I told her to disregard the IQ test. I had what was considered a pretty high IQ and I only had a B-minus average. Three and a half years later, my friend graduated early with honors. I dropped out of high school in my senior year. My daughter is four and a half years old. Will her test scores be correct? Test scores are not perfect. I will make sure my daughter knows that!*

*Dore D.*
*California*

## THE SITUATION ▪ Your Child Is Afraid of School or Daycare

**My four-year-old son has always been the clingy sort, and so I thought he might have a problem starting school. But it's gone beyond even what I had imagined. He cries bitterly every morning before I take him to nursery school and says he wants to stay home with me. Next year is kindergarten, and I am anticipating the worst. What can I do to help prepare him for "real" school?**

## WHAT THE EXPERTS SAY

What your child is experiencing isn't really a fear of school, but anxiety over separation from you. As you've already commented, your child is the clingy type, meaning he's probably always had trouble with separation. For those children, a fear of school is especially common. It should also be noted that this problem will not last forever. (See "Your Child Clings" in Chapter 6.)

You must not let your child avoid school or daycare no matter how loud he yells, or if he complains of stomachaches, headaches, or nausea, says Cynthia G. Last, Ph.D., professor of psychology and director of the school phobia program at Nova University in Fort Lauderdale, Florida. If your child is rewarded for missing school by being nurtured, you will be fostering undesirable behavior.

Of course, it's possible your child really is sick and needs to stay home. But let's face it, how long does it take to recognize the real thing from the psychosomatic, especially if your child's symptoms spontaneously disappear as soon as the bus pulls away (without him) and are never present on Saturdays, Sundays, or school holidays?

The school-age child needs to get out and gain experience with his peers and autonomy from his family, even if it is a difficult step, adds Alan S. Bellack, Ph.D., professor of psychiatry at the Medical College of Pennsylvania. You are not being cruel when you leave your child in the care of others. To make the transition easier for you and your son, try these tips from Drs. Last and Bellack.

- Take your child to the school before he's scheduled to begin. Whether he's entering preschool or elementary school, he needs to get familiar with the building and if possible, with the teacher he'll have.

- Read stories to him about going to school.

- Reminisce with your child about what it was like when you started school. If you were fearful, too, tell your child how quickly that feeling went away.

- Make sure he sees all the big kids going off every day on the school bus, especially if they're laughing and having fun together.

■ Talk to him about what he might be doing at school—story time, show-and-tell, learning letters and numbers, playing games.

■ Introduce your child to other kids who will be in his class before the fall term begins. You can get the names from his teacher. Then not everyone will be a stranger to him.

■ Try the gradual approach. If your son is in preschool or kindergarten, have him stay at school ten minutes the first day, an hour the second, two hours after that, until he is comfortable being there.

■ Stay with your child at first, but gradually wean yourself out of the picture.

■ Have him choose a favorite outfit to wear to school the first day, and perhaps a new pair of cool, big-boy shoes.

■ Don't moan and whimper about how much you're going to miss your son when he goes to school. That will only make him feel guilty and want to stay with you more.

■ Discuss his day with him when he gets home, and tell him how proud you are of him for being such a big boy.

The fears your child displays at going to school should be gone in a week or two, says Dr. Last. Or by mid-October at the latest, adds Dr. Bellack, especially when the problem is one of separation or adjustment to a new surrounding. You may need to step in, however, and seek help from his teacher, a psychologist, or the school counselor if the symptoms don't go away. Sometimes there are underlying stresses that need to be uncovered—a bully at school (see "Your Child Is Being Bullied" in Chapter 15), a problem with learning, etc.—that must be addressed if the problem is to be resolved.

## WHAT PARENTS SAY

*We had a hard time with our son when he first started school. He was so scared we thought he'd never make it to first grade. But we found a wonderful solution.*

*We had brought back a number of beautiful stones from Oregon. We told him that they were magic stones, and that he was to pick out one that he especially liked and it would protect him. He took it to school with him each day. In fact, he wouldn't leave home without it.*

*His teacher reported that she would see our son take out his stone and hold it or keep it on his desk when he was feeling a bit out of sorts. After a few weeks of carrying it every day, he no longer needed the stone for "protection."*

*Pam S.*
*Pennsylvania*

■

*My son, age four, was never truly afraid of school. He was more concerned about how I would manage at home without him, and so he kept refusing to go to school.*

*One morning, a week after school began, he inquired why I hated him now; what had he done wrong that I was sending him to this awful place? With tears in my eyes and a voice barely audible, I took him in my arms and told him I would always love him, that his school was the very best, and that it was important for him to go.*

*That was the day my heart truly ached. That was also the very first day my son enjoyed school! When I picked him up, he said to me, "It was fun. Can we do something special now?" It was obvious from his reaction that he was reluctant to give up our special time together, as I was. Now he genuinely loves school, and afterward we still go for walks, talk, paint pictures, or have quiet time together.*

*Cheryl R.*
*Ontario, Canada*

# CHAPTER 17

# BEDTIME
# ▪
# With and Without Bedlam

**THE SITUATION ▪ Your Child Has Nightmares**

How should I handle my daughter's nightmares? She's three and will occasionally wake up crying that "someone" is trying to get her. Sometimes I have to lie down in bed beside her to get her to go back to sleep, she's so frightened.

## WHAT THE EXPERTS SAY

A nightmare is a dream gone bad, and although you and your daughter both know that dreams aren't real, her fear certainly is. And the fear is what you need to focus on. "The best thing to do for nightmares is to handle them in the same way as you would if something real had frightened the child," advises Richard Ferber, M.D., director of the Center for Pediatric Sleep Disorders at Children's Hospital in Boston.

Hold your child, sit with her, even sleep with her. Though many experts will tell you not to allow your child to sleep in bed with you, Dr. Ferber (and we) believe that if that's what it takes to calm a child's fear, then that's what you should do. Just don't make a habit of it. Your immediate goal is to get the child back into peaceful sleep, and your long-term goal is to help her learn that while dreams can get scary, they're only dreams. If you always take her into your bed to "protect" her after her nightmares, she might begin to believe there's really something to fear.

Nightmares occur during the rapid eye movement (REM) stage of sleep, which is when we dream. It's not unusual for children to have a run of bad dreams during those times when they're reaching developmental hurdles. The little—or great—anxieties of the day brought on by potty training or speaking in sentences are translated at night into monsters or bogeymen pursuing them across a terrifying dreamscape. Horror movies or frightening TV shows can also become the stuff of nightmares.

Even infants can have nightmares. Though they may not be able to tell you they've had a bad dream, they'll seem startled or frightened.

The only time nightmares are something to worry about is when they occur chronically, says Dr. Ferber. A child who has nightmares night after night is more anxious than a child should be, and you'll need professional help in determining what daytime fears are pursuing her into dreamland.

## WHAT PARENTS SAY

*I try to remain calm and supportive when my children have nightmares, reassuring them that this experience will pass. In the morning, I quiz them on the situation and try to make light of it by suggesting the "monsters" they saw are good, not evil, as in the Good Witch in* The Wizard of Oz. *I also try making sure they are not exposed to frightening movies.*

*Deborah M.*
*Ohio*

■

*Comfort the child. Acknowledge how scary bad dreams can be. Touch the child's forehead and say you're filling him/her up with good dreams now.*

*Muriel H.*
*Pennsylvania*

■

*My daughter used to have terrible nightmares. I put a night-light in her room and found a cheap crystal pendant at a garage sale. I told her that if she wore this "magic" necklace at bedtime, it would help her control her bad dreams. We also started talking at bedtime to see if something had happened during the day to upset her. I explained to her that sometimes when things are bothering you, you have bad dreams. This seems to have helped, and now the only time we have problems is if she sees an especially scary preview for the latest slasher or horror film on TV.*

*Wanda R.*
*Illinois*


## THE SITUATION ▪ Your Child Has Night Terrors

**My five-year-old son woke up last night absolutely terrified, flailing around in his bed, his eyes wide open, like a scene from *The Exorcist*. We tried to talk to him to calm him down, but he didn't seem to hear us. When we tried to hold him, he just fought us off. After a few minutes, he lay down and went back to sleep. What happened?**


## WHAT THE EXPERTS SAY

You and your son just experienced what's called a night terror. It was probably more of a frightening experience for you because you witnessed it. Your son wasn't really awake and never knew anything was going on. Kids usually don't remember anything the next morning.

Your reference to *The Exorcist* is apt. Kids having night terrors often seem possessed. They may scream, moan, get out of bed and run wildly around the room, waving their arms, even talking. Though their eyes may be open, they don't seem to see you. While it's a scary sight, a night terror is usually a passing phenomenon in a young child's life.

Although some experts believe night terrors are uncommon—

occurring in only about 2 percent of all children—Dr. Ferber suspects they're more widespread. "If you ask people if their child had a night terror, most people will say no. But when you ask, 'Has your child ever screamed out during the night and when you go in, they're flailing about and don't seem to know you're there?' we usually find out that most kids have had an experience like that at one time or another."

Night terrors are quite different from nightmares. For one thing, they occur during an entirely different phase of sleep, usually during the first half of the night when a child has been sleeping deeply in a nondreaming state. Nightmares tend to rouse a child from sleep, but with night terrors, "there are elements of waking and deep sleep simultaneously," explains Dr. Ferber. We all have these partial wakings during the night. We may even open our eyes. But more often than not we simply turn over and fall back into deep sleep again.

Your first experience with a night terror should have taught you what *not* to do. Because the child isn't fully awake, he doesn't even know you're in the room. Holding or trying to restrain him rarely does any good, and if the child fights back, it may mean an injury to you. "Night terrors are an easy thing to make worse and not easy to make better once they're going on," says Dr. Ferber. Trying to wake the child or restrain him may actually prolong the episode, "whereas when you keep a quiet, calming voice and do very little, it will just run its course and then end," Dr. Ferber says. Once it's over, the child won't be afraid anymore, only sleepy.

He suggests simply watching the child, if only to allow yourself to get more comfortable with what occurs. If your child seems particularly active during these episodes, make sure the area is childproofed. And you may want to move him from a top bunk, if that's where he sleeps, although it's rare for children to injure themselves during a night terror. Once you see that your child is in no danger, you probably don't even have to go into his room when he's having a milder episode. By all means, warn his babysitters that your child may have a night terror after he goes to bed, and tell them to simply make sure he's safe while the episode runs its course.

Children who are overtired or on chaotic schedules have a greater tendency to have night terrors, so make sure your child gets enough sleep (daytime naps can help) and has a fairly dependable daily schedule.

Night terrors usually only occur once a night, sometimes as a momentary thing, other times lasting for five to fifteen minutes, sometimes longer if the child is stimulated. Children tend to outgrow them.

## THE SITUATION ▪ Your Child Sleepwalks

**I woke up the other night to find my daughter standing at the side of my bed. Her eyes were open but she didn't seem to see me. I figured she was sleepwalking, so I just guided her back to bed. It had never happened before. I'm worried that if it continues, she'll injure herself.**

## WHAT THE EXPERTS SAY

Sleepwalking may be the most active form of night terrors, and miraculously, small children rarely injure themselves during these nocturnal meanderings. Children who sleepwalk are partially awake. They may answer you when you speak to them. They may even use the bathroom if you guide them there. But when you ask them about it the next morning, they won't remember a thing.

To cope with sleepwalkers, make sure there's no clutter on the floors that might cause them to stumble and fall. Keep their bedroom doors closed (although that might not stop them) or use a security gate. Fortunately, most children who sleepwalk tend to be awake enough to negotiate through the house, although Dr. Ferber says it's best to find a way to keep them away from stairs (if only because they'll be climbing them in the dark, half-asleep).

Kids tend to outgrow sleepwalking usually by the time they're five or six. Though stress may contribute to both night terrors and sleepwalking, it's more often a passing phase related to development.

## WHAT PARENTS SAY

*For a few weeks when her father and I had just separated, my daughter got out of bed and walked around without waking up. Her eyes were wide open, but when I tried to talk to her, I realized she did not know what was happening. I tried to get her back into her bed and I was careful not to wake her. In the morning, she did not recall the incident. On the advice of her doctor, we just observed the frequency of the episodes and noted what had happened that day. In about three weeks, when she felt more secure in her new surroundings, she grew out of the sleepwalking problem. Her doctor explained that this frequently happens when there is some underlying disturbance. I talked to my daughter about our new surroundings and let her know that we were safe and secure and that I was here all the time while she was asleep. This seemed to be her concern, and she soon became comfortable and accepted her new room and our new home.*

*Dore D.*
*California*

## THE SITUATION ▪ Your Child Can't Wake Up in the Morning

I'm at my wit's end. My four-year-old daughter is almost always late for nursery school because I can't get her out of bed on time. She's still in a deep sleep at seven A.M., and it takes at least half an hour to rouse her. Any suggestions?

## WHAT THE EXPERTS SAY

First, you need to find out if she's getting enough sleep. Perhaps she needs to get to bed an hour earlier or needs an afternoon nap. Does she like her nursery school? Maybe she's reluctant to get up because she doesn't want to go. (See "Your Child Is Afraid of School or Daycare" in Chapter 16.)

If the extra hour or the daily nap doesn't work and she likes her school, she may have a not uncommon problem that has physiological roots. Psychologist Lynn Embry, Ph.D., who has studied this phenomenon, says the world is divided into two groups: the quick-to-wake and the slow-to-wake.

The quick-to-wake—those lucky morning people—experience a rise in both blood pressure and body temperature as the new day dawns. By the time the alarm goes off, they're ready to get up. But slow-to-wake people actually experience substantial drops in their blood pressure and temperature in the morning, more consistent with the metabolic slowdown most of us have at night. "That makes it very hard for them to get up," says Dr. Embry. "They're cold, they're irritable, and they're tired."

You can't change your daughter's physiology—she'll be slow to wake her whole life—but you can learn to work with it using Dr. Embry's wake-up technique.

The only equipment you'll need are warm blankets and a small radio. You should figure on waking up an hour earlier than your child every day, since the whole waking process takes forty-five minutes to an hour.

An hour before you want the child to get up, go in and cover her with warm blankets. Blankets warmed in the drier might be most effective. (Dr. Embry used electric blankets in her research, but many doctors now feel they are not safe for children.) What you're trying to do, says Dr. Embry, is raise the child's body temperature. Then turn on the radio, low volume, and tune in to a talk show. "You need something stimulating, something that changes enough and doesn't get too rhythmical," the psychologist explains.

Then go away for about fifteen minutes. "You can use this time to get ready for work or the day," she says.

At your second visit, turn up the volume of the radio slightly, and start touching the child gently. The child may make sounds but at this point won't be able to talk to you. "People who are slow to wake aren't able to make monosyllabic answers until about thirty minutes into the wake-up process," says Dr. Embry.

Allow the child to lie there for another fifteen minutes, then go back in, turn the radio volume up to normal, and help the child sit up. Rub her back gently, talk to her, and ask if she'd like some juice. Since her blood sugar is low, she'll probably need a little fruit juice at this point. After fifteen minutes or so, she should be able to get up and use the bathroom, after which she'll be awake.

## WHAT PARENTS SAY

*This was a major problem for my daughter. I decided to tell her that breakfast was at seven-fifteen A.M. (her school starts early— eight-fifteen) and that if she was up five minutes early, she could have five extra minutes of reading time at bedtime. But if she was five or ten minutes late, those minutes would be subtracted from her reading time. Now she usually beats me to the kitchen.*

*Cindy M.*
*Washington, D.C.*

■

*I've found that giving my two daughters their very own alarm clock and setting the clock fifteen minutes earlier than they have to get up gives them time to gradually get up and get going.*

*Connie H.*
*New York*

■

*Each of my two daughters takes a turn being held on my lap and rocked for a few minutes after they get up in the morning. It's a nice way to start the day, especially since they must wake early to go to the sitter. Now they are much less reluctant to get out of bed, and it gives them a little extra attention to get them through the day. And I've noticed they are more cheerful and even-tempered in the morning since we instituted our "morning rock."*

*Denise B.*
*Michigan*

**THE SITUATION** ▪ Your Child Won't Go to or Stay in Bed

Once a child is out of a crib and into a bed, how do you keep them there? My three-year-old son is up six or seven times an hour, after what's usually a small scene about going to bed.

## WHAT THE EXPERTS SAY

If kids are going to get into a power struggle with a parent, they'll usually choose one of three battlefields: the bed, the dinner table, or the bathroom. Why? Because there are three things you can't make a child do: sleep, eat, and poop. Short of resorting to child abuse, you really don't have a lot of control over some of the more basic bodily functions. Kids know this and they will use it.

What you need to do is avoid the need for your child to struggle by giving him some power. Bob Mendelson, M.D., and his wife, Lottie Mendelson, R.N., suggest that you make an effort to allow the child to make more choices during the day. Let him pick out what he will wear from two or three outfits you've preselected. Give him a menu for lunch so he can decide whether he'll have tuna fish on toast or peanut butter and jelly. Give him a say in the day's activities, asking a self-limiting question such as, "Where shall we go after we pick up your toys, to the park or the mall?" Then praise the good choices he makes. This allows the child to feel that he has some control over his life, which will do wonders for his self-esteem and short-circuit his need to throw his weight around at bedtime.

Let him help decide on a bedtime ritual, and stick to it: kisses and hugs all around, a small drink of water, assurances that teddy is in the bed, a short discussion of the day's activities, and a few songs before lights-out. Some kids like to hear stories, play quiet games, or pray with a parent. Some will nod off listening to music or story tapes.

While you've given the child some choices, you need to make some unvarying rules. The first, bedtime is at a specific fixed time. And the second is that she is to stay in bed until morning, except for a dire emergency.

Go through the bedtime ritual, then say good-night. Once. Says

Dr. Mendelson: "I advise parents not to see the child again until morning. By that I mean even if the child is gnawing on their kneecaps. You *ignore* the child until morning. Now these resistant children very often will be asleep in the hallway outside the parents' room. And that's fine. There's nothing wrong with that. They don't have to sleep in their bed." Of course, have your house totally childproofed and keep an eye on the child to prevent him from getting hurt.

Researchers at the University of Arkansas, in a study published in the journal *Pediatrics*, found that bedtime tantrums could be decreased if parents ignored the tantrums for longer and longer periods each night before offering their children comfort. Tantrums were also less frequent if parents allowed their children to stay up a little longer and filled up the time with pleasant bedtime rituals, such as reading or backrubs, then gradually moved bedtime back to its original hour.

You may have lulled your child to sleep as a baby or toddler whenever he awoke. Consequently, he never developed the self-soothing skills he needs to put himself to sleep. For help with that problem, see the experts' advice on what to do when a child wakes up or needs a feeding at night, later in this chapter.

One thing we've found in our experience as mothers is that it helps if the child is *tired* at bedtime. If you put your child to bed at eight P.M. and he doesn't fall asleep until nine P.M., maybe the later hour would be a better bedtime.

Of course, some reluctance to go to bed may stem from the child's fears—of the dark, of the "monsters" lurking in the corners of his room, even of his own nightmares. (For ways to deal with fears, see Chapter 8.)

It doesn't hurt to give in to your child's requests when he's afraid, but it does when you're involved in a battle over who runs the household. Even very young children can understand that there are set times for certain daily activities, and in fact, many children your son's age actually feel more secure on a schedule. Giving the child attention—or giving in, by allowing the child to either stay up or climb into your bed—will simply prolong the delaying tactics at bedtime. Your child needs to know that there are social rules everyone in the house abides by and that they'll be enforced. He also needs to know he is safe sleeping alone, away from you, something that will eventually foster a sense of confidence and independence. And you're not being selfish insisting on a little private time away from him either.

If all else fails, try this little technique that Lottie Mendelson says worked for her when her four children were little: "I was always so obnoxious at night, nobody really *wanted* to be with me."

## WHAT PARENTS SAY

*My three small children have their baths, hear some stories, then ask for kisses and more kisses. They still each get smothered with kisses, but then I blot my lips on three napkins and give each child one with a kiss from Mommy on it to keep under their pillows.*

*Debbie F.*
*New Jersey*

■

*Ever since he could get out of bed on his own, my son has climbed in with us in the middle of the night. I read up on the "family bed" and we tolerated the intrusion until he was four. But now he is allowed to bring a pillow and blanket and sleep on the floor in our room if he is "too scared to stay in bed." The thrill eventually wore off. He is five now and very rarely ventures in.*

*Sheila E.*
*New Hampshire*

■

*Don't lock a child in her bedroom. I did it once (for about one minute). She was screaming to get out, and to this day, she will not sleep with the door closed.*

*Susan S.*
*Pennsylvania*

■

*Make up a short and sweet special bedtime song that belongs to only one child (no sharing the song with siblings!). Use it only as you are carrying or leading the child to bed. Don't worry if you can't sing; to your child, no voice will be more beautiful than yours. Combine your song with lots of hugs and kisses, and end the song by saying "Good night" very quietly and gently. Most nights your child will be dozing off by the song's end.*

*Susan B.*
*Washington*

■

*To get my child to go to sleep, I tell her all the activities she has to look forward to the next day if she stays in bed.*

*Cheri M.*
*New Jersey*

■

*We told our son that when he wakes up at night, he may turn on his light and read for a few minutes, then he should turn his light off and try to get back to sleep. Giving him the responsibility really paid off. I heard him wake one night. He turned on the light, read for about three minutes, then turned off the light and slept soundly until morning. The mastery was all his, and he was awfully proud of the fact that he was dealing successfully with the situation.*

*Elizabeth D.*
*New York*

## THE SITUATION ■ Your Child Wakes Up or Wants a Feeding at Night

**My seven-month-old wakes regularly every night around two-thirty A.M. That's always been the hour of her nighttime feeding, so we give her a bottle. She's got two teeth now, and I'm afraid the nighttime feeding is eventually going to lead to tooth decay. How can I break her of this habit?**

**My fourteen-month-old daughter has been waking up at night, just as she did as an infant. We don't give her a bottle anymore,**

but we find she won't go back to sleep unless we rock her. We're exhausted. Help!

## WHAT THE EXPERTS SAY

Babies and toddlers who wake regularly during the night have been "trained" to do so, says Charles Schaeffer, Ph.D., coauthor of *Teach Your Baby to Sleep Through the Night* (Putnam, 1987).

Who trained them? Their parents. How? By rushing to their aid at the slightest peep with food or comfort.

Babies over four months old who "need" a night bottle or to nurse have simply gotten into the habit of feeding at night when they wake, says Dr. Schaeffer. They have learned that when they wake up in the middle of the night, as most people do, all they have to do is cry and a parent will rush in and rock or sing them to sleep or take them into their bed, "anything to stop the crying," says Dr. Schaeffer. Because their needs are always met, they never acquire the skills to soothe themselves back to sleep.

Both night feeding and night waking are habits that, in most children, take little time to break. But that little time can be mighty painful for parents who can't stand to hear their child cry. Dr. Schaeffer's technique, called the Quick Check Method, is not much different from the techniques experts recommend to eliminate a child's negative behavior. It's based on the theory that if you ignore it, it will go away.

What will help is to start off with the right motives. It's true that a baby's teeth can be damaged if the sugars in the milk or juice are allowed to cling to his teeth over the course of the night. At seven months, night feeding just isn't a healthy practice. Just as important, you know your child will be happier after a good night's sleep, something he's not getting if it's interrupted for a late-night snack or a conversation with you. And how you feel is important, too. Without adequate sleep, your health—both physical and mental—can suffer.

Before you attempt the Quick Check Method, make a commitment to follow the procedure for a minimum of three nights and to be absolutely consistent. You can't give in. If your child's crying disturbs you, go to a part of the house where you can't hear it, or listen to music with earphones. Consistency is the key to making Dr. Schaeffer's technique work, as Denise and her husband can testify; they used it—with success—on their son. Here's where to start:

- Establish a consistent bedtime and bedtime ritual and put the child to bed still awake. "You need to leave when the baby's eyes are open so she learns to fall asleep on her own," says Dr. Schaeffer.

- "If she cries, just go in after about five minutes and make a quick check to reassure yourself that she's okay. Then go in every twenty minutes or so after that to remind her of what she's supposed to be doing—sleeping," Dr. Schaeffer says. Make your visits quick and don't be sociable. You don't want to give the child any positive reinforcement for the behavior you're trying to eliminate.

- Do the same thing for late-night crying. Don't respond immediately. Wait five minutes. Then check on her. Instruct her to go back to sleep, but don't pick her up or act sympathetic or hostile.

- For the night feeder, the technique is the same, but you may want to cut back on the amount you feed at night rather than just going cold turkey. Gradually cut down on the time you breast-feed. Diluting formula or substituting water can also help, says Dr. Schaeffer. If your child doesn't lose interest in a night feeding of water, you'll know for sure she's not waking up hungry. She's just come to associate the feeding with falling to sleep.

- Keep a diary of the amount of time the child cries. This will allow you to see that you're making progress when it seems as if you aren't. Usually, says Dr. Schaeffer, the child cries the longest the first night and less each successive night.

Most kids take three to seven days to work out their sleep problems.

At times the Quick Check Method is not the right solution to a child's sleep problems. Nightmares, night terrors, and sleepwalking are three of those exceptions, and we've told you how to handle those elsewhere in this chapter. Dr. Schaeffer lists a few more:

- Medical problems, such as teething pain, diaper rash, colic, middle-ear infection, or other illnesses need to be treated. Before you let your child "cry it out," make sure he's not crying from pain.

■ Some medications such as antihistamines can keep children awake. Ask your pediatrician or pharmacist if your child's medications could be the cause of his night waking.

■ Constitutionally poor sleepers are children who simply don't need as much sleep as others. They will not respond to the Quick Check Method. Dr. Schaeffer recommends observing your child for signs of tiredness, keeping him from napping during the day, and working around his sleep needs.

■ If you have recently moved, or there has been a trauma such as a death or divorce, a child's sleep can be disturbed.

■ Some children are sensitive to ambient light and sound and have trouble dropping off and staying asleep. For these children, keeping their room dark and the house quiet will help them sleep.

■ Many kids going through a stage of separation anxiety or who are beset by fears may wake during the night and need a parent to comfort them. Dr. Schaeffer recommends that you do. Pull a chair up next to her bed and stay with her until she falls asleep, making it clear that this is something you plan to do only temporarily. On each successive night move your chair farther and farther away. If the child calls out, simply say, "Go back to sleep," in a normal (nor angry) tone.

## WHAT PARENTS SAY

*When our baby started waking up every half hour every night, our doctor suggested going in the first time to make sure he was okay, patting him and reassuring him, but not picking him up. Then, he said to let the baby cry after that for increasing amounts of time, occasionally checking on him as before. It worked!*

*Jennifer B.*
*Pennsylvania*

■

Our son woke up at twelve A.M. and at five A.M. at seventeen months. I cut the twelve A.M. bottle out, then I gave him less in the five A.M. bottle until he was down from eight ounces to three. Then I took it away completely. He cried the first two nights, then he was fine.

Cerene C.
New York

# PART·FOUR

# FOR
# PARENTS
# ONLY

# CHAPTER 18

# REALITY
·
# There Are No Perfect Parents

**THE SITUATION ▪ You Want to Have the Person You're Dating Sleep Over**

I've been divorced for over a year and have had quite a few casual dates. Now I'm seeing a man who is special to me, and I'd like him to spend the weekend at my place. My five-year-old son likes this man, too, but will his feelings for him change if this man starts sleeping with me?

## WHAT THE EXPERTS SAY

Not necessarily, but it's good that you're anticipating some possible fallout from this occasion. A child who has experienced his parents' divorce has usually felt a sense of loss and abandonment, explains sex therapist Shirley Zussman, Ed.D. He may be fearful, despite your reassurances, that he will lose you, too.

Ask yourself what kind of relationship your friend has with your son. Have they spent time together? Does he play games with your son? And how has your son received this attention? Does he seem genuinely fond of this man? Or does he seem cool, even rejecting of his friendly overtures at times? Remember, liking this man could cause your son to feel disloyal to his father, or he may fear that this new man will leave him, too.

Before the special weekend arrives, talk to your son about your plans. You don't want him to wake up Sunday morning to a surprise in mommy's bed. So ask him how he feels about having this man sleep over.

Once you make it clear that this man will be sleeping in your bedroom, address any concerns your child may have about your availability. Will he be able to come to you for comfort after a bad dream if there's someone else there? Yes. Will he be excluded from snuggling in bed with you in the morning? No. Will you still read him a bedtime story? Yes.

Your son may feel compelled to intrude into the bedroom to disturb your privacy, at which time you can let him know when it is appropriate to disturb you, and that he must knock before entering (a privacy rule that should already have been established).

You want your child to understand that having this man sleep over means he is very special indeed. That the probability of the relationship continuing is good, says Dr. Zussman. "Of course, no one can predict the future of any relationship, but children should not be exposed to a series of lovers who come and go. It could give them a sad model of the inconstancy of love and in addition, expose them to repeated feelings of loss, if attachments develop."

## WHAT PARENTS SAY

*If I have a girlfriend sleep over, she sleeps in the guest room. I feel it's important for children to realize by my example the values of adults sharing each other, commitment as opposed to casual sex mates spending one night and not being seen again by my children.*

*Henry P.*
*New York*

## THE SITUATION ▪ You Lose Your Patience Easily

Sometimes my four-year-old daughter's behavior makes me so angry I can hardly contain myself. In fact, I often blow my stack screaming at her as loud as she screams back. I feel so bad later after I calm down, but the damage has already been done. How can I learn to control my temper so I don't continue to frighten my little girl?

## WHAT THE EXPERTS SAY

You're already on the right track, because you recognize that you naturally have a short fuse. That doesn't excuse you from taking responsibility for your actions, however. It just means that you'll have to work that much harder to keep control of your temper. And it can be done.

First you must realize that it's not your child's fault that you lose your temper, says William Koch, M.D., child development specialist in New York City. *You* are the one out of control, not your child. If you have been lax in setting and enforcing limits on your child's behavior, then she will naturally test you until she finds out what those limits are, he explains. What's more, since kids learn by imitation, don't be surprised if your daughter becomes less tolerant of frustration and reacts with temper tantrums of her own.

You need to decide ahead of time (before you get angry) how you're going to handle specific situations and then do your darndest to be consistent about enforcing the rules, adds professor of pediatrics William Carey, M.D. Otherwise, it's going to be very confusing for your child if a specific behavior elicits no reaction from you one time and harsh criticism the next.

Ask yourself if you have reasonable expectations about your child's abilities, Dr. Koch says. Are you demanding, for example, that a two-year-old put his clothes in the hamper every night? If you are, then you will have to reset your priorities because a child this age simply won't do it. And you'll be turning up your frustration level if you expect him to comply.

When the parents' and the child's temperaments are in conflict with each other, however, the approach is a little different. You can't change the parents' or the child's temperament, Dr. Carey explains, but you can at least change the way the parents look at a situation and the way they handle it. This does not mean that the parents have to lie down and let the kids run all over them, he says. It means the parents find ways of handling the kids that are less stress producing.

The fact is, we all lose our patience with our children, and we're ashamed of things we've done, Dr. Carey points out. If you blow your stack from time to time, don't feel as though you've lost the battle to bring up your child well, he stresses. No parent is 100 percent perfect. If you're doing the right thing most of the time, that's as much as anybody can hope for.

And if you should have an inappropriate screaming fit at your child, go back later and apologize, adds Dr. Koch. This is not a sign of weakness, but rather an indication that you are human, that you make mistakes, and that it is indeed okay to make mistakes. Your child will learn that she can make mistakes, too, and that an apology will be accepted.

## WHAT PARENTS SAY

*We treat people outside of our family far better than we do the ones we love best. I am making a diligent effort to try to talk with my children the way I would talk with a friend. Instead of yelling at them to meet my demands, I talk with respect, and instead of accusing them, I speak in I-terms (I'd like to have you wash your hands; I'd be happy if you'd come home right after school). While we are still the authority figures in these young people's lives, that doesn't mean we have to be dictators. The way we treat them early on will reflect in the way they listen to us and talk with us, especially as they become teenagers and adults.*

*Phyllis M.*
*New York*

■

*Take a deep breath and give yourself a time-out. Declare a silent book-reading time or quiet time in your rooms. I walk out of the room and give myself time to cool off, and I tell my children this is what I am doing.*

*Linda U.*
*Pennsylvania*

■

*As a parent who was once a neglected child, I know I have to go that extra mile so as not to continue that destructive pattern. Little situations with my child sometimes trigger a childhood memory, and I have to work twice as hard to not do as my parents did—and not to be too soft, either. For example, every time my daughter spills her milk I remember spilling my milk and being hit for it. Children spill, big deal. I try to be sensitive to those things.*

*Julie G.*
*Wisconsin*

## THE SITUATION ▪ You Dislike Your Stepkids

I recently married a man with two daughters, who are four and five years old. My own child from a previous marriage is eleven and quite mature. I love this man very much, but I can't stand being around those two little brats of his. Even though they visit only every other weekend and for several weeks during the summer, I dread each occasion. Do people often have this reaction to their stepkids, or am I a "wicked stepmother"? Is it okay for me to stay in the background while they are so young and untamed? Is it possible that I will grow to like them eventually?

### WHAT THE EXPERTS SAY

Nowhere is it written that "thou shalt love thy new husband's children." There isn't even a law that says you have to like them. But they are a fact of your life as long as you're married to their father, and so it would be nice if you could reach a level of mutual respect and cordiality at the very least.

It could be that you started out with unrealistic expectations of what your blended family would be like, says Anne Bernstein, Ph.D., author of *Yours, Mine and Ours: How Families Change When Remarried Parents Have a Child Together* (W. W. Norton, 1990). The Brady Bunch existed only on television. In real life, you need to give yourself time to get to know one another, to figure out whom you're going to be in one another's life.

In your case, those two girls already have a mother and they don't need another one. That's not to say that you can't or won't have some influence over them. It could be that your dislike of these children stems from their obnoxious behavior rather than from inborn personality traits. In that case, simply getting rid of the disagreeable behaviors might naturally lead to a more harmonious existence for all of you.

To do that, you and your husband will need to set up house rules. Children can understand and accommodate to the fact that when they have two homes the rules and expectations may be different in each home, says Dr. Bernstein, who also specializes in stepfamily problems. It's okay to say, "I know that in your other house this is the way you do things, and that's fine there. But when you're here, this is what we'd like you to do."

The rules and limits you decide to set up should be agreed upon by both you and your husband. And they should be explained, implemented, and enforced by him, especially in the beginning of a stepfamily relationship.

You may also want to consider stepping back from the situation for a while. That is, when your stepkids are visiting, stay in the background and let your husband take complete care of them. They may be feeling somewhat displaced in his affection now that he's got a new love in his life.

Eventually, time will pass, the kids will grow up, and you will probably get used to each other's ways or at least call a truce. You may even grow to have a genuine affection for them. If, however, the situation continues to fester, if it begins to affect the relationship with your new husband (and it could if the two of you disagree about his kids, or there's an ex-spouse who is foolish enough to instigate trouble), you and your husband should consider getting professional counseling. The appalling fact is that nearly 50 percent of stepfamilies will deteriorate within the first five years. If you want yours to survive, don't let this situation get out of hand.

## WHAT PARENTS SAY

*My husband's ex-wife told his boys that now that Daddy has a new wife he won't have any time for them. When I learned about that, I went out of my way to make sure that the time they had with their father was not diminished at all. When my husband took his children to the movies, museums, or anywhere for that matter, I did not go along. I think they needed that special time with their father.*

*Lee T.*
*New Mexico*

## THE SITUATION ▪ You Sometimes Need to Discipline Another Person's Child (While the Other Person Is There)

A close friend of mine brought her four-year-old son to my house to play with my little boy. As we sat having coffee, I couldn't help but notice the bratty behavior her son displayed. He grabbed toys away from my child, threw them across the room, ran around like a wild person, and all the while my friend did absolutely nothing to contain him. I wanted to send this kid to time-out, permanently, but his mother obviously didn't find his behavior objectionable. I don't see how I can ever invite the two of them over again unless I can get her to understand my concerns. Is there some way to do that without killing our friendship?

## WHAT THE EXPERTS SAY

Maybe not. Your friend's parenting style is obviously different from yours, a fact you will have to deal with one way or another.

Overly permissive parents often have the mistaken idea that if you discipline a child and set limits on his behavior, you will somehow "break his spirit," says child development specialist William Koch, M.D. If your friend is open to it, you might explain to her why that child-rearing philosophy may actually be hurting her son. According to Dr. Koch, the strength of the personality is measured to some degree by the ability to internalize and live and work within a set of rules. A four-year-old child who is permitted to throw toys across the room today, for example, may become a sixteen-year-old who thinks it's okay to drink and drive.

Remember, a child who misbehaves terribly outside his home is probably doing the same thing inside his home as well, explains Dr. Koch. And so it's unlikely that a sudden attempt to curb his uncivilized display at your house will do any good. Nevertheless, you should offer your friend the chance to reprimand her son. If she refuses, ask her how she would feel if you attempted it. Reprimanding him on your own without your friend's permission could work in your favor or against it. The boy's mother may be relieved that you took the initiative, or she may be insulted and let you know loud and clear.

The possibility does exist that your friend is as uncomfortable with her son's wildness, and her inability to control it, as you are. If that's the case, she may welcome a heart-to-heart talk with you about the problem, says child and family psychologist Lynn Embry, Ph.D. Simply saying to your friend, "I'm uncomfortable with your son's behavior, and I'd like to know what we should do about it," could be all that's needed to start a friendly dialogue about discipline techniques such as time-out and rewards for good behavior.

There's a risk, of course, that you might lose this woman's friendship over this issue, Dr. Embry admits. If she says that her child's behavior doesn't bother her, you must make a choice. Do you want to risk the friendship over a disagreement in parenting techniques, or do you want to keep the friendship and limit it to meetings without the kids around?

## WHAT PARENTS SAY

*I will discipline another's child only when my son, my home, or my principles are being compromised. If the other parent is there and sees the inappropriate behavior (hitting, biting, fighting, etc.) and does nothing, I then explain that that behavior is not permitted around us. Period. Every time this has happened (very rarely), the other parent then took the initiative and disciplined her child.*

Quite frankly, I have found it difficult to remain close friends with certain people because of the way they treat their children. I have found that I am closer to friends and family who share my child-rearing philosophies.

Angela W.
California

■

My seven-year-old niece is sometimes bossy and pushy with my three-year-old son. One time, I got so annoyed with the situation that I just told my niece to lay off my son. My sister shot me a look of disapproval but kept silent. My niece gave me a look of disbelief that someone was actually imposing limits on her behavior. But she accepted my reprimand and stopped pestering my son. Although this tactic worked, I believe the next time it happens I would talk to my sister first and ask her to discipline her daughter. That's how I'd like another parent to handle it with me.

Eliot M.
Ontario

■

When a child does something or says naughty words not allowed in my house, I first touch the child on the arm or put my arm around him. Touching is important because it allows the child to know you are talking to him and still love him. Next, I express my feeling verbally: "Words like that make me sad." "Throwing the ball in the living room makes me upset." "Punching the baby hurts her and she doesn't like that." Be sure to stay calm and don't be afraid to explain your feelings. Also, give praise and tell about "good feelings" when appropriate.

Susan B.
Pennsylvania

## THE SITUATION ▪ You Need to Tell Your Child You're Getting Divorced

My husband and I are planning to separate. We're going to try counseling, but I'm pretty sure we're heading for a divorce. How can we reduce the trauma on our kids?

## WHAT THE EXPERTS SAY

You and your spouse are facing a difficult time ahead and so are your children, who, even though they're young, are already picking up the subtle changes in your relationship.

If there can be a rule of thumb about children and divorce, says Marcia Lasswell, Ph.D., a family therapist and professor of psychology at California State University in Pomona, it's that children "do about as well during a divorce as their parents do."

If your children hear you yelling or see you crying all the time, they're likely to feel that their security is threatened. If they see you adjusting fairly well, they'll adjust, too. Not that it won't be rocky. Sometimes young children experience sleep or behavior problems during or following a marital split. Toilet-trained youngsters start having accidents, and even school-age children may begin sucking their thumbs or returning to the comfort of a long-abandoned teddy. They may become depressed (see "Your Child Seems Depressed" in Chapter 5). A child may even associate the trauma with some mundane aspect of life that coincided with the split—"The day Daddy left, I ate at McDonald's. I'm never going to eat there again."

Many children are beset by "abandonment fantasies," says Dr. Lasswell. "They oftentimes think, 'If Daddy or Mommy gets mad and leaves, or if they don't love each other anymore, won't they leave me, too?' "

They may even fear the loss of the custodial parent and become clingy. "And sometimes they think they have to be extra good so that doesn't happen," Dr. Lasswell says.

Very young kids—two or three years old—will probably have the most trouble grasping the fact that daddy or mommy "doesn't live here anymore. They do something we call 'searching behavior,' " says Dr. Lasswell. "They really don't understand the person is gone. They're conditioned that daddy or mommy comes home at a certain hour, and they will look for that person. They will ask over and over 'Where is Daddy?' or 'Where is Mommy?' They may even look around the house sometimes."

Even slightly older children may not grasp reality at first. "What's frustrating to parents is that they think that once the children are told, that ought to be it, but the child may ask the same question a day or two later," says Dr. Lasswell.

The best thing you can do to reduce your children's trauma is to make them feel secure. That doesn't mean they can't see you crying sometimes. Simply explain that you're upset at the moment but you'll be fine and so will they. "The child's main concern at this point is his or her safety and security, and that is all they really want to know," says Dr. Lasswell. "If the parents are out of control and the children see this, they begin to think, 'Maybe I'm not going to be all right either.'"

They also need to know that they were not the cause of the marital breakup. "They need to be told, if not shown, that this is something between mom and dad," says Dr. Lasswell.

They may be concerned that the loss of a parent is permanent, or that the divorce will mean they will have to leave the neighborhood and their friends. Sometimes, divorce does bring a major change in family finances, and the custodial parent must move to more affordable housing. Too often, the noncustodial parent loses touch with the children, either because he or she finds it "too painful" to see them or because the custodial parent refuses to allow visitation. Allay their fears, but be honest if you know that a move is in the offing.

And it's important for you and your spouse to remember that you are divorcing each other, not your children. The parent-child relationship should remain intact and relatively unchanged no matter what is going on between two adults.

If dad is the parent who leaves, which is frequently the case in this society, be prepared for your child to be angry: at dad for leaving, at you for "making" him leave. Explain as simply and as often as possible that sometimes people who have loved each other can no longer live together, but that both of you love and want to be with your children.

The noncustodial parent should make an effort to see or talk to the children on a regular basis. You should try to establish as normal a routine as possible, especially if you have joint custody. If your children are going to call two places home, they have to feel at home in both places.

And be reliable. If you say you're going to call at seven P.M., make sure you call. If you tell your kids you'll pick them up for a romp in the park, be there. "One of the most heartbreaking memories I have is of my son, sitting on the curb outside our house, waiting for his father, who said he was coming but never came," recalls our friend Pat, whose four children ranged in age from thirteen to one when she was divorced.

"If you're going to date, do it away from the children until you're absolutely sure the child has adjusted and is doing all right," says Dr. Lasswell. "They have enough to adjust to without having to get used to someone else in mommy's or daddy's life."

Once you're confident the child can meet your dates, introduce them as friends. Don't try to involve your children in your new relationships at first. You'll be testing their loyalty to your ex-spouse, and you don't want to offer them a parent substitute who might disappear in a few months (or after the first date). "Then the child begins to get a history of people close to him leaving," says Dr. Lasswell. (See "You Want to Have the Person You're Dating Sleep Over," earlier in this chapter.)

By all means get counseling—for you and for the children. Breaking up a marriage and at the same time keeping a family together is tough on you. You may find yourself using your child as a therapist. Don't. "Talk to another adult, not your children," says Dr. Lasswell. "That's very important." Confiding your troubles to your child is asking him to take on more responsibility than he can at his age.

You might also find that you've got a short fuse. Ask a relative or friend to baby-sit occasionally so you can get a break. Never be afraid to ask for help when you need it.

## WHAT PARENTS SAY

*The worst thing during a bitter divorce is to lose your cool. What I did was create my own "mommy" time. Every night when I came home, I gave my baby son to a neighbor for about two hours. I then filled the tub with nice warm water, poured myself a glass of wine, and just relaxed. You'd be surprised how much that helped me un-*

*wind. On my days off I gave the baby to a neighbor and just went for a walk, window-shopped, went out to dinner (nothing fancy, even frozen yogurt by yourself is a treat).*

*I eventually started a support group of divorced women with small children. We took turns baby-sitting, made dates to go out (either with or without the kids), held small get-togethers, and were just "there" for each other.*

*Ann W.*
*New York*

## THE SITUATION ▪ You Disagree With Your Partner About Child-Rearing

**My wife and I agree on just about everything regarding raising our three kids, except for corporal punishment. She thinks it's barbaric and I don't see the harm in occasionally spanking a child. How do we resolve this conflict? We want to present a united front to our kids.**

## WHAT THE EXPERTS SAY

Though we tend to side with your wife, as do all the experts we've spoken to, the bottom line (no pun intended) is that your children probably aren't going to be harmed by having parents who do some things differently. Their teachers in school and their bosses at work aren't going to be stamped from the same cookie cutter either. Your kids are going to need to learn how to adjust to a wide variety of human styles throughout their lifetime. They might as well start at home.

How you punish may not be as critical an issue as why you punish. As long as you and your wife are of one mind as to what's right and what's wrong, you *are* presenting a united front to your children.

You're probably more favorably disposed toward spanking as a punishment because you were brought up in a home where you were spanked, "and you turned out all right," says Dr. Lasswell.

The problem, as the family therapist points out, is what spanking teaches children. "It teaches them that violence is an acceptable response," she says. It doesn't necessarily teach them that what they did was wrong and according to a number of research studies, may not even change their behavior. Besides, you want your children to behave well for instrinsic motives—because being good and moral and upright is a good thing—not because they want to avoid pain.

Unfortunately, few parents spank their kids dispassionately to teach them a lesson. More often than not, they strike out in anger, and there's always the risk that you can really hurt your child without meaning to.

As for your disagreement with your spouse, Dr. Lasswell says, as long as it doesn't develop into a power struggle that is played out in front of the children, it's probably not going to affect them.

You need to respect your spouse's point of view, even if it differs radically from yours. Negotiate a compromise—"I'll spank the kids for these situations when I see them arise, and you handle them in your way" or "I'll try your way for a few months and see what kinds of results I get."

## WHAT PARENTS SAY

*When we are disagreeing in front of our son, we try to give way to the other person and then talk about it later. It is better to give in even though you think your spouse is making a mistake than to fight in front of the child.*

*Bob H.*
*Michigan*

■

*My husband usually defaults to my judgment because I am the primary caretaker of our son (I'm a stay-at-home mother). Most likely I have dealt with the situation before and have found a way to deal with it that works. If my husband feels strongly about resolving the situation in another way, we discuss it then and there. Note that I said "discuss," not "argue." My son has the opportunity to see resolution of conflict. We almost always see the other person's rea-*

*soning. We're both open-minded people, and that is reflected in our
parenting.*

*Angela W.*
*California*

## THE SITUATION ▪ You Feel Ambivalent About Your Kids

**Is there something wrong with me? I know I love my kids, but
there are some days when I really don't like them. Some days I'm
so filled with love for them that they seem like the greatest bless-
ing of my life. Other days they seem like greedy, spoiled little
monsters, and I can't stand being around them. Does everybody
have times when they're not crazy about their kids?**

### WHAT THE EXPERTS SAY

Yes, and the ones who say they don't are lying. Think of it this
way: Do you *always* like the ones you love? Haven't there been
times in your marriage when you've thought fondly of your care-
free single life? Haven't you ever had days when you'd like.to
donate your parents to an orphan? When you toy with the idea of
making a childless couple ecstatically happy? And face it, there
are days when your kids aren't too crazy about you, either.

It's all part of the ebb and flow of love that characterizes even
the most stable relationships. Parents of temperamentally difficult children often struggle with this ambivalence on a daily
basis. Love generally wins out, but parents need to come to grips
with the negative emotions their child's behavior inspires in
them. If those feelings ever become violent or chronic, you'll need
professional help. But if they're fleeting, you'll need to learn to
accept them.

"Some parents just wish they had nothing but love for their
children and can't tolerate their feelings of anger, hatred, or disappointment," says Jerome Karasic, M.D., clinical professor of
psychiatry at the University of Southern California. "Some are

more accepting of their negative feelings. I remember hearing a woman analyst talking about wanting to throw her children into the barbecue on the Fourth of July because she had to leave a party early. That was enough years ago that I know the outcome of her parenting: one child is a prominent physician and the other is a very successful lawyer. It suggests that her being able to face her ambivalence had a positive effect.

"The negative feeling on the part of the parents is important because it stimulates the development of conscience in the child," says Dr. Karasic. "Not liking to be woken up in the middle of the night, not liking a kid to throw a tantrum in the middle of a supermarket—if you liked those things, the kids would never give them up."

It doesn't hurt to tell your child, "I don't like what you're doing." In fact, though you may be thinking, "I don't like *you*," putting it that way will help you separate the child from his actions, which are really what's bugging you.

Get used to feeling angry and maybe even hating a child at times. That will pass. But examine your anger. Does your child dredge up what you thought were long-lost animosities: "He tags along with me just like my brother did." "She whines just like my mother." You want to react to your child, not your memories of childhood.

Don't run away from your negative feelings. Accept them as normal, in you and in your children. Allow your children to express their animosity toward you. *I hate you* aren't the three little words you want most to hear from your little ones, but they're only words, spoken in a moment of rage. Share your feelings with other parents. You'll be surprised at the sighs of relief you'll hear, just before they launch into why they can't stand their kids either . . . sometimes.

If your resentment is prolonged, or seems to be based on what you see as a fundamental failing in your child, seek professional help before you damage his self-esteem. If you just need a break, give yourself a time out. Go out with your husband once a week, go out by yourself once a week. Go into your bedroom and close the door for however long it takes for your angry feelings to pass, especially if you think you'll do or say something you'll regret.

## WHAT PARENTS SAY

*I can remember sitting in the dark one morning with my infant son, rocking him and chanting softly. "I hate you, I hate you, I hate you." I meant it at the time. I hadn't slept for more than two hours a night for a week. I was convinced that having this child was the worst mistake I had ever made in my life. Shortly thereafter, I became convinced it was the best thing I'd ever done. But I have allowed myself to have both feelings, without guilt.*

*Donna R.*
*Utah*

## THE SITUATION ▪ You're Having Trouble Deciding About Returning to Work

**I told my employers that I would be back to work after a six-month maternity leave, but I can't bear the thought of leaving my son. I worked hard for many years to build up my career. I'm afraid if I stay home, I'll be throwing it all away. On the other hand, this may be the only child I have. How do I deal with this dilemma?**

## WHAT THE EXPERTS SAY

"If you're ambivalent about going back to work vis-à-vis staying home, it's going to be torture, *torture*," warns Susan Weissman, M.S.W., founder and executive director of the Park Center Preschools in New York City. "The guilt is overwhelming."

Approach your decision making in a businesslike way. First, look at your finances. "Economics are always going to be the answer," says Weissman. "It's almost easier for the woman who knows she has to go back to work. It's not a torturous decision. She knows she has to. It's the ones who have more choices that have the problem."

But if you have a choice, examine *all* your choices. Ask your employer about part-time work, job sharing, flextime, and working at home. For some women (alas, not many), those are viable compromises. Are you at a stage in your career when some time out won't affect you? Take a five-year vacation from your job. Keep in touch with your former coworkers and stay abreast of advances in your field and you may be able to slip back in once your child is in school.

We don't want to give you the impression that this is a simple decision to make. Some women's careers can be damaged by too long an absence from the work force. But feelings are involved, too. After the birth of a baby some women don't have the same emotional involvement in their careers as they once did. Neither do some men, who may find going back after paternity leave a problem, too—with fewer solutions. Men tend to have the bigger paycheck and despite the much heralded arrival of the "new father," are more stigmatized in the job market by a few years' hiatus in the nursery.

You need to take some time to examine your new feelings and what staying at home or going back to work might mean to you. Will your work be affected by your yearning to be at home with your son? Will you feel deprived if you're not there for his first steps or his first word? Will the loss of your career leave an important part of you unfulfilled? Do you think you might be a better parent if you're not with your child all the time?

Talk to other parents who have had to make this decision. But remember, it's your life. You have to live with the decision you make.

How you feel about your decision will be important. If your idea of motherhood involves being at home, baking cookies, and smocking blouses, you're likely to feel like a bad mother even if your child is happy and well adjusted at daycare. (In fact, studies have shown this.) Try to remember, as Sirgay Sanger, M.D., writes in his book, *The Woman Who Works, the Parent Who Cares*, "There is *no* contradiction between being a good mother and leaving a child in the care of another adult for part of each day."

On the other hand, don't succumb to the prejudice against stay-at-home moms, although if this is your choice, be prepared to deal with it. Anyone who has ever stayed at home to care for her children knows there's no job in the world, short of putting out oil-rig fires, that is more difficult. Mothers get their own holiday in this country, but they don't get enough respect.

If you find you're leaning toward going back, even part-time, one way to make it easier on you and your son is to find good daycare. Susan Weissman is the coauthor of *The Parents' Guide to Daycare*, an excellent resource to help you find the right caretaker for your child. Do you want—and can you afford—a live-in nanny, either an au pair or a trained nanny?

For infants and toddlers, family daycare is often the best choice. Look for a daycare provider with whom you feel comfortable. Sometimes, the woman who spends all day playing with and cuddling the children is a better choice than the one who teaches them French. Investigate daycare centers in your area. From our experience, they vary greatly. (See Chapter 16, "Daycare and School—The First Good-bye" for many ideas.)

"You should definitely have them in your home or have your child with the daycare provider or in the center a good few weeks before you go back to work, because that will allay an incredible amount of anxiety," says Weissman. "If you see that the caregiver is indeed working out, that the relationship is going to be a good one, you'll feel much better about your decision."

## WHAT PARENTS SAY

*I have decided to start back to work part-time. This way my son and I won't be shocked when we are parted. I need space to grow and my son needs this time and space also. A lot of people would love to stay home, but it's not easy. It's rewarding a lot of the time, but it's hectic. You also need time with the real world, to see different people. Working part-time makes it easier to balance everything. It gradually eases you into the swing of things.*

*Cerene C.*
*New York*

■

*How do I feel about my decision to stay home with my daughter? Ambivalent.*

*I miss contributing professionally to a field in which I worked for eleven years, but it is a special pleasure to read with my daughter and help her discover the world of books. I resent the empty stares and shallow conversation of those who think my brain went dead the moment I became a stay-at-home mom, but I take great satisfaction in exploring long-deferred interests such as gardening.*

*I hate being the wife of the boss instead of the boss, but I love being home for my child and teaching her songs and rhymes, who Grandma is, what a cardinal looks like, and where to find her toes. I miss the personal income, but we are not digging ourselves into a financial abyss.*

*Do I think I made the right decision? Absolutely. How do I view working moms? Sometimes with envy, sometimes with a sense of superiority, but usually with understanding. Everyone has to make a choice, and I doubt many find it easy.*

*Jessie W.*
*Maryland*

■

*If you're not sure, stay home. If it is a financial question, take a close look at those finances. Make sure you are absolutely honest about how much you* really *have left of a salary after paying for* all *work-related expenses, and* all *the things you will not need if you stay at home. Then see if you can do without more than you thought you could. I try to keep in mind what my husband's grandmother once said when we were discussing what some people felt they needed: "Those aren't needs, honey. Those are wants."*

*Heidi C.*
*Alabama*

# INDEX